THE ONES WHO GOT AWAY

OSPREY
PUBLISHING

All those Allied airmen left their homes, their families, and their countries to come and help us. We owed them all the help we were able to provide them.

Anne Brusselmans
A celebrated helper of evaders throughout the war who coordinated the activities of a network of safe houses in Brussels.

DEDICATION

To my grandson Axel, a lover of adventure stories: I hope you'll enjoy these tales of obstacles surmounted and challenges met, and that you will grow up and grow old never losing your love of adventure.

BILL YENNE

Mighty Eighth Airmen
on the Run in Occupied Europe

THE ONES
WHO GOT
AWAY

OSPREY PUBLISHING
Bloomsbury Publishing Plc
Kemp House, Chawley Park, Cumnor Hill, Oxford OX2 9PH, UK
29 Earlsfort Terrace, Dublin 2, Ireland
1385 Broadway, 5th Floor, New York, NY 10018, USA
E-mail: info@ospreypublishing.com
www.ospreypublishing.com

OSPREY is a trademark of Osprey Publishing Ltd

First published in Great Britain in 2024

A catalog record for this book is available from the British Library.

ISBN: HB 9781472858719; PB 9781472858689; eBook 9781472858702; ePDF 9781472858726;
XML 9781472858733; Audio 9781472858696

24 25 26 27 28   10 9 8 7 6 5 4 3 2 1

Maps by Bill Yenne
Index by Zoe Ross

Typeset by Deanta Global Publishing Services, Chennai, India
Printed and bound in Great Britain by CPI (Group) UK Ltd, Croydon CR0 4YY

MIX
Paper | Supporting
responsible forestry
FSC® C171272

Osprey Publishing supports the Woodland Trust, the UK's leading woodland conservation charity.

To find out more about our authors and books visit www.ospreypublishing.com. Here you will find extracts,
author interviews, details of forthcoming events and the option to sign up for our newsletter.

Contents

CONTENTS

List of Plate Section Illustrations

Andrée de Jongh, known as Dédée, was only 24 when she became one of the founders of the Comet escape line. She personally escorted more than 100 Allied airmen across occupied Europe, and made two dozen round trips through the Pyrenees herself before she was captured in 1943. She is seen here at Buckingham Palace when she was awarded the George Medal in 1946. (© IWM HU 55451)

The navigator aboard the B-17 called *Wulfe Hound*, 2nd Lieutenant Gilbert Schowalter, was shot down in October 1942, celebrated New Year's Eve in Paris with Dédée de Jongh, and spent most of January 1943 interned at the British Embassy in Madrid before reaching England. This photo of him in civilian garb was taken for use in his counterfeit identity papers. (USAAF)

William Whitman and Lee Fegette lived here at the Château de Breuil in the commune of Rozay-en-Brie, about 40 miles east of Paris, for two months from December 1942 to February 1943. (Author's collection)

Tech Sergeant William Whitman was the flight engineer aboard *Wulfe Hound*, a B-17 that was shot down in October 1942. He and fellow Texan Lee Fegette remained in northern France until April 1943, but they were back in England via Gibraltar by May. (USAAF)

Sergeant William Claxton "Billy" Howell was the tail gunner aboard a B-17 of the 381st Bomb Group, 533rd Bomb Squadron that was shot down over France on July 4, 1943. He was badly injured but finally reached a doctor in Paris. He later walked across the Pyrenees in the company of Sergeant Otto Bruzewski of the B-17 *Chug-a-Lug Lulu*. (USAAF)

Like many fellow evaders, Fred Hartung and Norman Therrien passed through the village of El Serrat in neutral Andorra as they made their way toward Spain and Gibraltar. (Nisse57, Wikimedia Commons, CC BY-SA 4.0)

This "Certificate in Lieu of a Passport" was issued to evader Sergeant
Norman Therrien by the US Embassy in Madrid in February 1943,
two months after he was shot down over France. Such documents
were necessary, as the evaders had ditched their American papers while
eluding the Gestapo in occupied Europe. (US National Archives)

A Hound in Wolf's markings. *Wulfe Hound* was a Boeing B-17F-27-BO
assigned to the 360th Bomb Squadron, 303rd Bomb Group. Damaged
during a mission on December 12, 1942, she was crash-landed in
France by pilot Lieutenant Paul Flickenger. She was the first B-17
captured by the Luftwaffe and restored to flyable condition, and was
operated by the Luftwaffe until April 1944 when she was ditched in
the Mediterranean. (Author's collection)

Shot down on August 17, 1943 during the "Black Tuesday" mission to
Regensburg, 2nd Lieutenant Martin Minnich was the copilot of the
B-17 *Our Bay-Bee*. Badly burned, he was cared for by the Belgian
underground and taken under the wing of the Comet Line. (USAAF)

The bombardier aboard the B-17 *Our Bay-Bee*, 2nd Lieutenant Henry
"Hank" Sarnow, hooked up with crewmate Martin Minnich shortly
after their aircraft was shot down on "Black Tuesday" in August 1943.
They evaded together, and thanks to the Comet Line were back in the
UK by November 23, 1944. (USAAF)

Anne Brusselmans (left) opened her Brussels home to fugitive Allied airmen
and coordinated the efforts of many safe houses sheltering as many as
50 airmen at any time. In November 1957, she had a surprise reunion
with one of her charges, Major Hank Sarnow (center), on the BBC
studio reality TV show *This is Your Life*, hosted by Eamon Andrews
(right). (USAAF)

Dating to the sixteenth century, the Château de Brax near Toulouse was
used during the occupation by the underground Groupe Morhange as
a fortress, torture chamber, and safe house for evading airmen. Among
those passing through its gates were 1st Lieutenant Bill Grodi and
members of his crew from the downed B-17 *Old Shillelagh*. (Didier
Descouens, Wikimedia Commons, CC BY-SA 4.0)

Shot down in January 1944, P-47 pilot 1st Lieutenant Joel McPherson
spent most of five months on the run with the Maquis in
southwestern France. His harrowing adventures culminated in his stint
as a getaway driver for a gang of Maquisard bank robbers. (USAAF)

Lieutenant Colonel Beirne Lay Jr was a prewar author, screenwriter, and
aviator who went on to command the 487th Bomb Group. After his
B-24 Liberator was shot down in May 1944, Lay evaded in northern

France until August, when he was able to link up on the ground with elements of General Patton's Third Army. He later co-wrote the novel *Twelve O'Clock High*. (USAAF)

On June 18, 1944, high on the crest of the rugged Pyrenees, evading airmen Lieutenant Joel McPherson and Lieutenant Gilbert Stonebarger crossed the border into the Spanish village of Canéjan. (Père Igor, Wikimedia Commons, CC BY-SA 3.0)

Flying with the 56th Fighter Group, Major Walker "Bud" Mahurin was the highest-scoring American ace in the European Theater through early 1944. He had 19.75 confirmed victories when he was shot down in March 1944. (USAAF)

Seen here as a US Air Force major in 1950, Jack Terzian was a lieutenant and a P-47 pilot with the 351 Fighter Squadron, 353 Fighter Group, when he was shot down over Belgium on May 22, 1944. He managed to evade capture until July, and he then escaped in a mass breakout of Allied airmen from a German freight car on September 3. His words at the time were, "then the party started." (USAF)

The crew of the 801st Bomb Group B-24 known as *C for Charlie*, piloted by 1st Lieutenant Henry W. "Hank" Wolcott. Back row, left to right: Bill Ryckman, Wolcott, Robert Auda and Wallis Cozzens. Front row, left to right: Dirvin Deihl, Richard Hawkins, Frederick Tuttle, and Dale Loucks. The aircraft went down in Belgium in May 1944 while on a secret Operation *Carpetbagger* mission. All but Hawkins escaped and evaded. (USAAF)

The pilot of a B-24 that he named *Mike*, after the mascot of Louisiana State University, 2nd Lieutenant Alfred Sanders was shot down over Belgium on May 28, 1944. He met Hank Wolcott four days later and they evaded together – sometimes in the company of Russian deserters, sometimes in the company of Belgian eccentrics – until they were betrayed in mid-August. (USAAF)

Prosper DeZitter was an infamous Belgian criminal and con man who collaborated with the Nazis. He set up a faux safe house in Brussels, into which he and his confederates lured dozens of Allied airmen before turning them over to the Germans – for a price. (Author's collection)

The dreaded Saint-Gilles Prison in Brussels was deliberately designed to have a foreboding, medieval appearance. Taken over by the Nazis in 1940, it was used mainly to house political prisoners pending transfer to concentration camps in Germany. It is still in use, and still internationally condemned for overcrowding. (Author's collection)

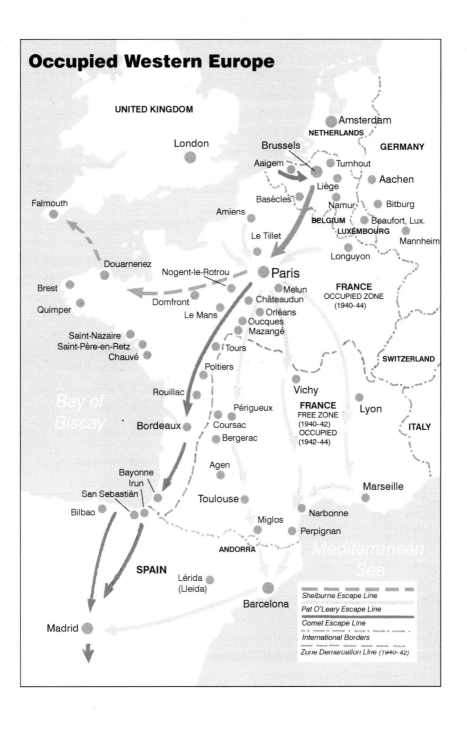

Occupied Western Europe

UNITED KINGDOM

London

Falmouth

Bay of Biscay

Douarnenez

Brest

Quimper

Saint-Nazaire
Saint-Père-en-Retz
Chauvé

Rouillac

Bordeaux

Bayonne
Irun
San Sebastián

Bilbao

SPAIN

Madrid

Amsterdam
NETHERLANDS

Brussels

Aaigem

Basècles

Amiens

Le Tillet

Nogent-le-Rotrou

Domfront

Le Mans

Tours

Poitiers

Périgueux

Coursac

Bergerac

Agen

Toulouse

Lérida
(Lleida)

Barcelona

Turnhout

GERMANY

Liège

Aachen

Namur

Bitburg

BELGIUM

Beaufort, Lux.

LUXEMBOURG

Mannheim

Longuyon

Paris

Melun

Châteaudun

Orléans

Oucques

Mazangé

FRANCE
OCCUPIED ZONE
(1940–44)

SWITZERLAND

Vichy

FRANCE
FREE ZONE
(1940–42)
OCCUPIED
(1942–44)

Lyon

ITALY

Marseille

Miglos

Narbonne

Perpignan

ANDORRA

Mediterranean
See

- - - - Shelburne Escape Line
- - - - Pat O'Leary Escape Line
━━━━ Comet Escape Line
·—·—· International Borders
— — — Zone Demarcation Line (1940–42)

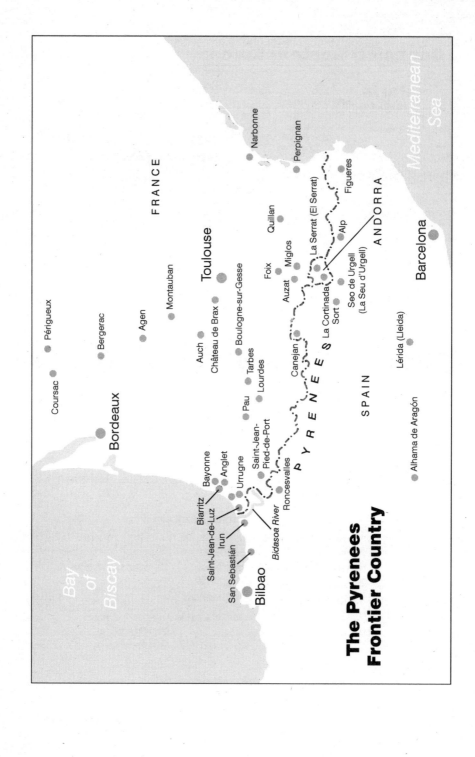

The Pyrenees Frontier Country

Mediterranean Sea

FRANCE

Narbonne
Perpignan
Figueres
La Serrat (El Serrat)
Alp
ANDORRA
Quillan
Miglos
Foix
Barcelona
Auzat
Seo de Urgell (La Seu d'Urgell)
Boulogne-sur-Gesse
Toulouse
Canejan
La Cortinada
Sort
Château de Brax
Auch
Montauban
Tarbes
Lourdes
Pau
Agen
PYRENEES
SPAIN
Lérida (Lleida)
Bergerac
Saint-Jean-Pied-de-Port
Alhama de Aragón
Périgueux
Coursac
Bordeaux
Bayonne
Anglet
Urrugne
Biarritz
Saint-Jean-de-Luz
Irun
San Sebastián
Roncesvalles
Bidasoa River
Bilbao

Bay of Biscay

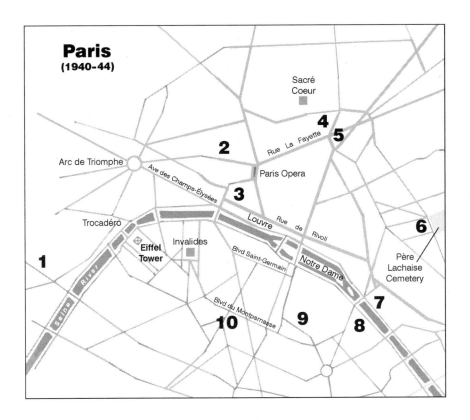

1. The Clapsons' safe house (63 Rue du Ranelagh)
2. Gare Saint-Lazare
3. Hôtel Le Meurice (German Headquarters)
4. Gare du Nord
5. Gare de l'Est
6. Monsieur Pirnaud's safe house (27 Avenue Gambetta)
7. Gare de Lyon
8. Gare d'Austerlitz
9. Mme Christol's safe house (4 Rue Edouard Quenu)
10. Gare Montparnasse

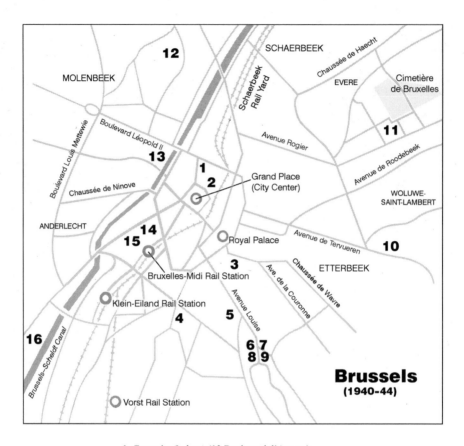

1. Germaine Leheys (13 Boulevard d'Anvers)
2. Hôtel Métropole (31 Place de Brouckère)
3. Anne Brusselmans (127 Chaussée d'Ixelles)
4. Saint-Gilles Prison (106 Avenue Ducpétiaux)
5. Prosper DeZitter's "Dog House" (16 Rue Forestière)
6. German SS Offices 1943-44 (347 Avenue Louise)
7. German Occupation Offices (418 Avenue Louise)
8. German SS Offices 1940-43 (453 Avenue Louise)
9. German Occupation Offices (510 Avenue Louise)
10. Allied IS9 offices after 09/1944 (218 Avenue de Tervueren)
11. Jeanne Frix-Claes (147 Avenue du Cimetière de Bruxelles)
12. Marcel van Buckenhout (226 Boulevard Emile Bockstael)
13. Philippe Vossells (85 Chaussée de Gand)
14. Alvier Willemsen (45 Rue Jorez)
15. Josse van Craenenbroeck (16 Place du Conseil)
16. François Delen (45 Rue des Fraises)

Introduction

These are stories of ones who got away, of intrepid airmen who eluded the prison camps of an enemy who controlled a continent.

These are war stories, not of great armies or even of platoon-sized units. These are stories of men on their own, or of bands of brothers in which the brothers numbered just two or three – all of them facing the challenges of occupied lands swarming with Germans.

The ones who got away, who slipped through Axis fingers in the European Theater, included more than 6,000 airmen from many Allied nations, though the great majority were from either the British Empire or the United States. In this book, though, our focus is on men of the American Eighth Air Force. The largest of the constituent numbered air forces within the US Army Air Forces, it was created specifically to conduct a strategic air campaign against the German industrial machine, and it came to be known as the "Mighty Eighth."

Of the 350,000 personnel serving with the Eighth, 210,000 of them were aircrewmen, of whom 50,000 were downed over occupied Europe. Of these, 26,000 men died and 21,000 were doomed to terrible years in brutal German prisoner of war camps. Only around 3,000 of those who were shot down were among the ones who got away. This book tells some of their stories.

Each airman had received training, or at least briefings, on the subject of "Escape and Evasion" (E&E). Perhaps the words ought to have been reversed. A man had to first *evade*, often repeatedly, before he could finally *escape*. The fact that fewer than one in 16 of all downed airman managed to get away is indicative of how perilously difficult this was. For those who did, it was partly because of a measure of cleverness and ingenuity, but mostly it was a matter of *luck*. It matters not how clever or ingenious a person is. When his luck runs out, it's game over.

Each of these unique stories is derived primarily from the personal recollections of individual Eighth Air Force evaders. All of the direct quotes, unless otherwise noted, are in their own words. These words, quoted from documents recorded when memories were still vivid and often written in each man's own hand, are part of Escape and Evasion (E&E) Reports produced when each airman made it back from occupied Europe. These after-action documents, nearly 3,000 of them, were filed, boxed, and shipped Stateside after the war. Eventually they came to reside in the collections of the National Archives and Records Administration (NARA), as part of NARA Record Group 498 (RG 498), which is entitled "Records of Headquarters, European Theater of Operations, US Army (World War II)."

The handful of stories included herein barely scratches the surface of what is contained in the folders – typed or handwritten on pages now brittle with age, but still almost literally dripping with sweat and tears, and certainly still crackling with the sparks of adrenaline from that extraordinary time so long ago.

These stories highlight men who came from all corners of the United States, and from all walks of life. There are city boys and farm boys. Among them are college students, accountants, factory workers, and a former semi-pro ball player. There is one man who had joined the Royal Canadian Air Force before the United States entered the war, and another who was a novelist and screenwriter who had previously had one of his scripts turned into a prewar Hollywood film.

Some of these tales seem themselves to be cut from Hollywood espionage thrillers, as we listen breathlessly to men shivering in fear while Gestapo officers scrutinize their forged identity papers on a train, or as they hide in the brush only inches from German troops.

We meet one pair of men taking cover during a Gestapo raid and crouching beneath the floorboards of a farmhouse in a situation reminiscent of the fearsome famous opening scene of Quentin Tarantino's *Inglourious Basterds* – although in our story, the two protagonists were accompanied by a platoon of Russian soldiers who had just deserted from the German Army. We find another pair jumping from a moving train to avoid a German checkpoint – only to board a different train and be cornered in their compartment by Gestapo officers.

There is the story of two men who bailed out over Germany, and had to evade capture in the heart of the Third Reich, where troops zealously protected the Fatherland, and where civilians were known to murder a downed airman, considering him a *Terrorflieger*, literally a "flying terrorist." After 100 anxious miles, they slipped out of the Reich, but still had 700 miles to go before they could taste freedom.

Some of the stories are poignant. One airman did the improbable and rode halfway across France on a bicycle. Riding through Poitiers, he passed the concentration camp where Romani people were interned. He recalled that as he passed, "a small child about four years old looking though the fence waved to me." The fate of the child had already been sealed.

Some stories border on the tragi-comic. While most of the downed airmen made contact with underground organizations, one man described how he fell in with a band of *maquis*, the disrupters and saboteurs who operated in the south of France. While with them, he was captured by the paramilitary, pro-German Milice Français. Imprisoned in a French jail, he decided to fake appendicitis because it was easier to escape from a hospital than a jail. The plan went sideways, and he woke up without an appendix – *and* convalescing in a German military hospital.

One American was on the verge of being arrested by the Spanish police as a smuggler on a snowswept mountain trail because he had no ID to prove he was an American. Luckily, he thought to show them his pocket comb with "US Army" stamped on it. This worked, and he was allowed to face a horrible blizzard alone, but *without* fear of prison.

Some downed airmen wound up fighting the Germans with the underground. One volunteered to take over operating the clandestine radio for a Belgian underground group in Basècles, Belgium, and soon became a trusted advisor to a Résistance leader. Another man found himself as the getaway driver for a band of *maquis* who attacked and looted the *châteaux* of French collaborators, and robbed banks to finance their activities – because nobody else in the gang knew how to drive.

What each of these men had in common was that one morning, he had climbed out of a real bed, eaten a hot meal, and gone to work in what was then one of the most technically sophisticated machines in the world.

During that day, each man cheated death – often by the skin of his teeth – then cheated the German war machine, again just barely, and reached an immense turning point in his life.

That evening, each man faced the uncertainly of a new life in a dark and dangerous new world, alone or in the company of just a few of his own, with none of the vast resources of the Mighty Eighth.

These are the stories of how each of these men, through cleverness, ingenuity, and *luck*, managed to beat the odds.

PART ONE

STRANGERS IN
A STRANGE LAND

Chapter 1

The Lay of This Treacherous Land

Their theater of escape and evasion began beneath the aerial corridor passing mainly through the air space of the Netherlands, Belgium, Luxembourg, France, and Germany. Through this corridor, the streams of Eighth Air Force fighters and bombers traveled from bases in Britain to targets within Germany, or German targets elsewhere in occupied Europe, especially France.

If an airman came down in an occupied country, he was surrounded by a population that was usually sympathetic, and often helpful – though not always. If an airman came down inside Germany he was, in the vernacular of the day, a *Terrorflieger* and liable to be killed, even by civilians. Everywhere, even in places that had welcomed Americans for generations, the rule of law was the rule of the Nazis, so locals aided airmen at their peril.

Just as Europe under the heel of the German jackboot was an alien world for the airmen who suddenly descended into it, the place was a strange land for those who had lived there all their lives. Since the German blitzkrieg conquests of April–June 1940, the people of Western Europe, their governments, and all aspects of their civil societies were no longer their own. The darkness of German occupation had descended quickly and completely across their lives and institutions.

The prewar governments of the Netherlands, Belgium, and Luxembourg escaped to Britain to become governments-in-exile, but their power had abruptly become more aspirational than real. The daily lives of their people were controlled by new masters in German uniforms and their local puppets.

France, which had been one of Europe's prewar Allied superpowers, suffered the dual humiliations of an almost overnight military defeat and a smothering military occupation. It had no government-in-exile, except in the person of General Charles de Gaulle, but almost no one – from Allied leaders to many French citizens – really took him seriously until the middle of 1944.

A third humiliation imposed on the French people was that the Germans allowed the creation of a French government – but a *puppet* government aligned with the Third Reich. The French Third Republic, which had existed for seven decades and was allied with Britain until France's defeat, was superseded by the État Français (French State). While this government ruled part of France, Germany imposed a direct military occupation across the north and west of the country.

A fourth humiliation was that Paris – the heart and soul of France for a millennium – was in the occupied zone, so the French administrative capital was relocated to the resort town of Vichy, and thus the État Français became known informally as "Vichy France."

The fifth humiliation came in November 1942, when the Germans extended their military occupation, and their pervasive presence, across the entirety of France.

The instrument of German victory had been its powerful armed forces, the Wehrmacht. While the Wehrmacht remained as the instrument of German military occupation, it was a parallel German organization which transformed all of occupied Europe into a police state.

The Schutzstaffel (SS), created in 1925 as a Nazi party bodyguard detail, had evolved into a million-man elite force answerable only to Reichsführer Heinrich Himmler and his boss, Führer Adolf Hitler. Dressed in their forbidding black uniforms, the SS touched all aspects of life inside Germany and in the occupied countries. Three of the four principal components of the SS were the Totenkopfverbände, which ran concentration and extermination camps; the Sicherheitdienst (SD), which conducted foreign intelligence operations; and the Waffen SS (Armed SS), a full-fledged elite army which operated in conjunction with – but outside the command structure of – Wehrmacht ground forces.

The fourth and most sinister element of the SS organization was its police forces. Most nefarious among these was the Gestapo – the Geheime Staatspolizei (Secret State Police). It spread its tentacles throughout Germany, as well as into the areas occupied by Germany. It was a constant source of fear and anxiety for those people who now found themselves strangers in their own lands, as well as for Allied airmen who became fugitives in these lands.

Meanwhile, though, just as the SS fielded its SD and its Gestapo, the Wehrmacht contained its own intelligence and secret police apparatus – the Abwehr. Commanded by Admiral Wilhelm Canaris, the Abwehr conducted both espionage and covert actions against Germany's rivals, occasionally in direct competition with the SD. The Abwehr also contained the Geheime Feldpolizei (GFP), a secret police component that rivaled Himmler's Gestapo.

The rival agencies both maintained a substantial presence in occupied countries, especially France, where they were involved in an ongoing turf war. In this book, we'll see the GFP and the Gestapo competing directly with one another over custody of specific captives.

Finally, within the complex tapestry of the occupation of Europe, there were the local collaborators, both inside and outside established police bureaucracies, whose heavy hand made life dangerous for their own fellow citizens, as well as for Allied airmen.

In France, for example, the nationwide Police Nationale was led by René Bousquet, an ambitious Interior Ministry bureaucrat who worked closely with SS-Obergruppenführer Carl Oberg, the commander of all SS and German police operations in France. In January 1943, Bousquet created the Milice Français (French Militia), a zealous paramilitary group known for torture and summary execution of opponents of both Germany and Vichy France.

An abhorrent example of Vichy collaboration was the expulsion to Nazi death camps of around 75,000 Jews – both French citizens and those of other nationalities. The French police also operated more than two dozen internment camps of their own.

Another illustration of Vichy collaboration, and a humiliation that stung a whole generation, was the infamous Service du Travail Obligatoire (Compulsory Work Service) program. Initiated by Vichy France itself in June 1942, the STO conscripted more than 600,000 able-bodied young men and women, who were shipped to Germany to work in German war materiel factories. The STO, like the parallel German slave labor programs, was designed to allow Germany to draft more of its own young men into the Wehrmacht. This naturally inspired many thousands of young French people to resist the occupation.

Meanwhile, there was another country in Western Europe, nearly as large as France, that was never occupied by the Germans and which played an essential role in the escape of Allied airmen. During World War II, Spain occupied a unique place among the nations of Western Europe. Things in that country were not what they might have been. Between 1936 and 1939, Spain had been embroiled in a bloody civil war between the left-leaning supporters of the Second Spanish Republic and insurgent Nationalists under General Francisco Franco. While the Republicans were actively supported by troops and aircraft sent by the Soviet Union, both Nazi Germany and Fascist Italy sent combat units to back Franco. Franco won.

Though Franco had not prevailed in the Spanish Civil War *without* the aid of Germany and Italy, the wily dictator decided to play it safe in World War II. He cautiously declined to join Hitler and Mussolini in the Axis alliance they formed with Japan in 1940. Franco did send an eventual 47,000 troops to fight alongside German forces in the Soviet Union, but he otherwise maintained Spanish "neutrality" throughout the war.

Amazingly, the Germans played along, and this played into the hands of Allied airmen escaping from occupied Europe. If an airman, or indeed any refugee from occupied Europe, reached the 250-mile-long border between

France and Spain – which lies almost entirely in the rugged Pyrenees mountain range – the Germans and the collaborating French police generally would not pursue them.

Spain allowed the airmen to make contact with the British or American consulates in Spain, which facilitated transit back to Britain via Gibraltar. This isn't to say that Spanish police agencies did not vigorously guard their borders, especially against *contrabandistas* – smugglers and black marketeers. As more than one undocumented airman found out the hard way, lack of papers would put him in a Spanish jail cell.

Between the authorities on both sides, and the rugged and often impassable Pyrenees, it was a difficult journey, an arduous trek far more easily described than accomplished. Nevertheless, these mountain trails became the most important escape hatch from occupied Europe for almost anyone who could make it.

Chapter 2

Herding Wildcats

Numbed by the suddenness of the German conquests in the summer of 1940, the people of France and Western Europe had at first acquiesced to the occupation, but gradually, driven by intolerable humiliation and day-to-day debasement, an active resistance was forming. This took many forms, not the least of which was a commitment to aiding Allied airmen who found themselves in the transformed land.

Internal, grassroots opposition to the German occupation of Western Europe took many forms. Despite a German crackdown and the real threat of summary execution or expulsion to concentration camps, there was a growing number of people determined to make the occupation difficult for the Germans. Passive noncompliance with the occupation was widespread, while active organized resistance took shape during the first year of the occupation.

Gradually, like-minded people banded together in a growing proliferation of separate and independent underground organizations opposing both the German occupation *and* collaborationist governments. These ranged from communists to military veteran groups to small *ad hoc* groups of men and women acting locally on their own.

Their activities ranged from theft of supplies, to publishing underground newspapers, to setting up clandestine radio stations for transmitting intelligence information to the Allies, to direct action, including sabotage and assassination.

Some groups were tightly disciplined, while others were loosely organized. Some cooperated with other groups to some degree, but usually they did *not* – for a variety of operational, security, and ideological reasons.

The phrase "herding cats" comes to mind when one thinks of efforts to coordinate groups from so many diverse backgrounds. The word "wildcats" comes to mind when thinking of the nature of the actions taken by some of these organizations.

In France, the term "la Résistance" was used, both as a generic term – as we use it in this book – and later in reference to the Conseil Nationale de la Résistance (National Council of the Resistance). It was finally formed in March 1944 as an umbrella coordinating group, but it never included all the resistance organizations.

Among the underground organizations which readers will meet in this book is Belgium's "White Brigade" (Brigade Blanche in French, or Witte Brigade in Flemish). Also known as the "White Army," it became active in aiding Allied airmen. It took its name as a sarcastic homage to the "Black Brigade," a paramilitary component of the pro-German Flemish National Union.

In France, one of the underground groups which caused the occupation and its collaborators continuous and nagging vexation was the colorful and loosely coordinated Maquis, which conducted widespread guerilla warfare, especially in the mountains and countryside of central and southern France. It took its name from the Corsican-Italian slang term for "bandits." Numbering as many as 40,000, the Maquisards were men and women from rural areas – as well as many who had transplanted themselves there from the cities, drawn to the colorful Robin Hood image of brigands of the forest. Most were young, and subject to conscription as slave laborers under the STO. And yes, to a large extent, they did imagine themselves as "bandits."

The Résistance groups, especially the Maquis, were given logistical support by the Allies in the form of air drops of supplies, especially of guns, ammunition, and explosives, as well as of radios. The British Special Operations Executive (SOE) was active in occupied Europe by 1941, but the United States Office of Strategic Services (OSS) was not on the ground in large numbers until 1944. Both SOE and OSS also inserted their own agents as radio operators and to provide technical training.

Despite the optimism of those in SOE or OSS command posts far from the action, the cats and wildcats of the Résistance were never fully herded, never fully merged or coordinated – either by De Gaulle and his committees, or by the Allies.

They and their families had been living under German rule since 1940. They had seen brutality beyond the pale of the Geneva Convention to

Comment on #849:

An increasing number of evaders are bound to fall in with the Maquisards, whose free ways, lack of discipline, and recklessness may be a shock to us. This story is a fair sample. Before condemning the Maquisards for a lot of brigands we must remember that for four years they have been hunted, tortured, and shot — which tends to break down notions of the sacredness of property. They are apt to treat ~~the~~ wealthy farmers and owners of chateaux as their ~~natural~~ enemies, as, indeed, is the case. ~~They are~~. But the Maquisards are on our side.

After debriefing Joel McPherson in July 1944, Captain Dorothy Smith of the US MIS penned this note cautioning USAAF airmen that the lawlessness of the Maquisards "may be a shock to us [but they] are on our side." (US National Archives) which armies of the signatories were *supposed* to subscribe. In short, the men and women of the underground, especially the Maquisards, saw the tactical situation in their own terms. They reacted and acted accordingly.

This is perhaps best summarized by the memorable words of Captain Dorothy Smith, one of the US Army Military Intelligence Service (MIS) officers charged with debriefing Eighth Air Force evaders upon their return to England.

In her memo of July 27, 1944, she wrote that an "increasing number of evaders are bound to fall in with the Maquisards, whose free ways, lack of discipline, and recklessness may be a shock to us. This story is a fair sample. Before condemning the Maquisards for a lot of brigands we must remember that for four years they have been hunted, tortured, and shot – which tends to break down notions of the sacredness of property. They are apt to treat wealthy farmers and owners of châteaux as their natural enemies, as, indeed, is the case. But the Maquisards are on our side."[1]

Chapter 3

Many Paths to Freedom

Throughout occupied Europe, within the underground organizations and among ordinary citizens, there was growing active support for the downed flyers. Without these people, and the risks they were willing to take, the escape and evasion of Allied airmen would have been far more difficult, or in most cases, impossible.

Just as organizations formed to resist and oppose the occupation, other organizations and escape networks formed specifically to support the evasion and escape of fugitive airmen.

As this book is the story of ones who got away, it is also the story of those who helped make this happen.

These stories include those of some of the hundreds of men – and at least as many women – who risked their lives to aid Allied airmen in occupied Europe during World War II. Their numbers included people from all trades, from nurses to doctors, from housewives to movie stars, from police officers to clergymen, from veterans of past wars to students. Despite living under the fear and privation of Nazi occupation themselves, they provided these strangers with food and shelter, as well as with medical aid and simple things such as civilian clothes that helped airmen conceal themselves from the common enemy.

As noted in Chapter 1, the goal for the airmen was to evade the Germans in occupied Europe and to escape from there, mainly across the Pyrenees into Spain.

The idea of an organized mechanism by which Allied airmen stranded in occupied Europe could be funneled through the Pyrenees escape hatch toward freedom germinated independently in separate places. As noted above, the escape line idea occurred spontaneously among civilians across occupied Europe, but it was also something that was being developed inside the British intelligence establishment.

The British Directorate of Military Intelligence – well known in popular culture for two still-active agencies, MI5 (domestic intelligence) and MI6 (foreign intelligence, aka the Security Intelligence Service, SIS) – had several other wartime "MI" organizations. One of these, formed in 1939, was MI9. It was a follow-on to a prewar idea to help escaping POWs. Under the leadership of Colonel (later Brigadier) Norman Crockatt, MI9 trained British personnel in the skills of escape from POW camps, but its mission evolved during the summer of 1940 to include aiding the escape of British troops who had missed the evacuation from Dunkirk, but who had managed to evade capture.

When the United States entered the war, MI9 personnel mentored the US Army Military Intelligence Service (MIS) in the formation of its similar MIS-X organization, which provided training and support in escape and evasion for United States Army Air Forces (USAAF) aircrewmen.

One of the most important people in MI9 was a man named Airey Neave. Commissioned into the Royal Engineers, he was deployed to France in early 1940 and was captured during the German onslaught. Imprisoned at Stalag XX-A, he escaped but was recaptured and sent to Oflag IV-C. Located in Colditz Castle, escape from this infamous prison was considered impossible. Nevertheless, Neave escaped from Colditz in 1941 and made his way back to Britain, where he was promptly recruited into MI9.

While Neave, who operated under the code name "Saturday," ran things from London, a young British diplomat named Michael Creswell took the name "Monday," and operated out of the British Embassy in Madrid. Creswell was the principal MI9 contact in Spain with the European escape organizations.

A colleague of Creswell's in Madrid was Donald Darling, whose code name was "Sunday." Darling had been recruited in 1940 by MI6, whose assistant chief, Colonel Claude Dansey, picked Darling because of his extensive knowledge of Spain and Portugal and because he spoke both these languages and French. Initially given a cover assignment as British vice consul in Lisbon, Darling went on to become one of the key players in getting Allied airmen from Spain into Gibraltar and back to Britain.

However, the most effective escape and evasion organizations were those that blossomed organically *inside* occupied Europe. They deliberately distanced themselves operationally from MI9 because their operatives were far better in tune with the reality on the ground, and better able to adapt to a constantly changing landscape. Gradually, MI9's role largely became one of supporting their activities logistically and financially – and taking charge of escapees once they had reached Spain.

While deferring much of the evasion assistance work to the indigenous lines, MI9 did operate some specialized escape routes of its own. The shortest means of transporting Allied airmen from France to Britain was directly, by sea or by air, but the German control of the coastline and airspace made this extremely hazardous. In 1943, Operation *Oaktree*, which attempted extractions from Brittany using Royal Navy high-speed motor gunboats (similar to US Navy PT Boats), failed due to German infiltration. Its evaders were then diverted to the lines across the Pyrenees. The idea was revisited in 1944 as the Shelburne Line, which succeeded in extracting a number of evaders.

Airborne extraction involved nighttime missions using the RAF's Westland Lysanders. These high-wing monoplanes had been designed as liaison aircraft, but were considered too big and too slow for the battlefield. However, their ability to land and take off on extremely short landing strips made them ideal for the kinds of clandestine operations inside occupied Europe undertaken by Britain's SOE, such as insertion and extraction of secret agents. Lysanders also did pick up a very small number of evading airmen (see Part Eight).

The indigenous escape lines were as complex and sinuous as creeping vines on a stone wall – which helped confuse the Germans and protect the escape networks. The two largest trunks among the sinews of these vines, and those best remembered in postwar folklore, were the Pat O'Leary Line (aka the Pat Line) and the Réseau Comète (Comet Line or Comet Network).

The Pat Line traced its origins to Lieutenant Ian Garrow, a British officer stranded in France in 1940, although after Garrow's arrest in October 1941 operations were taken over by Albert-Marie Guérisse, a Belgian army doctor who had escaped to Britain via the Dunkirk evacuation in 1940, but who went back to Europe under the auspices of British intelligence. Under the cover identity of Lieutenant Commander Patrick O'Leary of the Royal Navy, he used a faux French-Canadian pedigree to explain his accent. Despite the line's links to the British, it operated autonomously.

The Pat O'Leary Line generally funneled evaders from Belgium, the Netherlands, and northern France though its hub of safe houses in Paris before sending them south toward the Spanish border by train via Limoges and Toulouse for crossings in the central Pyrenees. These often passed through the land-locked independent Principality of Andorra. Other Pat Line routes ran farther east, reaching Marseille via Dijon or Lyon. From here, crossings into Spain took place through the eastern Pyrenees.

After Guérisse was betrayed by a traitor and arrested in January 1943, the activities of the Pat Line were assumed by one of its operatives, the unassuming Marie-Louise Dissard. A 62-year-old dressmaker and former local bureaucrat in Toulouse, she went by the *nom de guerre* "Madame Françoise." For this reason, the later incarnation of the Pat Line is often referred to as the "Françoise Line."

Madam Françoise lived with her cat in an apartment above her dress shop at 40 Rue de la Pomme in Toulouse, which she ran as a safe house for evaders. In turn, she coordinated a network of safe houses – including a suburban *château* – around Toulouse and across towns in southern France. These included Bergerac, where she relocated after her Toulouse apartment was compromised. She was dismissed by the Vichy French police as an eccentric, an image that she carefully crafted, and which probably saved her life.

A spin-off of the Pat Line was the Réseau Bourgogne (Burgundy Line), created by journalist Georges Broussine to pick up some of the pieces after Guérisse's arrest had compromised the Pat Line in early 1943.

The Comet Line, meanwhile, was the creation of a group of young Belgians led by 24-year-old Andrée "Dédée" de Jongh, the youngest daughter of elementary school principal Frédéric de Jongh, who called her *le petit cyclone*, a nickname that certainly described her. Belgian Lieutenant General Baron Albert Crahay, who later praised her in his postwar book *20 Héros de Chez Nous* (*20 Hometown Heroes*), wrote that "difficulties stimulated her."

Crahay told of her dramatic arrival at the British Consulate in Bilbao, Spain in August 1941. She informed Vice Consul Arthur Dean that she had just crossed the Pyrenees with two other Belgians who wanted to fight for the Allies, and a Scottish soldier who was an escaped POW. She added that they would be the first of many. She explained that there were British troops still hiding in Belgium and that she was setting up an escape line

THE ONES WHO GOT AWAY

to bring them out. All she wanted was for the British government to help with expenses.

A flabbergasted Dean insisted that she dare not risk her life again to repeat such an impossible trek.

"I am as strong as a man," she said, rolling her eyes, adding that she was a strong swimmer and hiker. "Girls attract less attention than men. My Basque guide will bring me back. If you help me, I can bring you other Englishmen."

The British were initially skeptical, even fearing that Dédée might be a German agent, but Michael Creswell drove up from Madrid, checked her out, and decided that she was genuine. Thus began the Comet Line.

One of Dédée's early associates was fellow Belgian Arnold Deppé, who had worked in the French town of Saint-Jean-de-Luz on the Bay of Biscay about eight miles from the Spanish border, and who had a sense of how to slip across undetected.

As with the Pat Line, the Comet Line used Paris as a hub, bringing evaders through there from Belgium and northern France. Joining in his daughter's enterprise, her father became the Comet coordinator in Paris, operating under the name "Monsieur Paul," or "Paul Moreau."

Among those who escorted evaders south from Paris were Dédée herself and fellow Belgian Jean-François Nothomb, aka "Franco." Dédée personally escorted more than 100 evaders between Paris and Spain before being captured by the Gestapo in 1943.

Among the Comet operatives were the members of the Dumon family of Brussels, Eugene and Marie (aka "Françoise"), and their two daughters – Andrée, aka "Nadine," and Micheline, whose *noms de guerre* included "Lily" and "Michou." All but Micheline were captured by the Germans, but she went on to become a legend. A 20-year-old nursing student when the rest of her family was arrested, Micheline immersed herself in the work of the Comet Line, from the train stations of Brussels to the safe houses of Paris to the mountain passes of the Pyrenees.

Some of Micheline's assets were her determination, her astute cleverness in reading people, and her youth. She was young, but she carried papers identifying her as only 16. Some people thought she looked as young as 12!

Whereas the Pat Line brought evaders south via routes in central or eastern France, Comet Line evaders traveled south through Bordeaux and Bayonne in the west. The final 20-mile leg of the Comet Line ran near the coast of the Bay of Biscay between Bayonne, France and the Spanish-Basque city of Irun on the border.

A Comet safe house was maintained in Anglet, on the edge of Bayonne, about eight miles from Saint-Jean-de-Luz, by Elvire de Greef, known as "Tante Go" ("Auntie Go"), who became an important figure in Comet Line activities. She and her husband Fernand were friends of Dédée's who had escaped from Belgium in 1940. When the Comet Line faltered after Dédée's arrest, Elvire de Greef and Micheline Dumon rebuilt it and kept it going.

Comet Line evaders typically traveled by train to the vicinity of Saint-Jean-de-Luz and made the rest of the journey on foot through the steep and arduous mountain passes. One of the most challenging obstacles here was the broad and turbulent Bidasoa River, which forms the international border in the western Pyrenees.

Because the routes across the western Pyrenees pass through the Basque country on both sides of the border, the Comet Line turned to the Basque *mugalari* ("border people") as guides. These guides, many of whom were smugglers familiar with these mountain trails, operated with great autonomy in their alpine domain. A favorite guide of Dédée's was Florentino Goikoetxea. A wanted man in both France and Spain at the time, he was much later awarded the French Légion d'Honneur (Legion of Honor decoration) for guiding 227 Allied airmen to safety.

Just as the escape lines maintained their operational independence from Allied secret services, they also distanced themselves from other underground and Résistance groups, never participating in sabotage or direct action against the Germans.

In contrast to the gun-toting Maquis, the motto of the Comet Line was *Pugna Quin Percutias* (Fight Without Arms).

PART TWO

RIDING THE TAIL OF A COMET

Chapter 4

Hounded Houndsmen

On October 16, 1942, 1st Lieutenant Paul Flickinger and his crew arrived at RAF Molesworth in Cambridgeshire with their B-17F, serial number 41-24585, to become part of the Eighth Air Force. The Eighth was still barely more than a work in progress. The organization that would one day be called "the Mighty Eighth" was, in effect, a mere "startup."

The Eighth had only just flown its first bombing mission – an attack on Luftwaffe airfields in the Netherlands – on July 4, 1942. To do so by Independence Day, the Eighth's 15th Bomb Squadron had to borrow a half dozen Lend-Leased Boston light bombers back from Britain's Royal Air Force (RAF). At least they used American-made aircraft.

The few B-17 Flying Fortresses that reached England during that July went to building up the 97th Bomb Group, which was to become the first operational heavy bomber unit within the Eighth. Launching a dozen Flying Fortresses, the 97th finally flew the Eighth's first heavy bomber mission against occupied Europe on August 17. The target was the Sotteville railroad yards near Rouen in northern France. Through August, the 92nd and 301st Bomb Groups took their place in the table of organization, and the 91st, 93rd, 303rd, 305th, and 306th followed in September.

The B-17 of Flickinger and crew was assigned to the 360th Bomb Squadron, 303rd Bomb Group – the "Hell's Angels." The crew named their aircraft *Wulfe Hound* (some references spell the name as *Wulf Hund* or similar variations), a moniker coined by Staff Sergeant Iva Lee Fegette, the flight engineer and radio operator. Then they painted a picture on the nose of an anthropomorphic Flying Fortress chewing on a German Focke-Wulf Fw 190 fighter.

On Saturday, December 12, 1942, *Wulfe Hound* took off from Molesworth at 10:30am, flying her sixth mission as one of 78 Flying Fortresses dispatched to strike a Luftwaffe depot at Romilly-sur-Seine, 70 miles southeast of Paris and 325 miles southeast of Molesworth.

Throughout the fall of 1942, as it was feeling its way into the new business of daylight precision bombardment, the Eighth confined itself to operations to targets in occupied France. These included transportation hubs, industrial sites being used by Germany, and the infamous U-Boat pens that the Germans built along France's Atlantic coastline. The first Eighth Air Force mission against a target inside Germany would not come until January 27, 1943.

By December 1942, a big factor in the success of precision bombing missions – and a huge frustration for Eighth Air Force planners – was the weather. If a target was blanketed with clouds and the bombardiers could not see the targets, there could be no precision strike.

Such was the case over Romilly-sur-Seine on December 12, so the bombers were ordered to divert to the secondary target – those railroad yards at Sotteville again. Between the weather and the Luftwaffe that day, only 17 bombers hit Sotteville.

On the flight deck of *Wulfe Hound*, Flickinger had gotten the abort message, but as he turned westward with the formation, the Luftwaffe pounced. Around 40 interceptors, Bf 109s and Fw 190s, piled on. Suddenly, it was the turn of the *Wulfe Hound* to be hounded by Focke-Wulfs.

The gunners in Flickinger's crew believed that they hit six of the attackers, but the Germans gave back for what they took. The bomber's number two and three engines were damaged. *Wulfe Hound* could no longer keep formation, so Flickinger dived to get into the clouds and escape, hoping to limp back to England on two engines.

As they dipped into the blanket of clouds at 8,000 feet, the number one engine began violently throwing off oil. Coming out beneath the clouds at 1,000 feet with one engine, Flickinger realized they were too low to bail out of the stricken bomber. He ordered everyone in the forward part of the aircraft to take cover in the radio compartment and brace for impact. The time was approximately 12:40pm.

"We made a crash landing and it was a beauty," recalled 2nd Lieutenant Gilbert Schowalter, the navigator, in his escape and evasion report.[2] "We all landed uninjured, happy and in a good frame of mind. We discussed how to dispose of the aircraft and could not find a way to do so. We discussed burning the plane, but did not have any incendiary bombs."

He and other crewmembers were very explicit in their later escape and evasion reports that they destroyed all the mission-related paperwork, and that they did likewise with radios and electronics. Schowalter specifically wrote that "the detonators went off on the IFF [Identification, Friend or Foe radio electronic] equipment."

Their Norden bombsight was presumably also thoroughly smashed, though it was not described in the reports. It remained so top secret that it went unmentioned even in official documents.

"About 15 French people came running up to us," recalled 2nd Lieutenant Jack Williams, *Wulfe Hound*'s copilot.[3] "They kissed and hugged us and told us to get away as soon as possible."

Sergeant Norman Therrien, the right waist gunner, could speak French, so he asked which way they should go. The consensus reply was "any direction but north." They had come down near the city of Melun, 60 miles due west of Romilly-sur-Seine, and 25 miles south of the center of Paris. The area to the north would be crawling with Germans.

The crewmen took off, running south toward the nearest wood. When they reached the cover of the trees, they stripped off their heavy flying gear and made a plan. Flickinger decided that they should split into pairs to be able to travel unobtrusively. The officers kept together in two of the pairs, the enlisted men in the other three. Flickinger was joined by 2nd Lieutenant Beverly Polk, the bombardier, while Schowalter and Williams joined forces.

Therrien and Sergeant Frederick Hartung, the ball turret gunner, paired off. The two sergeants had a lot in common. Both were both 23 years old, and both were from Massachusetts – Therrien from Haverhill, Hartung from Salem.

As the Massachusetts men made common cause, so too did a pair of Texans, 22-year-old Tech Sergeant Bill Whitman from Fort Worth and 24-year-old Sergeant Lee Fegette of McGregor, the man who had named *Wulf Hound*.

The two other sergeants, Kenneth Kurtenbach, the tail gunner, and waist gunner George Dillard, were not actually part of the *Wulfe Hound* crew. They were just filling in that day. Both men had arrived at Molesworth as replacements in October and had flown just two missions – aboard *Yardbird* of the 360th Squadron.

After a sober shaking of hands all around, the men of *Wulfe Hound* departed in opposite directions. Flickinger and Polk faired poorly, being captured within hours and sent eventually to Stalag Luft II.

As Therrien and Hartung recalled in their escape and evasion reports, they decided to walk due south, crossing a field and hiding out in a thick wood until after dark before they continued.[4] At about 8:00pm, they cautiously knocked on the door of a French farmhouse. When French-speaking Therrien explained that they were downed airmen looking for help, the family offered them food and assured them that there were no Germans in the immediate vicinity. With this, the Americans relaxed. They learned that they were near the small town of Villeneuve-les-Bordes, east of Melun, and that there was a *château* nearby at which they might seek shelter.

After about two hours with their benefactors, Therrien and Hartung continued their journey. Soon, in the distance, they saw the large *château*, probably Château des Bordes l'Abbé, which is today a luxury hotel, spa and golf club located on a 4,000-acre deer hunting property.

The people then living at the huge estate took them in, offering them a meal and a place to sleep. The two men remained here in these comfortable surroundings for four nights, spending their days in the attic and sleeping in the barn.

As they became acclimated to their new reality in occupied France, the two Massachusetts men began discussing their next moves with their gracious hosts. The object, of course, was to get to Spain and then to Gibraltar, and because they had money in their survival kits, they would be able to take the train. They were told that this would involve taking a local into Paris, then transferring to a through train toward Bordeaux and points south.

Appearing uneasy about exposing themselves in public in a land where the Gestapo lurked, they were told not to worry. They would have a guide. Living at the *château* was the 18-year-old nephew of the owners, who was himself in a precarious position. Hanging over his head was France's abhorrent STO program that was conscripting men of his age to work in German factories.

The people at the *château*, who naturally wanted their nephew to escape the long arm of the STO, asked the Americans to take the boy with them, suggesting that he would be useful. They agreed. On the morning of Wednesday, December 15, with the Massachusetts men of *Wulfe Hound* having been madeover in civilian attire, the three walked five miles north to Mangis, where they caught the train into Paris.

On the afternoon of December 12, having parted company with the other *Wulfe Hound* airmen, 25-year-old Lieutenant Gilbert Schowalter of Milwaukee and 23-year-old Lieutenant Jack Williams of Highland Park, Michigan headed into the nearest woods. Eventually they emerged into an opening where they dashed across a main highway and a parallel railroad. They continued westward along a stream and entered a deep forest.

Copilot Williams had been a military flyer for a year and a half, but his career had not started in the USAAF. Before the United States entered the war, he had quit his job as a tool and die maker to do as many young Americans had done – to go north to join the Royal Canadian Air Force (RCAF). In July 1942, after a year in the RCAF, he came home to join the USAAF. Showalter had been a college student when he enlisted in May 1942.

As they hiked, they heard the sounds of people and feared a German search party – but the voices they heard turned out to be Bill Whitman and Lee Fegette. Having once again picked opposite directions, Schowalter and Williams crossed another stream and headed back into the trees.

A while later, they heard the thunder of a pair of BMW motorcycles on the nearby highway. Flattening themselves into the ground, they watched as the German riders raced past in the direction of *Wulf Hound*'s crash site.

By 10:00pm Saturday evening, Schowalter and Williams had been in occupied Europe for less than 12 hours, but the exhaustion of the day, and fast walking through rugged terrain, had finally gotten to them. They stumbled into a farmyard, where the buildings seemed deserted. Schowalter used his survival kit flashlight to check the house. Nobody had been there for some time, but the airmen decided to bed down in the barn – just in case.

Having slept soundly until Sunday morning, they decided to stay put until it started to get dark. Throughout the day, they kept their eyes on another farmhouse about 500 yards in the distance. As they watched people coming and going, they decided that if they were going to make contact with civilians with the hope of connecting with the Résistance, this would be their opportunity.

"We knocked on the door and told them we were American flyers," Williams recalled, telling of a conversation that unfolded in sign language. Neither the Americans nor the French spoke the other's language.

"We walked in on the people who had just finished eating," Schowalter added. "There were five grown people and two children... One large man just looked [at us] and then came up and said he was Swiss. He made a great fuss over me. I showed him the [brass 'US' insignia] on my clothes and the man showed us all around the room."

"They told us to come in and sit down and have something to eat," Williams continued. "We had wine, meat and bread."

"They offered us their bed," Schowalter remembered. "But we said we would rather sleep in the barn. After much argument, we took the bed... After we had slept for a few hours, we were awakened. They said to come down and we would have to leave. They gave us food and we left with the large man and two other men."

By daybreak on Monday, December 14, the five had crept quietly through several small towns and past a large German military camp. At last, they stopped into the home of a couple named Garney. The wife spoke English and offered the travelers some red wine. She even uncorked a bottle of champagne.

Thus fortified, the Americans walked to the edge of Mormant, where they were introduced to an English-speaking former French army officer named Louis Lyon, who gave them a place to sleep and some civilian clothes. As Schowalter and Williams were finishing their breakfast on Tuesday morning, Lyon promised that someone would be coming who could help them.

At about 9:00pm that evening, after a long day of waiting and wondering, a man named George Reuter arrived in a truck to take them to the farm of a Monsieur Wall about seven or eight miles out into the country. As Williams wrote, "we stayed at this farm about three days [Schowalter says two], during which time they took very good care of us."

On the afternoon of Wednesday, December 16, by Schowalter's reckoning, Monsieur Lyon returned to the farm to take photographs of the two men for use in false identity cards.

The next day, Schowalter paid Reuter from his survival kit to buy rail tickets to Paris and points south for their escape to Spain. Schowalter noted that he "did not receive any change from the 2,000 Francs," adding that

"I told Mr. Lyon to speak with Reuter about the money and split it between themselves for the many, many favors they did for me."

Clearly, he underestimated how far they still had to go.

Late on Thursday, when the Americans sat down to share a few glasses of wine with Reuter while waiting for their train, it was almost one too many. Schowalter recalled that "we waited so long that we had to run to catch our train. We got into a carriage with about six other people and pretended to sleep."

Arriving in Paris after a rail journey of about 45 miles, Schowalter and Williams were taken to a church, where they were met by Monsieur Lyon, who had gone ahead to make arrangements. With this hand-off having been made, Reuter bade them *adieu* and slipped out of the church. They never saw him again. One hopes that he had picked up the bar tab.

Accompanied by a former captain who had been his superior when he was in the army, Lyon took Schowalter and Williams to the apartment of a woman whose nephew was, like Lyon, a former army officer. They arrived at around 8:00pm, just in time for dinner, at which they were joined by a young woman who had attended college in England. She spoke fluent English and was pleased to have a conversation with Americans who had been stationed in England.

The next day, Schowalter and Williams moved on to the home of yet another former French captain, where they stayed until Saturday, while, as Schowalter wrote, "the two captains and Lyon tried to find a method for our escape." By now, forged identity cards had been finished and were delivered.

As both Schowalter and Williams noted later, the two men were lucky to have a number of very determined people helping them. The apparatus to aid in the evasion of downed airmen was already a well-oiled machine.

Chapter 5

Christmas in Limbo

On Sunday, December 20, as he walked the streets of Paris, Gilbert Schowalter had a reminder of his former life with the Eighth Air Force. Had it been only eight days since he had heard the snarl of Wright Cyclone engines? It seemed longer.

He glanced up as his ears caught the unmistakable sound of "B-17s approaching Paris on their way to London [after a raid on German targets]. The people become very jovial and excited every time the Allied Air Forces come over their country."

He had no way of knowing what their target might have been, but today was the "make-up" mission for *Wulfe Hound*'s own of eight days before – the Luftwaffe depot at Romilly-sur-Seine, southeast of Paris. Sixty Flying Fortresses and a dozen B-24 Liberators had just put 167 tons of high explosives on the target.

Among the Flying Fortresses that Schowalter heard rumbling overhead was *Rose O'Day*, a B-17F piloted by 28-year-old, Philadelphia-born former pro football player John R. "Johnny" McKee. He had been a star catcher on the Villanova University baseball team a decade earlier, and later had a short career in the Canadian Football League. By the time that he enlisted early in 1942, though, McKee was living in Barrington, New Jersey and working in a shipyard.

After he finished flight school, McKee was assigned to command the aircraft that became *Rose O'Day* at Westover Field in Utah in August 1942. He and his crew had come overseas to Thurleigh in Bedfordshire in October and were assigned to the 367th Bomb Squadron, 306th Bomb Group, the "Reich Wreckers."

Today, though, as on December 12, the group was nowhere near the Reich and the wrecking was being done *to* the Americans. There were worse days yet to come – much worse days – but today, the Eighth Air Force suffered its worst losses yet. The flak and fighters over the target were vicious. Aboard *Rose O'Day*, Sergeant Carl Warheit in the ball turret took the worst of it and was killed. Over the intercom, the waist gunner, Staff Sergeant Darwin Wissenbach, reported that the tail gunner, Staff Sergeant Helmuth Roeder, had also been shot.

Before the formation reached relative safety with the escort fighters over the English Channel, 31 bombers were badly damaged. Six went down and one of those was Johnny McKee's *Rose O'Day*. They were north of Paris and passing through 15,000 feet when McKee sounded the bail-out alarm. He recalled waiting two minutes after the last survivor had left the aircraft before he jumped himself.

He came down in a plowed field just outside Creil, a tiny village of about a dozen buildings located 50 miles northeast of the French capital. More than a dozen women who had been working in the field gathered around to have a look at the American airman who drifted out of the sky. Using hand gestures, they told him that they had seen eight parachutes. This was good news, because *Rose O'Day* was flying with a crew of nine. Other than Warheit, whom McKee knew to be a fatality, everyone had at least escaped from the stricken aircraft.

As he later recalled, the women looked him over and went back to work as McKee buried his parachute and started walking west.[5] He came to a river, found a boat with which to get across, and continued on his way, avoiding houses and other buildings that he saw, until about a half hour past sunset, when he came to a substantial bridge across another river.

In the gathering dusk, he had not noticed at first that the bridge was being guarded by a lone German sentry. McKee froze.

Captured already, after just a few miles?

McKee swallowed hard and tried to think what to do.

Take off running?

Certainly not! That was an invitation to get himself shot.

The most unobtrusive thing to do was to make a right angle turn and amble away slowly. When he had gone about 600 yards, he glanced back at the German. To McKee's fright, the man had raised his rifle.

"He drew a bead on me, but for some reason, did not fire," McKee recalled.

Partly shielded by the ravine, he crouched down in the grass, watching and waiting. At last, the German lowered his weapon and walked away. As soon as his back was turned, McKee was on the run. After about two miles, McKee came to another river, where he met a Frenchman calmly fishing in the twilight.

Using sign language, McKee explained that he was an airman and asked for help. The man nodded. He would help him, but this would necessitate taking a road where more German sentries were posted. The man looked him over, and because it was hard to mistake him as an Allied airman, the man gave McKee his overcoat, let him carry the fishing pole and tackle, and told him to keep his head down as they passed the Germans.

After about two miles, the two men arrived at a small tavern, where McKee was given something to eat and a glass of wine. It seemed that the crash of the *Rose O'Day* had been the talk of the afternoon in the area. The man who owned the bar had been out a few hours earlier and had passed the local German barracks. There, he had learned that, like the women in the field, the Germans had counted eight parachutes. One of the eight men was dead when he was found, and the Germans had rounded up and captured six of McKee's fellow crewmen. This left one unaccounted for – McKee himself.

It was decided among his new friends that McKee should get some rest and resume his travels before German patrols resumed their search at dawn.

McKee traded his leather A-2 flying jacket for a raincoat and a beret, put on a pair of coveralls, and lay down to catch some sleep. It was about 10:30pm when the innkeeper woke him up, led him through the darkness to another river, rowed him across and bade him farewell. McKee was advised to make his way to Paris, where he could contact someone who could get him out of France, although in his escape and evasion report he gave no details of where in Paris he had been told to go.

Having crossed the river, McKee walked until about 2:00am, when he crawled into a haystack and fell asleep until dawn on Monday, December 21. He then walked south until he came to a fork in the road. He tried to ask a passerby which fork led to Paris, but he couldn't understand what he was trying to say with his elaborate hand gestures. The man did share some bread and wine before he departed.

Some time later, an old man appeared.

"He stood looking at me for about three minutes," McKee explained in his escape and evasion report. "Then he said to follow him. He took me to the home of a relative of his who had helped an RAF man four weeks previously. This RAF man had broken his leg."

Later in the afternoon, the mayor of the town, possibly Montfermeil, 25 miles south of Creil, arrived at McKee's safe house to see the American. He spoke English well and was able to assure McKee that he was "in good hands and would be helped."

As it was Christmas week, the promised help was not immediately forthcoming, so McKee remained for six days, enjoying Christmas dinner with his new friends.

During those six days, McKee went to visit the RAF man, who was possibly Sergeant William Greaves of No. 142 Squadron whose Vickers Wellington went down on the night of November 20–21, and whose own story generally coincides with McKee's.

In any case, the RAF man whom McKee met was by now nearly recovered from his broken leg. McKee explained that the topic of escaping occupied France dominated their conversation, adding that "the RAF chap was making plans to get back to England some way, either by submarine or airplane."

According to McKee, the two men "decided, after much discussion, that if these people did not move us within two weeks we would start out on our own."

Back on Sunday, December 20, the day that McKee was shot down, Gilbert Schowalter and Jack Williams were biding their time in a Paris apartment, listening to American bombers high overhead and waiting for Monsieur Lyon and Madame Garney to take care of forging their identity papers.

Late that afternoon, as McKee was 50 miles to the north staring down the barrel of a Mauser at 600 yards, there was a knock at the door of the apartment. Schowalter opened the door to a serious-looking man and woman, who identified themselves as being "from the old French intelligence service [the Deuxième Bureau, which was dissolved officially after France's defeat in 1940] and they asked us to give them any message that we wanted to be sent back to England [by radio]."

Schowalter said that he wanted his boss, Colonel James Wallace, commander of the 303rd Bomb Group, to know that all of the men from *Wulfe Hound* had survived.

The woman then took Schowalter and Williams to an abandoned apartment at 63 Rue du Ranelagh in the 16th Arrondissement, where, as Schowalter explained, they "spent several days; in fact we spent Christmas there... [we] met a Mr. and Mrs. Ted Clapson while we were there. They were British and did many favors for us... We were furnished an excellent Christmas dinner, consisting of champagne, chicken, eggs, and we were also given scarves and ties. One night, several days later, the [Deuxième Bureau] lady who had taken us there came back and said she had good news and we were soon to leave [for the Spanish border]."

On the evening of December 28, the two airmen were "turned over to the Belgian organization" in whose care they would remain for the remainder of their time in France. Having walked about two miles across Paris to the home of Madeline Noel, they were met by two "Belgian" operatives, whom Schowalter later identified as "Dedi and Franco."

Of course, the "Belgian organization" was the Comet Line, "Dedi" was Dédée de Jongh, and "Franco" was the code name of her associate, Jean-François Nothomb. Like the two Americans, Dédée and Franco were young people engaged in a very serious and potentially deadly business. All four were between the ages of 23 and 26.

Williams recalled Dédée and Franco as being much more suspicious of them than were the French Résistance people with whom they had interacted earlier. Indeed, at this very moment the Gestapo was working hard to infiltrate and compromise the Comet Line, and the utmost care was warranted. Dédée asked many questions, for instance wanting to know from where in the States they were from. Williams added that this conversation lasted until Madame Noel got home from work, whereupon the mood changed and they "had tea, a bath, and shared drinks."

When they awoke the following morning, Dédée and Franco were there to take Schowalter and Williams to a railway station photo booth to take headshots for a second set of false identification papers. For security reasons, they split up, with Franco taking Schowalter, and Dédée taking Williams. This project completed, the young Belgians dropped both airmen off at the home of a Madame de Serbonne and told them that they'd be back in "a couple of days."

Chapter 6

Undocumented Fools At Large

On Sunday, December 20, 1942, as John McKee of *Rose O'Day* was first getting his feet wet in French soil, and as Schowalter and Williams of *Wulfe Hound* were still waiting to travel into Paris from the countryside, two of their mates from the *Wulfe Hound* crew were already in the Pyrenees!

Norman Therrien and Fred Hartung were attending Mass at the Église Saint-Hilaire in the French village of Miglos. Located at an elevation of nearly a mile, the village is only about a dozen miles from the Spanish border – as the Pyrenees lammergeier vulture flies – but by mountain road, the distance is six times that.

How was it that the two Massachusetts sergeants had made it all the way here when the two *Wulfe Hound* officers had not yet even made it to Paris?

Perhaps it was the advice of the nephew from the *château* near Villeneuve-les-Bordes, whose incentive to run from a future behind German barbed wire was as strong as that of the Americans.

Mostly, though, it was the incredibly good luck of three men who did not know what they were doing. They had no idea how naive they were, and how dangerous their circumstances were about to become.

The trio had arrived in Paris by train around the middle of the day on Wednesday, December 16. The nephew suggested that they travel south by way of Tours and Bordeaux. He had been on this route before, so he knew the way – though he had not made the journey since the occupation. He was apparently oblivious to the fact that everyone needed identification papers, or that the Gestapo and the French police made routine checks aboard the trains.

Neither of the Americans had papers, or any identification beyond his GI dog tags, which were a fast track to a cell. The nephew had papers, but they showed him to be of an age that made him a candidate for immediate STO conscription. Had they been in the hands of the Comet Line or the Pat Line, they would have been with people who could have forged papers for them and told them what to do, but the trio were on their own, and making it up as they went.

Arriving at the Gare d'Austerlitz rail station in Paris, they discovered that the next through train to Tours was not until 5:45pm. Instead of hanging around the train station for several hours attracting attention, they decided to spend the afternoon in a darkened movie theater where they would not be seen. No mention was made in their later escape and evasion reports of which film they watched.

Traveling on third class tickets, they reached Tours about an hour before the curfew. Fortunately, there were no identification checks aboard the train or in Tours.

On the street, they stopped a man and asked him where vagabonds such as themselves might find a place to spend the night. The woman at the place where he directed them had food to offer, but nowhere for them to stay.

She was fearful of both the Gestapo and the French police, but she did know that there was a train leaving for Bordeaux at 1:30am. The fugitives had not even bothered to look at the departure board when they arrived at the station earlier.

They had tickets in hand by curfew time at 11:00pm, and since waiting for a train was not considered a curfew violation, they were not bothered at the station.

Despite his inexperience with wartime evasion, the nephew had good instincts. He had proven it with the darkened movie theater, and he did so again as they approached Bordeaux. The city was located in the coastal "Zone Militaire," heavily controlled by the Germans, so the nephew decided that they should not take a chance of being caught in that area, especially while on the train. He decided that they would get off the train in Libourne, about 30 miles short of Bordeaux, and make their way eastward.

By 7:40am on Thursday morning, they were on a train to Périgueux and feeling pretty good about themselves. However, they failed to take into account the demarcation line between the Zone Militaire and the part of France which had been nominally under Vichy control until a month earlier. The Germans had extended their occupation into all of France after the Americans landed in North Africa in November 1942, but the earlier internal checkpoints remained.

As Therrien recalled, just as they were starting to relax, "a Frenchman who was riding in our compartment must have seen though our disguises, for he told us that the Germans were checking all passengers through Montpon [25 miles from Libourne] which was on the line of demarcation. We went to the rear of the train, jumped off and started to walk in a semi-circle so as to cross the line and find another railway station. We walked for some time and finally arrived in Beaupouyet [eight road miles east of Montpon]. This was about 3:30pm."

They decided simply to approach the station master, tell him who they were and what they wanted to do – hoping that he would not turn them in. He didn't.

"He said he would sell us tickets to Foix [150 miles to the south] and from there, we could walk across into Spain," Therrien continued. "About 4:30 that afternoon, two French gendarmes asked us for our identification papers. Not having any, we had to tell them who we were and what we were trying to do. They let us go and told us to hide in the woods until train time. Our train left at 8:15pm."

It was not an easy ride. As Therrien recalled, they found themselves "in a compartment with two French gendarmes and a German officer and felt they knew who we were. As it turned out, they apparently did not… [They] left the train."

They arrived in Périgueux late on Thursday, December 17, tired and hungry – they had not gotten anything to eat since Tours – and feeling scuffed up from having jumped off the back of a moving train.

It was here that the young French nephew told them that he'd had enough of this adventure. Never mind everything else, the tension and fear overhanging the whole enterprise had been unbearable. It was like living inside an espionage thriller. The boy couldn't take it any longer.

"He thought, and so did I, that we were going to be caught," Therrien admitted. We are left to wonder what the nephew did next. It is likely that he continued his journey toward the Spanish border, probably relieved not to be encumbered by the two awkward Americans. It was his goal, after all, to get out of France to escape the STO.

After traveling through the night, the two sergeants rolled into Toulouse at 8:30am on Friday, December 18. They had several hours to kill before their train left for Foix, so they went to a barber shop to get a shave. As Hartung could not speak French, he "played the part of a deaf and dumb man."

When they tried to buy food, they discovered that ration cards were necessary for nearly everything, so they wound up with a package of barely edible cookies.

Leaving Toulouse just after noon, they were in Foix, with the snow-capped Pyrenees in the distance, by 3:00pm. They began walking south, as the Beaupouyet station master had recommended.

In Ferrières, they stopped at a house to ask for food, and were invited to dinner. As they were eating, the conversation naturally led to their being asked who they were and what they were doing.

As Therrien later related, he was in the midst of his usual explanation, when the "man of the house told us he was a German."

Both the conversation and the American heartbeats came abruptly to a halt.

It was one of those "pin drop" moments that had seemed to be haunting Therrien and Hartung with some regularity.

"We asked him what he was going to do," Therrien recalled, looking back at all of the visions of barbed wire, bludgeons and bullets that ran though his mind at that moment in the Pyrenees foothills.

One can imagine the sigh of relief when the man continued his reply. As Therrien wrote, "he was a German refugee. He had been chased out of Germany by Hitler because he was a politician. He fed us well and gave me a map, which turned out to be very useful."

After spending the night as guests of the former German politician, Therrien and Hartung were on their way into the mountains at 9:00am on the morning of Saturday, December 19. By 3:00pm that afternoon, they were passing through the mountain village of Capoulet, when they were abruptly stopped by a gendarme.

When he learned that they had no papers, he could have arrested them on the spot, but he did not. As Therrien wrote, he told them to "go back and think out some answer to our problem. We turned back and decided to seek the counsel of a priest."

Again, as in Beaupouyet the day before, their luck was with them. Maybe it was the Christmas spirit or his not wanting to wade into the paperwork that an arrest would require. Perhaps he felt a tinge of pity for these hapless, undocumented fools.

They had noticed the church in Miglos – the spire is impossible to miss if you are hiking through these mountains – so they went back there. The priest claimed that he knew of no mountain guide who could get them across, but he did give them some bread and fruit, and a place to sleep in the parish barn.

This is how Norman Therrien and Fred Hartung happened to be attending Mass at Église Saint-Hilaire in Miglos on Sunday, December 20. And it was at that service that they met a French family who took them in, fed them and gave them a place to sleep on their second night in Miglos. As Therrien recalled, when word got out that they were there, "almost everyone in the village came out and brought us food and wine."

Arguably even more important was that over glasses of Pyrenees cabernet and slices of cheese and cured meats, they had the benefit of volumes of local experience with hiking the mountain passes between Miglos and Spain. Actually, as they learned, the mountain trail from Miglos ran not to Spain, but to the 181-square mile neutral microstate of Andorra. This tiny land, which today is known to the outside world as little more than the answer to a trivia question, was known during World War II as a hub of smugglers and refugees doing as the *Wulfe Hound* sergeants planned to do – to escape from occupied Europe.

The distance from Miglos to La Serrat (El Serrat) in Andorra is only around 25 miles, but they were – and remain – arduous and challenging miles, especially in the dead of winter.

There was no road to Andorra. Indeed, the winding mountain road through Miglos ended – and still ends – just four miles away, at the village of Siguer. From here, the narrow alpine trail to Andorra leads up into the Pyrenees, along a windswept slope, with the 8,153-foot Redouneilles Peak to the west and the ice-covered lake Étang de Peyregrand below to the east. Modern mountaineering guides note an elevation gain of 5,246 feet between the trailhead at Siguer and the lake overlook. Today, this seven-mile segment of the trail is a popular, but strenuous, hiking experience that takes about four hours – in the summer.

Those of us who enjoy such alpine hikes make them without the most serious challenge faced by Therrien and Hartung. As the route was being described to them, they were cautioned that there was a large German garrison in Siguer, so it was imperative that they sneak through that town in the predawn darkness.

They left Miglos at 3:00am on Monday, December 21 with this in mind, and were on the trail in the Monday morning shadows.

Again, as on Thursday aboard the train to Périgueux, the two sergeants had just begun to relax with illusions of momentary respite from human obstacles, when suddenly, they rounded a bend and found themselves facing a pair of heavily armed French gendarmes, who ordered them to halt.

Unlike Thursday, there would be no jumping off the back of a train to escape. There was only the 1,500-foot drop down the steep cliff into the icy waters of Étang de Peyregrand. They were cornered – literally between the rocky slope of Redouneilles Peak to their right, and a very hard place at the bottom of the cliff on their left.

As he had done many times over the previous week, Therrien tried to talk their way out of a jam.

No, they had no papers – real or forged. They were Americans trying to reach Spain. As the conversation progressed, it began to seem that fugitive airmen were not high on the list of concerns for these gendarmes. They were hunting the smugglers who routinely used this route. Finally, they asked whether these two disheveled young men in French civilian clothes could *prove* that they were Americans.

No, they had had long since gotten rid of their American identification, as it could be a liability while traveling in occupied France. Sadly, the handcuffs came out, and the pall of a jail cell in their immediate future came over Therrien and Hartung.

Suddenly, though, Therrien thought of something!

He pulled out his pocket comb and handed it to one of the gendarmes, pointing out the "US Army" stamped on it.

Four men on a mountain trail breathed a sigh of relief. There may even have been a smile exchanged.

The Frenchmen calmly warned them that a German patrol went out on this trail each morning at around 7:00am, so they should make haste. With this, the gendarmes turned and continued back down the mountain toward Siguer.

The steepness of the trail increased as Therrien and Hartung climbed south toward Andorra. The snow was much deeper here, and the men got lost a couple of times trying to follow the trail. By the time they reached the summit, the snow was waist deep, and they were cold and wet.

They stopped here to catch their breath.

As Therrien wrote, they "were debating whether or not to go on when we discovered that we were standing next to a frontier marker, which was mostly covered by snow."

It was around noon on Monday, December 21. After nine harrowing days, and a dozen close calls, the two sergeants had just stepped out of occupied Europe!

Norman Therrien and Fred Hartung of *Wulfe Hound* reached La Serrat, Andorra on the afternoon of Monday, December 21, but finding the populace "not very friendly," they walked another two miles south to Llorts. Having found a generous family who gave them food and allowed them to dry their wet clothes, they walked another two miles to the village La Cortinada, where they checked into a hotel.

They still had 1,650 French francs, which the hotel changed into about 100 Spanish pesetas. It was a buyer's market for the hotel clerk, as the franc had in fact collapsed since the occupation in 1940, when this sum would have bought nearly 400 pesetas.

That evening at about 8:00pm, as the sergeants were trying to get some rest after their long day in the Pyrenees, there was a loud commotion in the hallway at the hotel. The Andorra police had burst into one of the rooms and were dragging two men out and down the stairs.

When Therrien asked someone what was going on, he was told that the men were "*contrabandistas*," or smugglers. In a country whose underground economy thrived on smuggling, their offense must have been more serious than the usual misdemeanor, and probably involved failure to make a payoff to someone.

Unfortunately, the police noticed the two Americans and began to question them. When Therrien gave them his practiced but truthful explanation, he was told that he and Hartung had to be out of the country by morning or the police would be back to take them into custody.

The two Massachusetts sergeants took this to heart, and by 2:30am on Tuesday, December 22, they were lying in a field near the border crossing at Sant Julià de Lòria. The frontier was heavily guarded, but by crawling through the field, they managed to get around the Spanish guard post and they were soon on their way to the Spanish city of Seo de Urgel, about six miles south of the border.

They were finally in Spain, and despite their exhaustion after hiking more than 30 miles through impossible terrain with no sleep for more than 24 hours, they were pleased with themselves.

But their luck had run out.

As they walked into Seo de Urgel on Avenguda de les Valls d'Andorra, they were stopped by two members of the dreaded Guardia Civil, whose reputation was of a police force that was anything but civil.

When they were asked for their papers, Therrien's attempted explanation, in French and English, got them nowhere with his Spanish audience.

This time, when the handcuffs came out, there was no sympathy for men who claimed without proof to be American.

After all they had faced, and all they had surmounted – through luck and initiative – Norman Therrien and Fred Hartung were about to spend Christmas 1942 swatting fleas in a dirty Spanish jail cell.

A week later, as their fellow *Wulfe Hound* crewmembers Schowalter and Walters were welcoming 1943 in Paris, Therrien and Hartung were staring hopelessly at the start of the new year through iron bars.

Chapter 7

A Menacing New Year

On Thursday, December 31, 1942, Gilbert Schowalter and Jack Williams of *Wulfe Hound* were quietly awaiting the new year in the Paris apartment of Madame Madeline Noel when Dédée de Jongh and Jean-François "Franco" Nothomb suddenly reappeared.

When the two Comet Line leaders had left the apartment on Monday, they had promised to be back in "a couple of days," and here they were – and they were bearers of good tidings. The forged papers for the two Americans were all in order, railway tickets were in hand, and as it was New Year's Eve, a celebration seemed to be in order.

Dédée had decided that they should mark the turn of the year by celebrating with dinner at a nearby cafe. They were joined by Dédée's parents, who were introduced as "Monsieur and Madame Paul," but who were actually Frédéric de Jongh and Alice Decarpentrie de Jongh of the Comet organization.

The Americans and the Belgians toasted the promise of 1943 with guarded optimism that they knew to be unrealistic, but hope springs eternal. They expressed some of that optimism for the dash to Spain that was about to begin. They toasted the recent American landings in French North Africa – Morocco and Algeria – which had occurred six weeks earlier, and smiled at how much this had perplexed the increasingly pessimistic Germans occupying France itself.

Schowalter would later comment on his impressions of the Germans whom he saw on the street in Paris, writing that "I was very much impressed by their slovenly attitude, and the shabbiness of the Germans' clothing... Their clothes were dirty and ragged and seemed to be very inadequate.

The soldiers all seemed to be very tired and worn out and their facial expressions are far from being happy… German soldiers realize that they are taking a beating [in North Africa, Russia, and from the skies over Germany itself] and admit it."

Williams added that he had "received the impression that enemy morale was bad. They feared American production and also the French people." He recalled speaking with civilians who had "witnessed the killing of numerous German soldiers by German officers for refusal to go to the Russian front."

Discussing how easy it had been for him and Schowalter to come and go – and even to dine out – in occupied Paris, Williams later said that Dédée and Franco "took us on a lot of sightseeing trips around Paris." Schowalter added that "the Germans certainly are not good detectives and the Gestapo is not made up of the super-men I thought they were."

The group finished their dinner before the bells of Notre Dame stuck midnight, and Franco and Dédée took the two Americans to the Gare d'Austerlitz, where they met Johnny McKee of *Rose O'Day*.

Two days before, as Schowalter and Williams were being "turned over to the Belgian organization" in Paris, a man from the same Comet Line organization had knocked on the door of the safe house north of Paris where McKee had spent the Christmas holiday weekend. Showing the same manner of suspicion that Schowalter and Williams were experiencing, he asked questions aimed at vetting McKee's authenticity. When the man was satisfied, he bundled McKee into his car and drove him into Paris.

With Franco as their escort, Schowalter, Williams, and McKee boarded a train before midnight, and were on their way toward Bayonne as the new year began.

At about 3:00am on Friday, January 1, while they were still aboard the train, Schowalter and Williams had their first frightening close-quarters run-in since the day their Flying Fortress went down. A French police inspector had decided to conduct an identity card check of the passengers.

There was no place to run, and no place to hide.

"It looked to me as if they had a tip about someone being on the train," Williams said. "But our cards were in order so he just went about his business." McKee later noted that the cop "seemed to have a very good idea as to who we actually were, but passed us without any comment."

On the morning of the first day of 1943, after a journey of nearly 500 miles, Franco and the three Americans arrived in Bayonne and were met by two women, one of whom was probably Elvire de Greef, Comet's "Auntie Go." The women took them to a cafe for lunch, and then to separate safe houses, where the exhausted men, who had been up all night, each fell asleep.

That evening, Auntie Go and her colleague took the Americans back to the train station, where they boarded a train to Saint-Jean-de-Luz, 16 miles from Bayonne.

A little more than a week earlier, Norman Therrien and Fred Hartung of *Wulfe Hound*, who had been making things up on their own, had approached the Spanish border through Toulouse and Foix, farther east, but the Comet route was a much more direct path from Paris.

McKee recalled that in Saint-Jean the three Americans were met by a man and two women, with whom they "walked from the station to the outskirts of the town, where we picked up a guide and he took us to a farmhouse in the foothills of the Pyrenees. He gave us a good meal as about 9:00pm we started to cross the mountains. It was very tough going all the way. About 2:00am, we arrived at a farmhouse, where we rested for about a half-hour and had some wine."

Assuming they followed the usual Comet route, the first of these farmhouses would have been in the small French Basque village of Urrugne, and the latter was probably Frantxia Usandizanga, a Basque woman well known for hosting evading airmen at her home.

Further details of the crossing by Schowalter, Williams, and McKee are muddled. Though other elements of their escape and evasion reports imply that they had all remained together, the accounts of the hike across the mountains differ, and none mention crossing the Bidasoa River that marked the border.[6]

McKee wrote that, despite the "tough going," they "continued on and arrived at our destination, which turned out to be a small village about 10 miles east of San Sebastian, at about 1:30pm," with the implication that this was on January 2 or January 3 at the latest.

Schowalter and Williams agree that their mountain guide, who was supposed to take them into Spain, abandoned them on the "first day," and that they did not reach any point near San Sebastian for five nights. In any case, with heavy winter snow on the trails, it would have been "tough going" indeed.

And they were lucky. Less than two weeks later, when Dédée herself brought three British airmen on this same route, things did not go well. On January 14, they departed from Frantxia Usandizanga's house, headed for the border, just four miles away. However, their usual ford of the Bidasoa

River was compromised by heavy runoff, so Dédée and the airmen doubled back to Frantxia's to spend the night.

On the morning of January 15, they found the house surrounded by German troops. The assumption was that they had been turned in by one of the workmen on Frantxia's farm. Everyone was arrested.

Dédée de Jongh returned to Paris, but this time to become an inmate at the infamous Fresnes Prison, which had been appropriated by the Gestapo to incarcerate – and torture – French Résistance operatives and foreign espionage agents.

Chapter 8

Unexpected Detours

Gilbert Schowalter, Jack Williams, and Johnny McKee arrived in San Sebastian during the first week of January 1943. They were deposited by their Comet Line handlers in a safe house where they remained for about a week, unaware of Dédée de Jongh's arrest. Schowalter recalled that he still had 1,000 francs in his survival kit. He decided that he had no longer had need for French currency, and gave this, along with his maps of France, to the Comet man as a parting gift.

The three Americans were picked up by a Mr Graham of the British Consulate in Bilbao, who took them to the British Embassy in Madrid. They assumed that the hard part of their escape was behind them and that they would be processed expeditiously.

They were wrong.

They were going nowhere any time soon.

Williams explained that they were "quartered in a small building in the rear of the Embassy which had several cots for sleeping. There was also [another] small building where two Spanish women cooked our meals. The British Red Cross gave us clean clothes, soap, tooth brushes, tooth paste, and shaving articles. We were also paid 35 pesetas a week for buying things we wanted such as wine and coffee."

While on the embassy grounds, the Americans met several evaders from the British Army and the Royal Air Force, and received several visits from a British Army major named Haslam. Schowalter noted that the British military attaché at the embassy, General William Wyndham Torr, never visited them, but that he often sent his wife or – separately – his 15-year-old daughter.

Parenthetically, both Torr and Sir Samuel Hoare, the British ambassador to Spain, did have bigger fish to fry that week. They were at this moment busy keeping tabs on a visit to Madrid by the infamous SS-Oberführer Walter Schellenberg, head of foreign intelligence for the Sicherheitsdienst (SD). Prime Minister Winston Churchill had explicitly ordered Hoare and Torr to "keep Spain neutral," and an official visit by Schellenberg almost certainly involved coaxing Francisco Franco toward a cozier relationship with Hitler's Reich.

Schowalter also recalled being interviewed by Michael Creswell, the MI6 agent code named "Monday," who "asked several questions about the [Belgian] organization and seemed to know all about it." He certainly did.

Schowalter told Creswell that he wanted "to be taken to the American Embassy but was politely refused." At the time, the British were so skittish about harboring Americans that the airmen were told that they must claim to be Canadian if asked their nationality, and they were given false names and paperwork to match. Of course, Jack Williams *was* a Canadian veteran, with a year of service in the RCAF before he joined the USAAF. Nevertheless, Haslam insisted that he now use the Canadian *nom de guerre* Sergeant Jack Roger.

Captain Babcock from the American Embassy did make a surreptitious visit, but as Schowalter pointed out, "he never offered to give us clean clothes, nor did he look after us in regard to cigarettes, etc. He made it very emphatic that I could not go over to stay at the American Embassy, visit it, or even have a look at it. He claimed that only three people from our Embassy knew that we were in Madrid, and furthermore they were too busy helping French people escape."

The Americans – with their counterfeit Canadian names and papers – now found themselves folded into the general flow of refugees from occupied Europe who were passing through Spain.

In his escape and evasion report, Johnny McKee wrote that Haslam took them out to dinner at Hotel Nationale on Saturday night, January 16, and that on Sunday morning, he took them to the train bound for Gibraltar. Schowalter recalls that they were in the "midst of a large group of Poles, French and [German] Jews."[7]

When they finally reached Gibraltar, the large assorted group remained together as they were all deloused and loaded aboard the British transport ship RMS *Ormande*, which had been used just two months earlier to land Allied troops in North Africa.

Growing impatient as they waited to join a convoy headed north to Britain, Schowalter wrote that he had "stayed on the ship for two nights and two days without any change of clothes, money, cigarettes or anything and never permitted to consult our American officials on the Rock [Gibraltar]. I sent word ashore that we definitely wanted to leave the ship and see some member of American forces on shore. My wishes were granted shortly before the ship set sail."

Schowalter's appeal passed through British channels, reaching the ear of MI6 man Donald Darling, who knew that American airmen were not supposed to have been lumped in with civilian refugees.

Darling immediately came to get the men and turned them over to US Army Lieutenant Colonel Carl Holcomb, who was in charge of the care and feeding of detached American personnel passing through Gibraltar. He got the men clean uniforms and put them up in American officers' quarters for a good night's sleep.

At 1:30am on January 26, Gilbert Schowalter and Johnny McKee joined two other officers – one US Navy, one British Army – and boarded a USAAF C-47 of the 60th Transport Squadron bound for Britain. Jack Williams did not make the flight. He had landed in the American hospital at Gibraltar with acute tonsillitis.

At 8:45am, the C-47 landed at Portreath in Cornwall, where Schowalter and McKee spent their first hour back in Britain being deloused again. The C-47 then took them on to the RAF field at Hendon in northwest London, from which they were escorted directly into the center of the city.

Rather than being taken to the Eighth Air Force headquarters (code name Widewing) at Bushy Park in the London Borough of Richmond, they went directly to 20 Grosvenor Square in the heart of London, which was the headquarters of Lieutenant General Dwight Eisenhower, the commander of all United States Army Forces in the European Theater, and recently named as Supreme Commander of Allied Forces.

There was intense interest at the highest levels in hearing the story of some of the first men to escape from occupied Europe. As noted earlier, of the nearly 3,000 documented debriefings of Eighth Air Force airmen who evaded and escaped, Schowalter, Williams, and McKee were E&E Nos.8, 9, and 10.

Three days later, in rainy Gibraltar, Jack Williams had recovered from his tonsillitis and was looking for his own ride back to England. An officer at the operations center at the airfield directed him to the pilot of a B-24 who was planning to leave as soon as the weather cleared. He invited Williams along for the ride, adding that there would also be a civilian passenger.

She turned out to be Hollywood starlet Carole Landis, who was returning to England after being part of a USO tour of American bases in North

Africa. Mainly a B-Movie actress, she had recently appeared in *Moon Over Miami* with Betty Grable, and like Grable she became known as one of the leading American GI pinup girls of World War II. Three weeks earlier she had married her second husband, Captain Thomas Cherry Wallace, an Eighth Air Force instructor pilot in England. Now she was on her way back from Algiers to rejoin him.

With Williams and Landis squeezed in with the crew, the B-24 took off at 2:00am on January 29, landing at Portreath at 8:30. The evading airman and the actress had breakfast together and went out to the flight line where a deHavilland general aviation aircraft was available to take them to London.

Williams checked it out and decided that it was not airworthy, so, as Williams explained, "being very anxious to get to London, Mrs. Landis [sic] and I motored over to another field, 20 miles from Portreath where a government C-47 cargo plane was waiting to take off for London."

They landed at Hendon at 3:30pm and went their separate ways. Jack Williams, like Schowalter and McKee three days earlier, was met at Hendon with orders to report to Eisenhower's headquarters on Grosvenor Square.

Landis went on to appear in a dozen further films, including *Four Jills in a Jeep*, a Hollywood movie set reenactment of the 1942 USO tour. She divorced Wallace in 1945, married her third husband the same year, and had a stormy, failed affair with actor Rex Harrison that caused her to take her own life in 1948. Wallace remarried in 1946, served in the Korean War, and later worked for the General Tire company in Venezuela. He was gunned down by gangsters in the backyard of his house in Caracas in 1968.

In his escape and evasion report, McKee was highly critical of the treatment that the American airmen had received in Madrid, wiring that "the American Embassy should take care of all US personnel escaping from France. Instead of paying us 35 pesetas for buying coffee and wine, they should have it there. The British authorities should have let us get in touch with the Americans instead of shipping us out on a boat in the harbor without clean clothes or money."[8]

The processing of escapees and evaders was still, and would remain, a work in progress.

After weeks of Comet handlers on the continent, Schowalter, Williams, and McKee were soon assigned a USAAF intelligence man to guide them into the next phase of their careers. On February 3, Captain Richard Nelson of the Eighth Air Force A-2 staff formally requested that they be "placed on detached service in order to visit all fields occupied by the Eighth Air Force" in order to share their experiences on the run in occupied France.

Chapter 9

In Hostile Hands

As inconvenient as life in Spain had been for Schowalter and Williams, things were much more challenging for fellow *Wulfe Hound* crewmen Norman Therrien and Fred Hartung. They were spending New Year's Eve in a Spanish jail while Schowalter and Williams were enjoying champagne with their Christmas dinner in Paris.

The two sergeants from Massachusetts, who had successfully crossed France without identity papers, and managed to traverse the Pyrenees in waist-deep snow, had been busted as smugglers – because they had no identity papers. Undocumented men picked up on a smuggling route into Franco's Spain had no rights, and certainly no friends among Spain's dreaded Guardia Civil.

On New Year's Day 1943, Therrien and Hartung were transferred to the prison in Lérida (in Catalan, Lleida), from which they were finally able to get a message to the US Embassy in Madrid. On January 16, they were released into the custody of the Ejército del Aire (Spanish Air Force), who put them up at the Grand Hotel in Alhama de Aragón. Clean sheets at last!

They were moved to the US Embassy in Madrid on February 10, where papers identifying them as American military personnel were finally drawn up. Therrien's "Certificate in lieu of a Passport," dated February 11 and signed by Willard Beaulac, counselor of the embassy,* is still in the folder with Therrien's escape and evasion report, E&E No.14, in the files of the US National Archives.

*See p.3 of the plate section.

They reached Gibraltar on February 21, where they were debriefed and processed by Colonel Holcomb while waiting for their flights back to England. Norman Therrien and Fred Hartung reached England on March 4 and March 15 respectively.

Among the other *Wulfe Hound* crewmen, pilot Paul Flickinger and bombardier Beverly Polk were prisoners of war, as were the two substitute gunners, Kenneth Kurtenbach and George Dillard. These two sergeants, who were only filling in on the crew for one mission, had managed to evade capture for almost two weeks, but were captured by the Gestapo in Dijon on Christmas day.

By February 1943, all of *Wulfe Hound*'s crew were either in German custody, or safely out of occupied France – except two. Bill Whitman and Lee Fegette, the two sergeants from Texas, were still less than 20 miles from where the Flying Fortress had crash-landed two months before!

After parting company with Schowalter and Williams in the deep woods on their first day in France, the two Texans had slept in barns, been scolded for trespassing, and had found a helpful Polish family, refugees from Germany's 1939 invasion, who gave them food and civilian clothes.

On the third day in France, back in December 1942, they had finally made contact with the organized Résistance, though it was only by accident. They wandered into the vegetable patch of a man whom Fegette identified in his escape and evasion report, E&E No.32, as Maurice Ployer. He yelled at them and gestured for them to go away, but responding with sign language, they calmed him down and explained who they were. When at last they had made themselves understood, he relaxed and brought them food and cigarettes. He then phoned a friend in Paris to come get them.

After two days with Ployer, a man in a five-passenger Renault collected them and took them to a safe house just outside Paris. On December 22, they were inexplicably moved back to the country again, this time to Rozay-en-Brie, some 40 miles from Paris and only 20 miles from where they started.

As *Wulfe Hound*'s two Massachusetts sergeants had had their *château* stay at Domaine des Bordes l'Abbé a week earlier, the Texans now found themselves living in a huge, towered, and turreted mansion called Château de Breuil in Rozay. Whitman and Fegette, in their escape and evasion reports, described the place as being like an "Englishman's hunting lodge [with] 100 rooms."[9]

The owners were apparently not around, but Ployer's nephew, Paul Pichard, and his wife Marie, who were the caretakers, made them feel at home. For nearly two months, as Ployer, his wife, and his daughter came and went, this *château* was the Americans' world.

Life at Breuil was like a British drawing room mystery, complete with an eccentric cast of characters – from a tall, well-dressed Argentinean, to "Big Jean" from Paris, to the local police chief with Résistance ties. All of this was, of course, set against the backdrop of the constant dread of a Gestapo raid that never came.

The curtain finally came down on this theatrical experience on February 15, 1943. Whitman and Fegette were abruptly driven back to Paris, this time supplied with counterfeit identification papers.

They thought they were making their exit, but it was merely the exchange of one long, improbable drama with another. They remained in Paris until April, staying at various safe houses, but settling in for about a month at the home of the colorful "Madame Cara," who had a sideline giving French language lessons to young German women. While the two Americans busied themselves in one end of the house, Madame Cara was in another, teaching French phrases to the daughters of the Nazi elite of Paris!

As at the Château de Breuil, Madame Cara's expansive home was filled with an intriguing supporting cast. For example, one of those who made an appearance was a Russian pilot whom Fegette identified – and possibly misspelled – as Abraham Konieniko. The improbable presence of a Soviet airman in Paris in 1943 certainly teases us with the possibility of an interesting story that may someday be revealed in more detail. Coincidentally, there is a twenty-first-century Russian cosmonaut and International Space Station veteran named Mikhail Kornienko.

While in Paris, Whitman and Fegette were at last taken in by the Comet Line organization. They spent at least one night with Comet operative Lucien Fouard, who told the Texans to say "hello" to Johnny McKee, whom he had hosted in December 1942.

They were taken to meet Robert Constant Aylé, head of the Comet Line for northern France, who questioned and vetted them, and took a look at the identity papers they'd been given at Château de Breuil. When he discovered that these were already out of date, Aylé took the Americans to a department store photo booth to get pictures for a fresh set of papers.

Soon, familiar Comet names reentered the *Wulfe Hound* evader narrative. Jean-François Nothomb, aka "Franco," who had shepherded Schowalter, Williams and McKee south to Bayonne, now stepped in to do the same for Whitman and Fegette. Later, toward the end of March, the two were introduced to another Belgian, who introduced himself as "Monsieur Paul," and whom the Texans called "Mr Belg." Of course, "Monsieur Paul" was the alias of Frédéric de Jongh, the father of Dédée de Jongh, who had aided Schowalter and Williams.

Dédée's arrest in January had thrown the whole Comet organization into distraction and this delayed the process of getting Whitman and Fegette out of Paris. Frédéric was certainly distracted, as Dédée had been incarcerated at Fresnes Prison on the edge of Paris, and throughout March and April he was consumed with desperately trying to raise bribe money to get her out. He was never successful.

There were also delays because, after Dédée's arrest, the Comet network had been compromised, so Nothomb left his evaders in Paris while he went south to survey new escape routes.

For more than three months, Fegette and Whitman remained in Paris. After a month with Madame Cara, they were bouncing from safe house to safe house, sometimes together, sometimes separately, not knowing where or when they would be moved next. The purpose was to frustrate the Germans who might be trying to locate safe houses, but it was also a frustration for the Americans.

At last, on Tuesday, April 27, 1943 things changed. As Fegette wrote, they "got new identity papers from Franco and Mr. Belg, went station, went train, went to Bordeaux, 11:30am."

As Nothomb had done with Schowalter, Williams, and McKee on the first day of the year, he came aboard as their Comet handler. Also joining them was Englishman Sergeant John Curry, a fighter pilot with RAF No.165 Squadron, who had been shot down on February 9.

On April 29, as they departed Bordeaux for Bayonne, they took separate compartments on the train because they would be passing into the coastal "Zone Militaire," where the Gestapo would come aboard to scrutinize papers.

When the time came, and black uniforms appeared in the passenger coaches, tense moments ensued. None of Nothomb's little band knew what was happening to the others. Each man cast a furtive eye toward the window, fearing that the next thing he saw would be someone he knew being dragged off the train.

Their worst fears did not materialize, and Nothomb made it to Bayonne with his Allied airmen. That night, they arrived in Saint-Jean-de-Luz to begin their crossing of the mountains by foot. By the evening of April 30, Nothomb had introduced them to Florentino Goikoetxea, the criminal and smuggler or *contrabandista* who was the most trusted and reliable of Comet's Basque mountain guides. As Bob Dylan later wrote, "to live outside the law, you must be honest."

Nothomb and Goikoetxea had recently surveyed new escape routes through higher mountain passes into Spain's eastern Navarre province. Whereas the jumping off point for the old routes had been the French Basque border town of Urrugne, the new ones now led through the Spanish Basque village of Erratzu around 20 miles away.

In comparing their ten-hour nighttime crossing of the Pyrenees to the detailed descriptions of fellow *Wulfe Hound* men Therrien and Hartung, there are both similarities and contrasts. The driving rain and mud of April were no less miserable and perilous than the drifting snow of January, but at least Fegette and Whitman had the services of the Comet operatives. They reached Spain on May 3, and Nothomb soon had them lodged at a hotel overlooking Bay of Biscay beaches in San Sebastian.

A van from the US Embassy collected Fegette and Whitman on May 6, and they spent the next two weeks in Madrid. Their escape and evasion reports share few details of those weeks, but by May 21, they were in Gibraltar being debriefed by Donald Darling of the British SIS and USAAF Major Grady Lewis. On May 25, they boarded their flight back to Britain.

With all the *Wulfe Hound* crewmen accounted for, one might be tempted to close the file on the events of December 12, 1942. However, there was one important loose end – *Wulfe Hound* herself.

In most of the incidents covered in this book, the aircraft at the center of the story ended the first act as a debris field. Not so *Wulfe Hound*. Paul Flickinger and Jack Williams had done such an admirable job of getting her down into a safe crash landing that she survived virtually intact. When German troops took charge of the crash site after the crew left, Luftwaffe engineers were summoned.

In all theaters of World War II, obtaining intact examples of the other side's major aircraft types was an important intelligence coup. In 1942, early days in the war between the Luftwaffe and the Eighth Air Force, finding such a B-17 Flying Fortress was a cause of celebration for Germany's air arm.

Wulfe Hound was dragged out of the mud and taken to a nearby Luftwaffe field to be patched up. Restored to flyable condition, she was the first Flying Fortress to be "brought back to life" by the Germans. According to the

Aircrew Remembered website, Flickinger himself was forced to fly the aircraft to the Luftwaffe base at Leeuwarden in the Netherlands for further repairs, and to be repainted with German insignia. The website notes that the first flight with a Luftwaffe crew came on March 17, 1943.

Wulfe Hound was then flown to the Luftwaffe engineering center at Rechlin, north of Berlin, where new German aircraft – as well as captured enemy aircraft – were flight-tested and evaluated. Initially, the aircraft was used to help develop tactics for intercepting and defeating American Flying Fortresses, but she was later transferred to Kampfgeschwader 200 (KG 200), the Luftwaffe's special operations squadron, in September 1943.

With KG 200, she participated in various clandestine operations where an American Flying Fortress would be useful as a decoy or deception. She was forward deployed to the Mediterranean, where she operated out of the secret base at Wadi Tamet in Libya, being used to conduct reconnaissance missions over Allied troop concentrations.

In an article on the 303rd Bomb Group website (303rdbg.com), Mario Schulze writes of a Flying Fortress seen in April 1945 Allied reconnaissance photos of the Luftwaffe field at Oranienburg, 20 miles northwest of Berlin. He believes that this aircraft was the former *Wulfe Hound*, and that she was damaged in an April 10 air raid, coincidentally by her old outfit, the 303rd Bomb Group.

After the war, this location was used by the Soviet Air Force, and was abandoned as an airfield by 1994. In 2008, when the area was being redeveloped as a business park, an explosives mitigation service unearthed metal scraps related to the long history of the area as a military airfield. Among these were several items bearing serial numbers, and according to Schulze, there was an engine nacelle hatch with the serial number 41-24585. This was from the exact Boeing B-17F that was known as *Wulfe Hound*.

Chapter 10

Long and Winding Roads

The Comet Line had survived the arrest of Andrée "Dédée" de Jongh in January 1943, but for her, life during the ensuing war years was a living hell. At first, the Germans underestimated Dédée's importance within the Comet Line, assuming someone so young and slight of stature could not possibly be the major Comet driving force.

In his 1983 book *20 Héros de Chez Nous* (*20 Home Town Heroes*), General Baron Albert Crahay quoted her as saying "the questions they asked me proved to me that they were still groping, although they had established an organizational chart of our network that was not so badly done, after all. I applied myself to prove to them that this scheme was false, that they had not understood anything and provided them with a host of details, false of course, which ended up making them lose their head."

While this meant that Dédée never faced an executioner, the Germans had developed the theory that her father was the real leader of the Comet Line network, and he had a price on his head of a million Belgian francs ($400,000 in today's dollars). Frédéric de Jongh was arrested in June 1943, five months after his daughter, and executed in March 1944.

Dédée was arrested by the Gestapo, but she was also interrogated by the rival Geheime Feldpolizei (GFP), the secret police arm of the Abwehr, the military intelligence branch of the Wehrmacht. Ironically, Dédée's life may have been saved by the bitter bureaucratic rivalry that existed between the Gestapo and the GFP.

As she later told Crahay, "I am convinced that the Abwehr hastened to send me to Germany, in order to put the Gestapo in a dead end, or, at the very least, to prevent them from extracting a confession from me by means of procedures to which I do not know if I would have been able to resist them."

After being jailed at Fresnes Prison, near Paris, she was moved to Germany. She spent time at the notorious Ravensbrück concentration camp, the women's prison operated by the SS at Fürstenberg, north of Berlin, where Frantxia Usandizanga, the Basque woman with whom she was arrested, was also imprisoned. Frantxia was killed, but Dédée survived and was later moved to the Mauthausen concentration camp in Austria.

By the time that the Germans figured out that Dédée de Jongh was more than what she seemed, she had become merely one among thousands of inmates scattered throughout the vast networks of Nazi camps.

"I existed only in the form of a number," she told Crahay, "lost in a multitude of equally anonymous numbers and, provided I moved a little, it became difficult for the Gestapo to get hands on me."

Upon her release in 1945, she was celebrated by those whom she had aided during her Comet years. The British government brought her to London, where she was greeted by the king and queen and awarded the George Medal for "acts of great bravery" by a civilian in wartime. Among other honors, she received the American Medal of Freedom, the French Légion d'Honneur, and in 1985, King Baudouin of Belgium made Dédée a countess.

Dédée's young colleague, 23-year-old Jean-François Nothomb, alias "Franco," had assumed a leadership role in the Comet Line organization, continuing to shelter and shepherd Allied airmen. This lasted for only a year. He was arrested *en route* to Brussels in January 1944. A German military court handed him a death sentence and sent him to the concentration camp at Bayreuth, a sub-camp of the notorious Flossenbürg camp, pending execution. Luckily, this order was still pending when the Americans liberated the camp in May 1945.

Dogged by ill-health resulting from the horrific conditions of his incarceration, Nothomb returned to Belgium, where he was reunited with Andrée de Jongh. She was also feeling the debilitating effects of years of mistreatment and malnutrition. They became engaged to be married, but soon went their separate ways.

In 1949, he opted for the priesthood and joined the order of the Little Fathers of Charles de Foucauld. He spent time as a missionary in the Venezuela and the United States, but was summoned to Rome in 1974 to work as a liaison between the order and the Holy See. Nothomb found life as a bureaucrat unappealing and left the priesthood in 1980. He later married a much younger Italian woman, and passed away in 2008 at the age of 89.

After breaking up with Nothomb, Andrée de Jongh studied nursing and went to Africa to work in leper colonies. In 1959, she met the novelist Graham

Greene, whom she told that she had wanted to cure leprosy since she was a teenager – and that if she had "delayed any longer it would have been too late." She eventually returned to Belgium and passed away at the age of 90 in 2007.

———

It was common Eighth Air Force practice for evaders to fly no further missions over occupied Europe because if they were shot down and captured, they might reveal information about the escape line people who had helped them. Lee Fegette, late of *Wulfe Hound*, was among the few exceptions. Records of the 303rd Bomb Group for Combat Mission No.6 note that "after spending a restless year in the United States, [Tech Sergeant] Fegette came back to Molesworth and was dispatched on 26 additional combat missions… with his old 360th Bomb Squadron as a radio operator with various crews."[10]

Having gone down with *Wulfe Hound* on the 303rd's Mission No.6, Fegette returned to the air 22 months later on the group's Mission No.254 on October 7, 1944 aboard the B-17G known as *The Red*, piloted by Lieutenant Verne Nafius. The mission was a long one, a 1,300-mile-roundtrip, deep penetration mission to Dresden.

Fegette flew his final mission on April 14, 1945, three weeks before the war ended, crewing with Lieutenant Robert Fowler aboard the B-17G *Old Cock*. As recalled in the records of the 303rd (cited above), the targets for the day were "German pockets of anti-aircraft and artillery positions and strongpoints covering the Gironde estuary on the French Atlantic coast… defense pockets that were denying the Allies use of port facilities in the Bordeaux, France area."

Almost exactly one year earlier Lee Fegette and Bill Whitman had been passing through Bordeaux on a train as helpless fugitives dodging the Gestapo. Now Fegette was back as part of a 1,278-bomber strike force designed to make the Germans feel the helplessness of their lost cause.

Fegette, the man who went back to the Eighth, left the service for a career with Texas Power and Light, while fellow Texan Bill Whitman stayed in, retiring as a major general in 1961. Both of these Texans who evaded together in 1942–43 ended up back in the Lone Star State and both passed away there in 2007. The two Massachusetts men from the *Wulfe Hound* crew ended up on opposite sides of the United States, Norman Therrien back in their home state and Frederick Hartung in Belleview, Washington. They died in 1993 and 1994 respectively.

While the *Wulfe Hound* men led later lives outside the limelight, John R. "Johnny" McKee of *Rose O'Day*, who evaded capture alongside Williams and Schowalter, would soon be squarely in it. Promoted to captain in March 1943, McKee went on to serve as a group operations officer with the Eighth Air Force, leaving the USAAF as a lieutenant colonel at the end of the war.

Having played baseball for Villanova back in the mid-1930s, McKee returned to the national pastime, landing a job on the coaching staff of the Pittsburgh Pirates under manager Billy Herman. Accounts on the sports pages during the 1947 season refer to him as the "bullpen coach" for the Pirates. According to the Pittsburgh *Post–Gazette*, both McKee and fellow coach Zack Taylor were let go by the Pirates on October 23, 1947, after Billy Meyer replaced Herman as the manager.

Thereafter, McKee sought his fortune out west, where he divided his time between working as a race horse trainer and a Hollywood career. He never made it big in the film business, but he did land a lot of roles. Though most of his work was as an uncredited extra, he appeared in over 150 films and television shows between 1948 and 1983, about a third of these being released between 1949 and 1954.

Early in his career, McKee received billing for a couple of baseball movies – as catcher Bill Baxter in *Angels in the Outfield* (1951), and as Hunch Harrison in *The Kid from Left Field* (1953). His wartime connections landed him an uncredited role as an operations officer – which he actually had been – in the great Eighth Air Force film, *Twelve O'Clock High* (1949). He portrayed the fictional Captain Symington in another iconic air force movie, *Strategic Air Command* (1955).

With the 1950s and early 1960s being the golden age of the Hollywood Western – on the big screen and on television – McKee's experience with horses landed him roles in many of these. In 1956, he was Brad Putnam on *The Roy Rogers Show* television series, and he had roles on *The Virginian*, *Laramie*, *The Texan*, and one episode of *Bonanza*. He appeared in several episodes of *Wagon Train* between 1959 and 1963. Later in his career, he was seen on *The Six Million Dollar Man* and in 1977 he portrayed Admiral William Leahy opposite Gregory Peck in the title role of *MacArthur*. McKee later retired to Vineland, New Jersey, where he passed away in 2013.

We are still waiting for Hollywood to discover Dédée de Jongh for the major motion picture that her memory deserves – perhaps to include the dynamic trio of Schowalter, Williams, and McKee.

PART THREE

THE MAN ON THE BICYCLE

Chapter 11

May Day Over Saint-Nazaire

It was the first day of May in 1943, and in hindsight it was to be a notable day for the alignment of stars who would later be part of the popular lore of the Eighth Air Force. Across southern England the sun rose to the rumbling of Wright Aeronautical R-1820-97 Cyclone radial engines from the wings of hundreds of Flying Fortresses.

From Bassingbourn in Cambridgeshire, the B-17F Flying Fortresses of the 91st Bomb Group lifted into the skies. Among them was the one piloted by 24-year-old Captain Robert "Bob" Knight Morgan of Ashville, North Carolina. Who knew when he named his bomber *Memphis Belle* after his girlfriend, Margaret Polk of that Tennessee city, that this aircraft was destined to become an icon of popular culture.

By May 1, Bob Morgan, his crew, and the *Memphis Belle* were already on their way to cinematic stardom thanks to Academy Award-winning director William Wyler, who was producing a documentary about them.

The idea was for a film about the first bomber crew to complete a full 25-mission combat tour. This day was to be their Mission 22. In fact, the *Memphis Belle* crew would reach the 25-mission milestone, but would miss being the first by a week. Nevertheless, Wyler's film went ahead and enjoyed a successful release in 1944, and the *Memphis Belle* achieved immortality.

From Thurleigh in Bedfordshire, among the Flying Fortresses of the 306th Bomb Group rising into the morning sun was an unnamed B-17F piloted by 1st Lieutenant Lewis Johnson. It would become notable on this day for the unlikely hero manning its ball turret on his first-ever operational mission.

Staff Sergeant Maynard Harrison Smith of Caro, Michigan, who was nicknamed "Snuffy Smith" after the cartoon character, was a bitter, abrasive character generally disliked by those around him. Just a couple of weeks shy of turning 32, Smith was much older than his crewmates, and he might not have been there at all but for the fact that he had enlisted in the Army as a means of getting out of serving a jail sentence. That said, today, May 1, 1943, was to mark the crowning moment of the entirety of Snuffy's 73 years. Today, he would become the first enlisted man in the USAAF to earn a Medal of Honor.

From Molesworth in Cambridgeshire, the 303rd Bomb Group launched 19 B-17s. Each of them took off with its bomb bay crowded with a pair of 2,000-pound bombs. They flew in a "V" pattern, with the last aircraft on the right rear corner of the "V" being *Black Swan*, piloted by 1st Lieutenant Jay Sterling. His navigator, 23-year-old 2nd Lieutenant Harry Edwin Roach, Jr. of Philadelphia, the subject of our narrative, was about to begin the adventure of a lifetime.

The aircraft from these three groups were part of a 78-bomber strike force headed for the great German U-Boat pen complex at Saint-Nazaire on the French coast, 350 miles south of the Eighth Air Force bases in England. It was a target that the men of the Eighth knew all too well. This was Bob Morgan's fifth time.

After the Germans defeated France in 1940, they undertook a rapid construction program to build these massive, reinforced concrete pens at Brest, La Pallice, and Lorient as well as at Saint-Nazaire. From here, U-Boats would have direct access to the Atlantic Ocean from which to conduct unlimited submarine warfare against all forms of Allied shipping across the Atlantic – and down the Eastern Seaboard of the United States.

As they were sinking more than half a million tons of Allied shipping every month, the U-Boats were creating a crisis for the Allies, especially for the

British, with their heavy dependence on imported food and fuel. U-Boats were seriously compromising the British economy. There was pressure from all sides, especially the British government, to use the Eighth against the submarine pens. They were seen as ideal for this mission because of the precision theoretically possible with the Norden bombsight. However, as the pens were protected by hardened roofs that were as thick as 25 feet, they were virtually indestructible.

Nevertheless, Lieutenant General Dwight Eisenhower, the commanding general of United States Army Forces in the European Theater, pointedly told Major General Carl "Tooey" Spaatz, the commander of the USAAF in the European Theater, that he considered the crippling of the German U-Boat threat "to be one of the basic requirements to the winning of the war."

In the forward fuselage of *Black Swan*, navigator Harry Roach checked the twin side-firing guns in the nose and scraped away a small patch in the thick frost that had formed on the inside of the Plexiglas in the frigid temperatures at 22,700 feet. Seven 303rd Bomb Group bombers had turned back or had not made it into the formation, so the group was down to just a dozen aircraft.

"For some unknown reason, my 'intuition' told me to attach my chute pack to my harness, which I did in a spare moment," wrote Roach in his escape and evasion report.[11]

It was a long and uneventful flight until they reached the initial point of their bomb run near Nantes, about 30 miles east of Saint-Nazaire. Then, all hell broke loose.

The antiaircraft fire, for which Saint-Nazaire was notorious, was deemed "moderate" but "accurate" in the 303rd Bomb Group's Combat Mission No. 32 after-action report. However, it was the Luftwaffe's Fw 190 interceptors that seriously plagued the 303rd that day. German installations on the Atlantic coast were under the able protection of the Luftwaffe's Jagdgeschwader 2 (JG 2) "Richthofen" fighter wing, then commanded by Oberstleutnant Walter "Gulle" Oesau.

"I heard a terrific bang as a [20mm] cannon shell passed about three feet behind me and hit the rear of our number three [right inboard] engine nacelle," Roach recalled. "We fell behind our formation. The Fw 190s, which had remained at a safe distance, became very nervy and came at us from all directions. Everyone was shouting on the interphone… A brazen, yellow-nosed Fw 190 came parallel with us. He seemed to stall there. I let him have the works [with a machine gun]; he dropped down but I could not see whether he had been damaged or was on fire."

Another German interceptor made a head-on pass, against which the top turret was the only defense, because Flying Fortresses were not fitted with forward-firing nose guns – until the later B-17G variant.

Luftwaffe records indicate that a Flying Fortress matching *Black Swan*'s description and markings was claimed at 11:24am that day by Unteroffizier Rudolf Gehrhardt of JG 2. It was his only victory claim. He was himself shot down and badly injured two weeks later.

With one engine knocked out for sure, Roach felt *Black Swan* going into a shallow dive. On the interphone, he heard Arthur McCormick, the ball turret gunner, report that the number three engine was also "smoking like mad."

Roach then heard pilot Jay Sterling order bombardier Dave Parker to jettison the bombs. He noticed that Parker, who was sitting just a few feet away, had not seemed to hear, so Roach tapped him on the shoulder and relayed the order.

"By this time, I could tell by the sound that we were going [down] at a helluva rate and the ship was shaking terrifically," Roach observed. "I smelt smoke out of the catwalk [though the bomb bay behind him] but could not see any flame."

He could see the 303rd formation above and, through a break in the heavy cloud cover, Saint-Nazaire was visible about 15 miles ahead and below. Given the state of things in his aircraft, he figured "it was time to get out."

As he stood to pull off his oxygen mask, *Black Swan* lurched to the right, throwing him face down on his navigator's table. Simultaneously, something hit him in the left leg, but when he looked down, "there was no [bullet] hole in the coveralls, so I thought it was okay."

Roach made it to the bomb bay, from which he planned to jump from the stricken aircraft, but the bomb bay doors were closed and it took him several tries to get the door release mechanism to work.

Black Swan was now spinning, and the centrifugal force threw Roach away from the opening. He finally crawled forward and went out head first, but found breathing "extremely difficult" because of the altitude and the exertion of getting the doors open.

"On falling out, the harness and chute pack appeared to be two feet away from me," Roach remembered. "Yanking the ripcord I was violently stopped and the harness was very painful to my back. There were still a couple [of] fighters around [and] I was thankful they did not attempt to make a pass at me... What was left of the ship, that [which] looked like the wing and forward part of the fuselage went spinning way off to my right.

Evidently the gas tank exploded... a great deal of debris was falling down... a giant piece of stabilizer, I suppose, was directly above me but it went past me at a safe distance."

Though Roach wrote in his escape and evasion report that he saw no other parachutes, the 303rd Bomb Group Combat Mission No. 32 after-action report states that "*Black Swan* was seen to explode over the sea with four parachutes observed, three after the aircraft blew up." These three belonged to copilot John Neill, bombardier Dave Parker, and flight engineer Powell Griffin. The other six crewmen, including Jay Sterling, didn't make it.

Black Swan was one of two aircraft that the 303rd Bomb Group lost that day. Bob Morgan later described the May Day operation as a "bad mission from the start" because the clouds were so thick that hardly any bombardiers could see the target and they could not drop their ordnance. Morgan's 91st Bomb Group lost only one aircraft, but the 306th lost three, one over Saint-Nazaire and two over Brest – because of a navigational error.

The usual mission plan for exiting strikes against Saint-Nazaire was to fly a northwesterly path until opposite Land's End in Cornwall, the southwest tip of Britain, and then to turn east. However, the lead navigator made a serious mistake and led the formation into an eastward turn 200 miles too far south on May Day.

As they sighted land, the bombers began their usual descent to 2,000 feet – but instead of Cornwall, the land was German-occupied Brittany, and they were bearing down on Brest, heavily protected by antiaircraft emplacements and interceptors. The skies were suddenly filled with the black carpet of flak, so the low-flying aircraft descended with the idea of slipping beneath the altitude at which the antiaircraft shells were fused to explode. As many as 20 Luftwaffe fighters jumped the bombers as soon as they cleared the flak.

From inside his cramped ball turret, Snuffy Smith returned fire until the electrical system failed and he could no longer operate the turret. He crawled out of his cramped space to find the center of the aircraft's interior space engulfed in flame. Impulsively, he fought the flames instead of bailing out, as a couple of men did. As a result, Smith saved the Flying Fortress and his fellow crewmembers who had remained with the aircraft, thus earning his Medal of Honor.

Chapter 12

Lines on the Map

Harry Roach had escaped an aircraft that was beyond being saved. He came down hard and fast in an open field, further hurting his sprained back. The wind was blowing hard enough that it caught the parachute and started to drag him, but he yanked the bottom-side shroud lines and spilled the air.

After getting things under control, he rolled his parachute around his Mae West life vest and hid the bundle in some brush. Putting his revolver into his pocket, Roach walked toward two farmworkers whom he had seen in a nearby field.

Almost certainly to protect their identities, Roach named no names in his otherwise very detailed 1943 escape and evasion report. However, the blanks are filled in by a Chemin de la Mémoire (Path of Memory) plaque in the tiny village of Morandières, near where Roach came down. The *Black Swan* marker was installed in 2015 by the Communauté de Communes du Sud-Estuare (Community of Municipalities of the South Estuary).

From this plaque, translated by Danielle Moreau, we know that the two men were Clément Bideau and Jean Leray. They came at him carrying pitchforks, but saw the blood running down his face from a cut between his eyes, and relaxed. When he told them he was an American, they called him "*camarade*."

They led him to some woods nearby, where they helped him dispose of his high altitude boots and his heavy flight suit. He also gave them his revolver, knowing that in any confrontation with the Germans, it was better to be unarmed than hopelessly outgunned.

Bideau, Leray, and Roach were soon joined by more people, identified in the Sud-Estuare plaque as including members of the Pasgrimaud family, and Bideau's mother, Clémentine, who brought food.

Roach recalled that he took out his pack of Chesterfields and offered cigarettes to his "*camarades*," adding that "they went wild-eyed" at the sight of American cigarettes.

As they smoked, one of the men pointed out Roach's location on his survival map, indicating that Morandières, where they were, was a suburb of the larger town of Saint-Père-en-Retz. They were about 20 miles south, across the mouth of the broad Loire River estuary from Saint-Nazaire.

At last, Roach parted company with his new friends and headed south. After about a half hour, he met a boy who recognized his uniform and took him to a house where the people gave him a well-worn civilian coat and shirt, along with a cap and trousers. He was then treated to a "couple shots of white cognac which was extremely strong."

As he continued on his way, "feeling better" from the cognac, Roach began to see smoldering fragments of *Black Swan* scattered through the surrounding fields. The section containing the bomb bay door through which he had dived was upside down among some trees. The inner sections of both wings were still attached, and one of the tires from the main landing gear was perfectly intact and partly lowered. The other was missing. He did not venture too close, as the wreckage was surrounded by onlookers, both curious civilians and German troops.

He stopped at another house, later identified as the home of Joseph Monnier, where he asked for a drink of water. As he was savoring it, there was a rumble nearby that was immediately recognizable as the sound of motorcycles – a German patrol looking for survivors of the crash. Monnier told Roach to crawl under the bed, while the family dashed out the back door. The roar of the BMWs grew louder and louder, but the Germans passed without stopping.

As soon as the sound disappeared into the distance, the American airman was out from under the bed and headed in the opposite direction as fast as he could scramble. He continued cross country at first, but found that the deep furrows of the recently plowed fields slowed him down, so he switched to an asphalt road. After a time, the passing of a truck loaded with German soldiers made him nervous, though he went unnoticed in his civilian garb.

Nevertheless, he decided to get off the road.

Exhausted, and with his back still hurting, Roach crawled into some bushes and fell asleep. When he awoke the sun was starting to go down on a very eventful Saturday. It had been nearly 12 hours since wheels-up at Molesworth.

Deciding that he should find a place to spend the night, he continued walking until he reached what he described as "a small town with a large church." He had arrived in Chauvé, a town of around 1,300 people situated five road miles south of the crash site. The town's Église Saint-Martin has a steeple that is visible from some distance.

In the gathering dusk, Roach approached a man, Antoine Trigodet, working in the garden of the rectory. He explained as best he could that he was an American airman who needed something to eat and a place to sleep. His prayers were answered. He wrote that he "had a good dinner with the priest and with use of a dictionary, we had a conversation."

"I could hardly get out of bed," Harry Roach wrote of his first morning in occupied France. "[But] after breakfast the priest and a sister massaged my back."

The rector of the church, identified by the Sud-Estuare plaque as Jean-Baptist Serot, made contact with the Résistance on Roach's behalf, and he also summoned "an English-speaking woman" later identified as Madame Michaud, who came from Pornic, a coastal town west of Chauvé. When she arrived late on Sunday morning, she told Roach that he was "very fortunate" to have evaded capture "and was in a good place to hide."

She went on to say that many people, obviously including the Germans, had seen three or four parachutes from *Black Swan*, and that one of his fellow crewmen – it turned out to be the top turret gunner, Sergeant Powell Griffin – had been injured and had been taken by the Germans to a military hospital in Pornic.

Roach was a very lucky man. He may have had a sore back, but he also had a bed to sleep in, breakfast, a massage – *and* his freedom.

Roach wondered about the other members of the crew. How many had escaped? If there had been only three or four parachutes, then he knew that most of the ten-man crew must have died. Much later, he learned that the other two parachutes belonged to John Neill and Dave Parker. French civilians had come to Neill's aid, while Parker hid out on his own. Both men, like Roach, greeted Sunday, May 2 as free men, but their luck would soon run out. Neill was picked up by the French police and handed over to the Germans. Parker made contact with sympathetic civilians, but he was spotted by a pro-German collaborator who turned him in.

On Monday, May 3, Harry Roach's benefactors brought him a newer, less ragged, change of clothes and a bicycle. On his map, Madame Michaud pointed out the city of Agen, and scribbled the address of a Mademoiselle Vigier, with whom he was to make contact. Agen was more than 350 road miles to the south, between Bordeaux and Toulouse. The next day, Tuesday, May 4, Roach's back was feeling well enough for him to begin a long bicycle journey into the unknown.

On his first day, following directions given him by his Résistance friends, Roach cycled south for about 30 miles to Legé, a modest town of about 3,500 people. Here, he made contact with another priest who taught English in a school.

"The [school] building stood on the other side of the town," Roach wrote in a notebook of recollections that he compiled later while in Spain, and which is contained within his escape and evasion report at the National Archives. "The town was infested with German soldiers and I had great difficulty in keeping from running over one of them with my bicycle. The building was on a street that the Germans were also quartered. I went into the yard and asked a priest in the garden for the 'English professor.'"[12]

Roach and the "professor" had an early dinner, at which the unexpected American explained his situation.

"It was dangerous for me to stay for more than one night," Roach was told. "The children, students and all, would be put out if I were caught. The Germans wanted the building for a barracks and only needed an excuse. At dinner, I learned a great deal of the difficulties of the French people… the next morning, the priest walked me to the edge of the town and I started off again."

The priest handed the traveler an automobile road map. As Roach later explained, "the safest route was traced on it, avoiding all towns for the time being."

On the evening of Wednesday, May 5, he stopped at "an isolated farmhouse," but the people said they had no room. The door closed in his face. He rode on to the next farm, where he was taken in. They offered him a place to sleep, and joined him in "the usual after dinner dictionary conversation."

As it grew late, he was shown to "a large feather bed," but he found it hard to sleep. As he later wrote, it was coming to be that "every night it was just a matter of rest." Sleep had become elusive.

after dinner dictionary conversation.
that next night I had a large feather
bed but for some reason I was not
able to sleep and every night it was
just a matter of rest.
the next day I expected to cross
the line of occupation and start
toward Spain. Late in the day
I reached the large town of Poitiers
which was infested with soldiers.
had trolley cars and a few charcoal
burning automobiles. the people looked
very much inclined to be poor.
On leaving the town by following
road signs I passed a concentration
camp, a small child about four
years old looking out the fence
waved to me as I went by.
Stopping a a farm house they let
me sleep in their barn. I learned of
a barrier in the road about four
miles down and with my map the

The navigator aboard the B-17 called *Black Swan*, 2nd Lieutenant Harry Roach, was shot down on May 1, 1943 and evaded capture as he rode across much of occupied France on a bicycle. This page from his hand-written recollections tells of his ride through Poitiers on May 6, when a little boy of about four years of age waved to him from behind the barbed wire of a concentration camp. (US National Archives)

By Thursday afternoon, Roach had reached the city of Poitiers, 120 miles southeast of Legé. As had been the case at Legé, he found Poitiers "infested with [German] soldiers," again using the term that compared the occupiers to vermin. Many French people would probably have agreed, but there was a difference. They had to live with the infestation. Roach was just passing through – or so was his intention.

Recording his observations in his notebook some weeks later, he wrote that Poitiers "had trolley cars and a few charcoal burning automobiles. The people looked very much inclined to be poor. On leaving the town by following road signs, I passed a concentration camp, a small child about four years old looking out the fence waved to me as I went by."

Chapter 13

Bombard Our House With Chocolate

Late on Thursday, May 6, 1943, Harry Roach stopped at a farm, asking for a place to spend the night. He was told he was welcome to find a place in the barn. The next morning, over breakfast, his hosts told him that he was about four miles from the former demarcation line between occupied and previously unoccupied France. There was still a German checkpoint on the road, but they showed him on the map how to dodge it.

Roach successfully avoided the German roadblock, but was caught by a torrential rainstorm moving in from the Atlantic. As on the previous night, he stopped at a small farmhouse and was offered a place to sleep in the barn. In the meantime, he was invited into the house for dinner, and was able to dry his shoes by the fire.

After a supper of thick soup with brown bread and a glass of "weak wine," a man from a neighboring farm dropped by and offered Roach a cigarette. As his pack of prized Chesterfields was long gone, he was pleased to have a smoke. Finally, it was time to head out to the barn. Rain was still pouring and it was growing very cold. Roach recalled shivering for eight hours.

The rain began to diminish on Saturday as Roach continued to pedal south. He had developed a momentum and was making good progress. By watching distance markers that he passed, he estimated that he was averaging about 90 kilometers each day. Though the Germans technically occupied this previously unoccupied zone, their troops were many fewer and much farther between than they had been in the north. He was finding it much easier to relax.

He was aware that many French cops collaborated with the Gestapo, but somehow they seemed less threatening. That is, until he noticed that a gendarme on a bicycle whom he had passed in the last village had started to follow him.

What had he done to arouse suspicion? Had the man seen through his disguise? Maybe it was just that Roach was an unfamiliar face, a stranger who did not belong.

He dare not panic or do anything to present a red flag. The best course of action was to just keep pedaling, though he did increase his speed ever so slightly.

The gendarme continued to follow him – through the town, out of the town, and into the countryside. Roach dared not glance back, but he did sneak a look on a curve now and then. Gradually, the distance between the two riders increased, as though the cop was getting tired. Finally, when Roach glanced back, he was gone. The American airman breathed a sigh of relief and kept riding south.

As the shadows of the trees across the road grew longer, Roach began scouting for another farm at which to spend the night. He had a routine and this was part of it, but his luck from previous nights now eluded him. "I tried three places and nobody would have me," he complained.

It was after 9:00pm and getting dark when he came around a corner and spied a cheerful-looking building.

"I came upon a small inn at the side of the road with no adjacent buildings," he later recalled in his notes. "The people evidently catered to traveling people before the war and spoke a few words of English."

They served up some fried potatoes and beefsteak, along with wine and hand-rolled cigarettes. Roach shared some of the small amount of chocolate that he had in his survival kit, which became a topic of conversation the next day.

Their dialogue that evening had naturally turned to the occupation and how eager the French people were for the Americans to land in France and liberate them. They hoped this would come soon, but no one, including Roach, could guess that it would be more than a year.

"With a good night's rest and the sun out in the morning," Roach was feeling cheerful as he arose on Sunday.

"Hurry up America," one of the people at the inn said as their guest climbed onto his bicycle, reminding him of their conversation about the invasion.

As Roach later recalled, another of his new friends at the inn handed him a package containing two sandwiches, "asked me to bombard their house with chocolate sometime, and said goodbye."

Roach calculated that he was now a little less than 90 miles from Agen. Since he'd gotten an early start and the days were long, he decided to try to make it all on one day. Pedaling for 13 hours, he passed through cities such as Bellac and Limoges, which he found crowded with German troops.

He later wrote in his escape and evasion report that as he was cycling a few miles southeast of Bergerac, he saw a Luftwaffe air base under construction. He noted four hangars and 16 buildings that looked like barracks. The site had been a civilian airfield taken over by the French air force in 1939 as a training field, and the Luftwaffe had been using it for the same purpose. It would be heavily damaged by the Eighth Air Force in March 1944.

When Roach finally reached Agen late on May 8, he began searching for the address that Madame Michaud had given him for Mademoiselle Vigier, but there was a problem.

"Two streets had almost similar names," he recalled. "As luck would have it, I went to the wrong one first. It was Sunday afternoon, and it was a large building [so] I decided to go to the back entrance as many German officers were standing around the front. Upon opening the door, I saw it was a cabaret, just alive with [German] soldiers."

Roach decided that the best thing to do was to go to the house next door and simply ask for Mademoiselle Vigier. It was an ill-considered idea that could easily have gone very wrong, but nevertheless this was a choice that may have saved him.

"The people did not know her," Roach discovered, not unexpectedly. "The large, stout lady who answered the door got all affected and nervous when I told her I was an American. By this time, I had acquired enough French to explain my situation. She ran out of the house, leaving me with two other people. At first I thought she was calling the gendarmes, but the people explained that we were friends."

Finally, the woman who ran out of the house returned with a woman named Mademoiselle Rickenback, who was fluent in English. She then helped sort out the conundrum. The address that Roach had been given was 9 *Place* de la République, but he had wound up next door to that same number on *Boulevard* de la République. While the former street is a quiet side street, the latter is still a busy thoroughfare. Coincidentally, the building at 9 Boulevard de la République, the establishment that Roach found to be a cabaret catering to German officers, was still operating as a night club and discothèque as late as 2019.

The women then escorted the American to the correct address, a modest two-story, stuccoed brick building on a hard-to-find street less than 300 meters from the cabaret.

At last Roach met Mademoiselle Vigier – but she told him that he could not stay at her house. Mademoiselle Rickenback then came up with an alternate plan. She knew someone who had a relative, and it turned out he was able to help. After a short walk down a series of very narrow streets, they arrived at the home of Monsieur Jean Thibaut at 17 Place Carnot, where Roach was shown to a room which he found to his liking.

Luck had smiled on the wayfaring stranger. Had Roach gone to the right address first, he would never have met Mademoiselle Rickenback, and might well have been out of luck.

"I was [told] to stay [at Place Carnot] until they could contact an organization to assist me," Roach wrote. "By this time, quite a few people knew I was there and they brought food and [ration vouchers] to the house; also cigarettes and a few books to read. With the food ration[ing] it was impossible for one family to feed me for long. A half pound of bread per day, a liter of wine per week, and four packs of cigarettes per month. No milk, except for children."

He did not mention a chocolate ration, which was not even on the list of approved and available goods.

Roach recalled in his notebook that he remained as a guest of Monsieur Thibaut and his wife for nearly three weeks, though he did get out and about, surreptitiously moving about in his civilian clothes, observing the goings on in the city. He mentioned in his escape and evasion report that he began seeing and hearing increased Luftwaffe activity overhead after the final surrender of German and Italian forces in North Africa on May 13. He added that he had heard there were about 5,000 German troops in Agen in early May when he arrived, but that "gradually they were being shipped out. By the 30th of May it was considerably noticeable."

During his time with the Thibauts, he was visited by Father Patrick Kelly, a Catholic priest from County Down in Northern Ireland, who promised to make arrangements with "the organization" to get Roach across the border into Spain.

The priest also promised to produce false identity papers for the airman. Father Kelly never came through on the latter pledge, but Mademoiselle

Vigier reappeared and handled it. She took the small passport-sized headshots that Roach had in his survival kit, and returned a few days later with papers identifying him as "André Dubon," a deaf and dumb brush maker. This faux disability would allow Roach, whose French was very poor, to avoid speaking if questioned by the French police or the Gestapo.

On Saturday, May 29, things began moving quickly. Mademoiselle Vigier arrived to tell him that he was to board a train for a two-hour trip to Bordeaux. He later wrote that he traveled in a first class compartment, and that there was no identity paper check.

"Instructing [me] to keep my mouth shut, a strange man took me to the train," Roach recalled. "I sat in a compartment with women and German soldiers. The man left the train. I was being watched by a different man so I sat quietly until we reached [Bordeaux]. Here, he motioned to follow him and we took a streetcar ride."

The man took him to a large house, where a meeting of a French Socialist group was in progress. Afterward, Roach was passed off to a third handler. Whereas the first two had been very reticent and serious, this man was just the opposite.

"The man who took me seemed very happy to do so," Roach wrote. "He continually had a big grin on his face… He was definitely against the *Allemands* [Germans] as he had spent a year in a German prison… [As] we started toward the railroad station, he explained all the sights of interest in French, and I understood some of it. [He] insisted that we stop at a couple of cafes to drink a beer."

Thus fortified, they finally reached the train station, where they boarded a third class car for a two-hour ride to Foix, about 50 road miles from the Spanish border. Here, the man took his American friend to his home.

"He explained that he had another house outside the town and I was to stay there by myself for two nights," Roach noted. "He brought me food and two books. I played cook for two days which was enjoyable after my three-week sojourn [in Agen, where the Thibauts did the cooking]."

On the third evening there was a rendezvous at a cafe where a young boy was to escort Roach by bus into the country, where he was to stay on a farm until it was time to make the border crossing into Spain.

"After a couple of drinks, we went on a two-hour bus ride [with] more Germans to look at," he wrote. "Upon reaching the town, the boy took me into a cafe for three aperitifs. From there, we went to his house for supper. They had a great wine cellar and we sampled many wines. His brother spoke a little English, so we went to the cafe for the evening."

The following morning, a young law student named Jean Soem showed up at the farmhouse to take Roach to his house. Here, he met an English-speaking woman who translated the details of Soem's plan to take a group of people across the Pyrenees in three days' time. Even with this explained, Roach was hesitant about joining Soem's traveling party.

Nevertheless, the three of them got along well. As Roach remembered, he "stayed at his [Soem's] house until the wee hours of the morning drinking cognac and talking."

Roach eventually went back to the farmhouse, where he awoke on Wednesday, June 2, "feeling good about getting the information about how they intended to cross the mountains. I decided to go with them."

Roach had not yet used any of the 2,000 French francs that he had in his survival kit, having depended upon the generosity of the French people whom he had met, but he was now about to open his wallet. He bought a pair of "hob-nailed hiking shoes" and heavy socks from a man named Monsieur Maynard. Most of the money, though, would go to pay the mountain guide.

Soem had explained that most of their trip would be made under cover of darkness, and two nights later, they assembled at the trailhead around midnight. Including their lead guide and two of his deputies, there were around 40 people, all of them men, except for one woman. Roach was the only one who was not French.

"The rendezvous reminded me of a small army," he later wrote, painting a picture of the scene in the moments before they started. "Some of the men were French army men, one French pilot, and the rest were avoiding German labor conscription," he wrote. "A very ragged looking bunch. A few were armed as if we met any German patrols on the mountains they were to be knocked off. These patrols usually consist of two men and they also have vicious police dogs with them. To my surprise, a couple of the men had lived in north France and could speak some English. My friend [Soem] could speak Spanish and a few of the others spoke German, having been in German prison camps."

Roach went on to say that they began at a rapid pace, as the beginning was said to be the most dangerous part of the trek.

"It was very dark and hot and we just stumbled consistently," he remembered. "Often times, we practically crawled, but the guide knew every bush and tree and did not let us rest very often. In the morning after walking eight hours, we stopped in the woods, but nobody slept… by this time my legs were very stiff."

Part of the reason for resting among the trees was that the Luftwaffe patrolled the French side of the Pyrenees, looking for groups exactly like this one. However, the guide knew their routine, and the party was under way as soon as the Messerschmitts had passed.

A short time later, they stopped at a small stone farm house, where they were joined by a man and his wife. They had been making the crossing with another group, but he had hurt his ankle and they had waited eight days for him to recover, and for another group to pass by on the same trail.

The next night, that of Sunday June 6, was the most difficult of the journey. As Roach described it, the mountains were "very steep and treacherous, no paths, just rocks to climb. By this time, we were very high and had a great deal of snow to contend with."

Roach wrote that Soem proved to be "a very sturdy fellow," happy to shoulder the weight of a heavy pack that he and Roach took turns carrying.

The following morning, after hiking continuously for 12 hours, they made a brief rest stop at one of the small stone huts that serve as refuges from blizzards in the Pyrenees. The temptation was to collapse into a long and well deserved slumber, but their guide prodded them to keep moving because he wanted to get across the border as soon as possible.

The going continued to be rough, as the next leg of the trip involved climbing a steep, snow-covered mountain side. The sun was out now and it was very hot despite the ice. The glare off the snow fields was blinding.

Somewhere, high above and beyond these glistening, icy cliffs lay their escape hatch from occupied Europe.

Chapter 14

Perils of the Pyrenees

When Harry Roach, young Jean Soem, and their exhausted group reached the snow-covered summit of the Pyrenees, their guide, who had been prodding them incessantly, finally acquiesced to a lunch break. The American was able to look around at his surroundings.

"It was a beautiful sight to see a lake down in the valley and the frontier beyond it," he recalled. "Another two hours and we were sitting on [another] mountain top on the frontier. One man had injured his ankle and it took six to carry him up this last mountain. My right knee was swollen and I could not assist."

Roach recalled that as soon as he took his first steps inside Spain, he lay down and slept for an hour. He had been walking for 30.

"The route now was directly down a snow-glacier, which I enjoyed very much," he wrote. "My hob nail shoes enabled me to slide down at a good speed without falling, with the aid of a baton. Upon reaching the valley, which is now in Spain, we followed the river. Everybody's spirit was good so we walked until midnight."

When they had crossed the border, the party split up. Coming off the steep mountain snow into the rocky foothills, they no longer saw it necessary to band together for mutual support.

There were some who could travel faster than the others, so they kept moving when others stopped to rest. Roach and Soem were initially among 15 people in such a group, though this contingent splintered into even smaller groups over the next few days.

Late on their first night in Spain, this group came upon a shelter cabin, where another party had been spending the night. They coaxed this party into abandoning the house to get an especially early start on their next day's traveling, and made themselves at home.

Harry Roach slept for a precious four hours on a wooden bench in the small stone hut, and then took his first bath in more than a week in a nearby stream. Talk now turned to the days ahead. Fear of the Gestapo and being thrown into a German stalag were now behind them, but they still had to be careful of the Spanish police.

As the escapees from occupied France had learned from the guides and others familiar with the politics of the Pyrenees, reaching Spanish territory would not mark an end to their trials, but only a change in the nature of their challenges.

The *carabineros*, the Spanish border guards, had a reputation for coming down hard on *contrabandistas* in these mountains. They usually gave the Allied evaders a pass if they had believable paperwork, but they were known to shoot first and ask questions second. It was best not to cross paths with them.

That morning, to avoid such a confrontation, the guide urged Roach, Soem, and the others to scramble a safe distance up a nearby mountainside while the morning patrol made its way past the cabin on their daily circuit. The hours dragged by, and when no such patrol had appeared by 3:00pm, the men decided they were not coming. As if on cue, though, two *carabineros* appeared just as they had started down the trail.

"They took a couple of shots at us, and we decided to give up," Roach recalled of their anticlimactic surrender.

With carbines at the ready, the two *carabineros* approached the men, demanding papers and explanations.

One of the men, either Soem or another man who spoke Spanish, concocted a fanciful tale of their being French Canadians. This would explain the French surnames on their forged papers, and the presence of men such as Roach, who spoke English. Amazingly, the two Spaniards bought the story and told them to be on their way.

In retrospect, it seemed like they had slipped through the confrontation easily, but they soon realized how narrow their escape had been. As the terrain became more open, they could see farther ahead on their own trail, and they could make out another trail snaking across an adjacent hillside. On this trail was another *carabinero* patrol, and they were putting another group under arrest. Possibly these people were smugglers, or maybe they were just unlucky travelers with their papers not in order.

Having hiked about four hours from the place where they had slept, Roach's party reached a point from which they could look down on the small Catalonian town of Alp. By now, the group consisted only of Roach, Soem, the French pilot, a French army surgeon, and another young man. Roach later speculated that they "were the only five [from their original traveling party] who had not been picked up [by the *carabineros*]."

Their destination was another town about eight miles from Alp where Soem had a contact who could help them. To avoid further *carabinero* encounters, they decided to get off the trail and stay in the hills rather than going though Alp and risking being seen.

Circling around the city was no easy task. After leaving the trail, they found themselves wallowing through the brush, slashing their hands on thorns. They were still ensnarled in this jungle as the sun went down, so they spent a miserable night among the brambles.

"We tried to sleep but it was terrifically cold," Roach recalled in his E&E Report No.44. "One man had a bottle of shaving lotion which he drank to keep warm. One mouthful was enough for me to decide it was no good."

In the morning, they struggled on, but after passing another small town, they decided to take their chances on the road that ran though the valley below.

Within a few hours, they had finally reached the town where Soem's contact lived and had located his address. Roach does not name this village, but it was probably Belver de Cerdanya, the only large town within an eight-mile radius of Alp.

It was decided that they would go to the local police station and have Roach ask to telephone the American Consulate in Barcelona. For some reason, possibly because there was no phone connection, the police loaded the disheveled travelers into a van and drove thcm 60 miles west to the small mountain town of Sort, from which Roach was able to get the American Consulate on the phone.

The man at the consulate, the first American with whom Roach had spoken in more than a month, promised to send cables to Roach's wife and parents, and promised to meet him at the police station in the larger city of Lérida.

Although their three-hour drive down out of the Pyrenees foothills to Lérida on Thursday, June 10 was uneventful, a surprise awaited the tired travelers. The four Frenchmen found themselves under arrest – and only the timely arrival of the man from the American Consulate saved Roach from the same fate.

Chapter 15

New Lives, Later Lives

Harry Roach's life abruptly changed. The man from the consulate, who was a Spanish national, took the American shopping for badly needed new clothes, and for city shoes to replace his hob nails. With his fresh wardrobe, Roach was checked into a hotel in Lérida, where he had "the best meal I'd had in a long time… better than England."

The consular official departed, leaving the American with enough spending money "to now lead the life of a king."

Among other things, he strolled down to a stationery shop called Sotos, and bought a 40-page Competidor-brand spiral notebook. On Saturday, June 12, two days after arriving in Lérida, he sat down, perhaps at a sidewalk café or back at the hotel, and proceeded to jot down his recollections of everything that had happened to him during the preceding two weeks.

On June 19, another man from the consulate arrived to collect him. Harry Roach said *adiós* – or *adéu* if he had picked up some of the local Catalan dialect – to this comfortable provincial capital and began his journey home. After a night in Zaragossa, he was in Alhama until the evening of June 25, when a consulate car came to take him to Gibraltar. By the afternoon of Tuesday, June 29, Lieutenant Harry Roach was back with his 427th Bomb Squadron, 303rd Bomb Group in Molesworth, via a stopover in Bristol where he learned that he was the only member of the *Black Swan* crew to have evaded capture.

What then of the others whom we mentioned at the top of this section who were part of the May Day mission over Saint Nazaire?

Maynard "Snuffy" Smith, who had valiantly fought that fire and saved the B-17 piloted by Lewis Johnson, had cut it close. The aircraft's fuselage broke in two pieces upon landing. Amid all of the heroism that was going around in the Eighth Air Force in those difficult days, Snuffy might not have been singled out if not for a writer for *Stars and Stripes*, the GI newspaper, named Andy Rooney. An article by Rooney, who later had a long and celebrated career as a CBS-TV commentator, made Smith hard to ignore.

In a ceremony on July 15, 1943, Smith received the Medal of Honor personally from Secretary of War Henry Stimson, who was in England touring American bases and secretly briefing Winston Churchill on the Manhattan Project.

Bob Morgan and the crew of the *Memphis Belle* completed their 25 missions and flew the aircraft back to the States to become the centerpiece of a triumphant publicity and war bond marketing tour. Released in 1944, William Wyler's documentary of the same name made the *Memphis Belle* a household name. Having achieved minor celebrity status, Morgan transitioned into the B-29 Superfortress and participated in the strategic air campaign against Japan. He remained in the Air Force Reserve until 1965 and was a popular figure on the air show circuit until his death in 2004. The *Memphis Belle* herself survived the war and was eventually sold as surplus. After going through a number of civilian owners, she has been on display at the National Museum of the US Air Force in Ohio since 2018.

The fragments of Jay Sterling's *Black Swan* were long ago scrapped, but in 1984, a monument to her crew was erected near the crash site along Rue Beau-Soliel, a county road passing through Morandières. As noted earlier, the Path of Memory plaque describing the crash was installed adjacent to the monument in 2015. There is a short residential street named Impasse Black Swan in the nearby village of Saint-Père-en-Retz.

Harry Edwin Roach, Jr, never flew another combat mission, given Eighth Air Force practice not to return evaders to flight status because they knew too much about evasion routes and the people who ran them. Instead, he worked briefing aircrews on what to expect if they were shot down.

In 1944, he returned home for flight training. He wanted to be a pilot. He remained in the USAAF as it became the independent US Air Force in 1947, and made the transition from piston-engine aircraft to jets. Sadly, it was in a jet cockpit that his life came to an early end. On October 1, 1954, the Lockheed T-33 trainer that he was piloting crashed at Sioux City, Iowa. He was only 34. By coincidence, Sioux City was the home town of Jay Sterling, the pilot of *Black Swan*, who died in France on May 1, 1943.

In 1984, Roach's son, Harry E. Roach III, who was just nine years old when his father died, traveled to France to spend two months revisiting the places where his father had been and meeting the people who had helped him along the way. He was on hand for the dedication of the *Black Swan* monument.

PART FOUR

BLACK TUESDAY BOYS

Chapter 16

Inside the Third Reich

Tuesday, August 17, 1943 was a milestone moment for the Eighth Air Force and its strategic air campaign against the Third Reich. The missions flown that day were among the largest and most complex to date. They were also a stunning reminder for the Eighth of the deadliness of German air defenses. This is how the day came to be known among the men of the Eighth as *Black* Tuesday.

August 17 also marked the one-year anniversary of the first mission against occupied Europe flown by the heavy bombers of the Eighth. Back in 1942, it was just a dozen Flying Fortresses of the 97th Bomb Group, then the only operational bomb group in the Eighth Air Force. Led personally by Brigadier General Ira Eaker, commander of the Eighth's VIII Bomber Command, they targeted railroad marshalling yards in northern France. A year later, the Eighth was now routinely launching missions with more than a hundred heavy bombers, and they were now striking targets deep inside Germany.

But this came at a cost. The more aircraft that went out, the more individual aircraft – each with ten men aboard – there were that never returned. And the deeper they went, the higher the toll exacted by German flak gunners on the ground and Luftwaffe interceptors in the skies.

The August 17 operation was big, and also complex. The latter came in its being a double mission. Bombers would be funneled into a pair of target cities, each directly associated with aspects of the German arms industry – Regensburg and Schweinfurt.

Regensburg was where Messerschmitt, the great German planemaker, manufactured the very Luftwaffe interceptors that caused the Eighth Air Force so much grief. Nearly 60 percent of all Luftwaffe fighters were Messerschmitt Bf 109s, and the company produced more than 10,000 of them at their plant in Regensburg, nearly a third of total production.

Schweinfurt's stock in trade was even more vital to the German war industry. Schweinfurt was the center for production of anti-friction bearings – ball bearings, roller bearings, etc. Every motor in every aircraft and every vehicle that flowed into the German war machine needed bearings, so Allied strategic planners called this a "bottleneck" industry. It was one which, if removed from the supply chain, would negatively affect a myriad of other industries. Most of Germany's bearing factories, or *Kugellager*, were located in or near Schweinfurt.

Schweinfurt and Regensburg were obvious targets involving missions more easily said than done. Both were located in Bavaria in southern Germany, more than 400 miles from Eighth Air Force bases in Britain. This put both cities at the limits of the effective range of bomb-laden American aircraft, and substantially beyond the range of fighter escorts.

As this author wrote in *Big Week: Six Days That Changed the Course of World War II* (2012), these cities were "like a tempting piece of fruit hanging on a limb beyond a precipice, just out of reach, easily seen, but untouchable without considerable peril. Regensburg and Schweinfurt presented a level of danger beyond what had yet been experienced by the Eighth."

The operation involved a total of 375 B-17 Flying Fortresses in two contingents. The Schweinfurt strike force was the 1st Bomb Wing, commanded by Brigadier General Robert Williams, who led 230 bombers from nine bomb groups. The Regensburg force, the 4th Bomb Wing commanded by Colonel Curtis LeMay, included bombers from seven bomb groups.

The price that would be paid on Black Tuesday was unbearably high, so high that Eighth Air Force planners wondered how they could sustain such losses going forward. Out of 375 bombers, 60 would be shot down and many were so badly damaged that they had to be written off. To put the loss of 60 into perspective, imagine the survivors who pondered 600 empty bunks where friends had slept the night before.

Our story here is a reminder that not *all* of those empty bunks represented men who were never coming back.

Flying out of Ridgewell in Essex, 381st Bomb Group contributed 20 B-17 Flying Fortresses to the Schweinfurt mission and lost nine, nearly half. It was the highest loss rate suffered by any group that day. Two of those that went down were *King Malfunction II* of the 381st's 532rd Bomb Squadron and *Chug-a-Lug Lulu* (formerly known as *Widget*) of the 535th Bomb Squadron. The former aircraft's nose art was a cigar-smoking gremlin wearing a crown, while the latter's depicted a monkey drinking beer from a wooden barrel.

On this Tuesday that became so black, the 532rd was the lead squadron in the 381st, the low group of the 1st Bomb Wing. At the controls of *King Malfunction II* was 1st Lieutenant Jack Painter. As was often the case with lead bombers, the copilot, 2nd Lieutenant Everett Ragan, was flying in the tail gunner's position so he could observe the formation behind them. On the flight deck opposite Painter, in Ragan's place as copilot, was 1st Lieutenant Robert Elmer Nelson, the 381st Bomb Group operations officer, who was acting as deputy group commander for the mission.

Over Aachen, Germany, about 250 miles from their base at Ridgewell in Essex and about 190 miles short of Schweinfurt, the group slid into a corridor of heavy flak set up to bracket bomber formations as they passed through this slice of German airspace. Next, as their fighter escort had to turn back, the bombers came under what Nelson later described as "the worst fighter attack I had ever seen."

The Luftwaffe reception committee numbered around 300 interceptors, including those of Jagdgeschwader 11 (JG 11), whose Bf 109G-6 fighters had just been armed with Werfer-Granate 21 air-to-air rockets.

"Scarcely did one group of enemy fighters withdraw before another took its place," wrote historian Arthur B. Ferguson.[13] "The Luftwaffe unleashed every trick and device in its repertoire... In some instances entire squadrons attacked in 'javelin up' formation, which made evasive action on the part of the bombers extremely difficult. In others, three and four enemy aircraft came on abreast, attacking simultaneously. Occasionally the enemy resorted to vertical attacks from above, driving straight down at the bombers with fire concentrated on the general vicinity of the top turret, a tactic which proved effective."

As both the number one and number three engines aboard *King Malfunction II* were knocked out, Nelson reached down to feather the props before all the oil was lost. With two engines out, the bomber could no longer keep up with the formation, and as they fell behind, the interceptors piled on. Painter and Nelson decided that they would "dive to the deck" to get away.

When the number two engine was finally shot out, Painter "put the ship into a steep, fast dive, taking evasive action" as he went. The German fighters chased them down from 20,000 to 17,000 feet before breaking off from this hopelessly crippled aircraft to continue hunting.

"I thought the controls were shot out because we were out of control," Nelson remembered in his escape and evasion report.[14] "However, at 10,000 feet we leveled off."

When Painter gave the order to bail out, the navigator, 2nd Lieutenant William Keays, was the first out from the forward part of the aircraft. Nelson waited for the bombardier, 2nd Lieutenant Lloyd Duke, and the flight engineer, Sergeant Matthew Kowalski, to jump before he abandoned the bomber. He then glanced back and saw Painter right behind him.

"I fell into a spin as soon as I left the aircraft," Nelson recalled. "But by holding my legs stiff in front of me and pulling my arms tight to my side, I stopped the spinning motion."

He delayed pulling the ripcord until he guessed he was at about 7,000 feet above the forest below. The idea was to have the parachute canopy visible from the ground for the shortest time possible.

Looking around, he counted seven parachutes as he watched *King Malfunction II*, one engine in flames, tip into a steep dive. Though Nelson did not know it at the time, Jack Painter never managed to escape the aircraft before it hit the ground. His body was found still aboard.

Below him, Nelson saw a road leading through a meadow between two patches of forest. The nearest parachute to him was that of Sergeant Raymond Genz, the right waist gunner – who was being shot at by a German farmer with a rifle. The airmen had been briefed ahead of time about the general helpfulness of Belgian and French civilians and the hostility of those here in Germany. They were known to be brutal to the downed Allied airmen whose bombers had brought terrible destruction to German cities.

Nelson came down with his parachute had snagged in a tree, leaving him dangling about 30 feet off the ground. Finally, Nelson swung himself against a tree trunk, grabbed it, and was able to climb down uninjured. By this time, he could see Genz running toward him through the trees.

Being only about a quarter mile from the farmhouse belonging to the man with the gun, they decided that time was of the essence. They left Nelson's parachute where it hung, ditched their heavy flying gear, and took off running. They had gone about 300 yards when they heard a loud crash ahead of them. Looking up, they saw Sergeant Norman Whitman, the left waist gunner, coming down into a tree, and get hung up as Nelson had been.

"Take your time," they shouted urgently as they watched a panicked Whitman thrashing about. Finally, he got to a tree and grabbed hold of it, but as he unfastened his chute, he lost his grip and fell about 40 feet, his back striking the ground. When Genz and Nelson reached Whitman, he clearly had the wind knocked out of him and was in pain. They guessed that he had probably broken some ribs. As they pulled off Whitman's flight gear and were getting him ready to travel, Sergeant Allen Kellogg, the ball turret gunner, arrived on the scene, limping from his own injuries.

The airmen made their way to a stream that they heard gurgling nearby, and filled their water bottles. All but Whitman took some benzedrine – as if the adrenaline rush of the past half hour was not enough.

They paused and caught their breath. No more than ten minutes had passed since Nelson and Genz had landed. High above them, the stream of Flying Fortresses headed toward Schweinfurt was still visible.

The question on everyone's mind was "what now?"

Deciding that they would look for a place for the injured Whitman and Kellogg to hide, they worked their way for about 100 yards along the stream as the thick brush gave way to a series of open meadows and farm fields. They followed the edge of the woods until they stumbled into a ravine that offered good possibilities for concealing Whitman and Kellogg.

"We stayed with them for an hour, examining our escape kits for first aid equipment," Nelson remembered. "No one of us had the presence of mind to remove the first aid kit which was attached to [each] parachute. We discussed returning to get one, but knew the trip was too risky."

It was decided that Genz and Nelson would explore the surrounding countryside for a better hiding place. They calculated that they had come less than a mile from where their parachutes had brought them, so it was certain that their ravine was within the search radius of German troops hunting for them.

Promising to return before midnight, Genz and Nelson headed out to survey the area. They walked south along the edge of the woods, being careful not to venture into the open where they might be seen by the farm workers laboring in the surrounding fields. When they reached the road which Nelson had seen as he was descending beneath his parachute, they heard people coming up the road shouting, so they buried themselves in some nearby blackberry brambles. Soon, the noisy group appeared. Marching up the road was a formation of very young men who appeared to be part of a Hitler Youth group. No sooner had they passed, than another, similar bunch came. Through the afternoon, the two Americans saw several more. If they were meant to be searching for the bomber crewmen, they missed two by just a few feet.

Around dusk, they left their hiding place and returned to the ravine. After communicating through a set of prearranged low whistles, they managed to find the well-hidden, but damp and cold, Whitman and Kellogg in the darkness.

Nelson and Genz decided to move their shivering comrades up to their hiding place in the brambles near the road, and from there they moved into a field, where they could bed down on some bundled sheaves of grain.

Though everyone was exhausted – Whitman and Kellogg had nearly passed out as they made their way up the hill from the ravine – nobody could sleep. They gobbled more benzedrine, chasing it with some Horlick's malted milk balls, and sat down to come up with a plan.

They got out their maps and tried to calculate where they were and to decide where they were going. Having passed Aachen in their aircraft, they knew they were somewhere between there and Mannheim, where the bomber stream had a scheduled turn. In fact, they were only about 35 miles southeast of Aachen, near the village of Munstereifel.

They guessed that they were east of the Rhine and that they would have to cross it to get to France – but they were wrong. They had actually landed 20 miles *west* of the great river. In any case, they knew that a southwest compass heading would take them in the direction of the French border.

Once in France, they would at least be out of Germany, but not quite out of the proverbial woods. They would still have more than 700 miles of occupied France between them and the Spanish border. For this reason, they decided that it would better to try to make for Switzerland, which was only about 150 miles from the French border.

In his escape and evasion report, Nelson wrote, "I knew that four were too many to travel together, especially when we were in enemy country and two of us were injured... and Kellogg was blacking out every few minutes."[15]

Whether or not he phrased it exactly this way in their conversation that night, all four of the men recognized the elephant in the room. Whitman and Kellogg had already decided to opt out of continued efforts at evasion.

"The two sergeants realized they were in no condition to travel," Nelson recalled, "and stated that the next morning they would go out on the road and give themselves up to military personnel. We discussed this with them from every point of view so they wouldn't misunderstand our leaving them."

It was about midnight when the two pairs of crewmen from *King Malfunction II* said their farewells.

Kellogg and Whitman were captured the following day. Kellogg was incarcerated at Stalag Luft IV at Tychow in eastern Germany (now Tychowo in Poland), while Whitman went first to Stalag Luft VIIB in Moosburg, and later to Stalag Luft XVIIB in Krems, Austria. Both survived the war and were repatriated.

Painter was the crew's only fatality, and all but Nelson and Genz were soon captured.

Chapter 17

Desperate Fugitives

For those 381st Bomb Group Flying Fortresses that did manage to battle their way into the skies over Schweinfurt on August 17, 1943, the churning, concussing mass of flak and fighters was horrific. When he finally exited the target area just after 2:00pm, 1st Lieutenant Lorin Disbrow, at the controls of *Chug-a-Lug Lulu*, breathed a sigh of relief. The worst was over, he thought.

He was wrong.

Around 3:30pm, while Disbrow's 535th Bomb Squadron formation was about to exit German air space on a heading toward Brussels, the Luftwaffe interceptors that had mauled them earlier in the day – downing aircraft such as *King Malfunction II* – hit them again. The oil system of *Chug-a-Lug Lulu* was shot up and the number three engine was hit. Disbrow tried to feather the windmilling propeller, but could not and *Chug-a-Lug Lulu* began to lose altitude. As the aircraft dropped out of the formation, the Luftwaffe jumped them. Stragglers were easy prey. The number four engine was hit, and then number two.

Watching all this from the vantage point of his position as the top turret gunner, Tech Sergeant Otto Bruzewski recalled in his escape and evasion report, "there was nothing left to hold us up and we started down."[16]

Bruzewski's interphone had been destroyed, so he never heard the order to bail out. He continued to fire .50-caliber rounds at Fw 190s until Disbrow shouted up to him over the din of the battle to abandon ship. He pulled on his parachute and left *Chug-a-Lug Lulu* at around 10,000 feet. He could see Disbrow and another gunner jump right after him.

Waiting until he was well away from the hazard of getting the parachute tangled in the props, Bruzewski finally yanked his ripcord. Dangling beneath his silk canopy, he could see *Chug-a-Lug Lulu* in her gradual descent, still being pecked at by Focke-Wulf Fw 190s. Around him, he counted nine parachutes, most of them close to the ground. He had been one of the last out.

He took off his thick gloves and watched them fall away. Then he pulled off his helmet, oxygen mask, and throat mike "and watched them fall, one by one." He had no more need for any of these things.

Far below was a network of roads threading though patches of forest. There were people all over the roads. "I thought I had very little chance [to avoid capture] for I believed we were still over Germany."

Bruzewski landed gently. His parachute was snagged in some tree branches, but he was only a few inches from the ground. As he unfastened himself and discarded his heavy, insulated high-altitude pants, he could see people coming toward him through the underbrush, so he ran.

He crawled under a fence and concealed himself from the crowd of civilians that swarmed after him, searching the wood for about two hours. "Once, a man stood two feet from my face," Bruzewski recalled. "I stared at him through the grass but he never saw me."

By dusk, the crowds had finally gone away, and Bruzewski emerged from his hiding place. He brushed himself off and decided to head south on the nearest road, hoping eventually to reach the French border.

He passed quietly through a sleeping village and continued south only to find himself lost. His wanderings took him back to the same village – *three times*. At last, he found that his compass needle had gotten jammed. "It was daybreak before I got straightened out, and I did not feel that it was safe to travel further [in the daylight]."

With this, he hid himself in the brush in a dry ditch near the rectory of a small church and fell asleep, exhausted.

During that same warm summer night that Otto Bruzewski was running in circles, Robert Nelson and Raymond Genz, late of *King Malfunction II*, were making their way through the rolling farm fields of the Rhineland, hoping to appear unobtrusive. As a gunner, Genz wore coveralls, which made him look at first glance like a factory worker, but Nelson's khakis and brown leather A-2 flight jacket made him stand out as someone who was definitely *not* a German civilian.

A native of Gresham, Oregon, the 26-year-old Nelson had joined the USAAF two months before Pearl Harbor. As an officer, he outranked Genz, who was three years his senior. Genz had joined the service just after Pearl Harbor. His home town was McGrath, Minnesota, a small town of 140 people situated in a rural landscape about 80 miles due north of the Twin Cities, a town about the size of those which he was to see in Germany over the next several days.

It was quiet, except for the crickets, and the world at war seemed a world away.

As they walked, they probably commented on the similarity of this landscape to those with which they were familiar back home. They paused to pick some apples as they walked through an orchard, and later discovered that they were in some kind of park, with "wide clean footpaths and picnic grounds." Having decided to take a cigarette break at a picnic table, their feeling of detachment from the reality of war had to have been remarkable.

As they moved on, they passed through a kale field and stopped at a stream to refill their water bottles. Discovering that they were walking through fields of turnips and potatoes, they "filled every available pocket with them."

They came upon a small village and circled wide around it. They could hear dogs barking, though it did not seem that the dogs had noticed the two Americans. Bypassing another village, their southwesterly hike brought them into a thick forest. They found an old wagon road, but they decided to abandon it in favor of following their compass on a straight course. As they were tired, and it was too dark to start plowing through the dark forest, they decided to conceal themselves and get some rest. At about 7:00am, after three hours of sleep, they resumed their hike, discovering a narrow trail through the deep woods. By now, though, their course was taking them more south than west.

Two hearts missed a beat at the sound of a slight rustling in the brush ahead. They stopped in their tracks as some deer crossed the trail and disappeared into the shadows.

The Americans later began seeing what looked like a series of observation towers, similar to the fire lookouts in the national forests in the United States. These seemed to be unoccupied, but Nelson and Genz were careful nonetheless. After a while, they figured out these were stands used by deer hunters. This was confirmed by climbing into one and finding it filled with shell casings.

At one point, they heard people talking and peered through the trees to see a cement blockhouse with an antiaircraft gun on top and a German sentry with his back to them. They gave this obstacle a wide berth, keeping a wary eye on the man.

When they finally reached the far edge of the forest, there was no one around so they made a dangerous daytime dash through a field toward another forest in the distance. They were just congratulating one another on their luck when they heard someone coming. About 200 yards away, coming up the same trail they were about to take, they saw a German woodcutter with an axe across his shoulder – *and he saw them.*

"Assuming a nonchalant swagger, we made a right-angle turn away from the path," Nelson recalled. "As soon as we thought we were out of his sight, we ran until we were on the opposite side of the woods. Spread before us was a wide, open valley. A village lay at the bottom of the slope in our path. Where the thick brush by the wood's edge was shaded by trees, we stopped to rest."

Planning to start out again at nightfall, the Americans enjoyed some of their apples and raw turnips, and spent the afternoon of Wednesday, August 18 taking naps.

As Nelson and Genz passed through a succession of valleys and forest, they passed some nearby workmen, who did not notice them, and saw a woman with some dogs herding cattle in one of the fields. Nelson reported that the dogs "disregarded us, no matter how close we came to them. They were well-trained to stay with the cattle."

Just before dark, they heard the footsteps of someone on the nearby trail, someone coming ever closer. Nelson and Genz crouched down and held their breath, remaining perfectly still as their friend the wood-cutter passed just 15 feet away.

After he was long gone, they ate a couple of the Horlick's lozenges and a square of chocolate from their survival kits, and stepped out into the gathering darkness of their second night in Germany.

By about 2:00am on Thursday, they had gone about five miles when they found themselves in another grain field and decided to make beds of some of the bundled sheaves and rest until dawn. As they continued their hike, they reached another deep forest, one more wild and rugged than those of the day before.

As the sun came up, they came to a paved road. Several bicycles and a couple of small cars passed, but it was not a busy thoroughfare. Beside the road was a signpost announcing the name of the next village. They could not find it on their map so they assumed that it was too small.

In fact, they were lost.

They were going the right direction, but they still incorrectly believed themselves to be *east* of the Rhine River.

Late Thursday afternoon, they came to a stream, where they washed their socks as well as themselves. As they were eating blackberries and waiting for their socks to dry in the warm August sunshine, it suddenly dawned on them that all of the streams they'd seen flowed eastward. It was now clear to them that they were actually *west* of the Rhine. France was much closer than they had thought!

Early on their third morning, Friday, August 20, Nelson and Genz reached a valley "which we dared not cross in daytime," because it was filled with fields and pastures, with farmworkers and people with dogs herding cattle. Across this valley lay "a large smoky city," with another about ten miles farther on.

Nelson made no mention of whether he identified these from his map. There are several medium-sized cities a two-day walk southwest of their original flight path that might match the description. One of these may have been Bitburg, as their route did take them near it.

They spent the day sleeping and resting, and successfully made it across the open space, a distance of about ten miles, at dusk. By now, they had mastered the routine of crossing valleys mainly under darkness, circling wide around villages, and resting in woods where they could find concealment.

For the most part, they were able to avoid people. They had a scare early on Saturday morning as they were waking up and brushing off their clothes. A passerby paused to watch them as they continued what they were doing. The Americans got up slowly, ambled into the woods, and as soon as they were out of his sight, they started running. As they reached a cement factory with no one around, they squeezed through an unlocked gate, ran out the other side, and kept running all morning.

They spent Saturday afternoon concealed near a wheat field where people were working, and the evening picking apples in a nearby orchard. They tried to put a few miles behind them that night, but for the first time since they'd been in Germany, clouds moved in and obscured the moonlight. Because of this, they wound up walking on roads, where they saw several people walking in the other direction. As Nelson recalled, "none of them paid any attention to us, although we passed within a few feet of them."

They traveled about three miles and had begun crossing a clearing when two rifle shots suddenly rang out.

The men stopped, remaining motionless in the moonless darkness.

Who was shooting?

Were Nelson and Genz their targets?

When would the third shot come?

Chapter 18

Shipwrecked Brothers

On Wednesday, August 18, 1943, as Nelson and Genz of *King Malfunction II* were warily circling an antiaircraft site in a dark German forest, Tech Sergeant Otto Bruzewski, top turret gunner of *Chug-a-Lug Lulu*, was waking up, assuming he was in Germany.

Looking around the overgrown ditch where he had spent the night, Bruzewski was like a shipwrecked sailor, washed up on a desert island. He had arrived disoriented in a strange and unfamiliar place that was actually between Boirs and Tongeren in Belgium, about 40 miles west of the German border.

He had found no drinkable water and his own water bottle was empty, so he made do with some apples and pears from nearby trees, and ate some chocolate and Horlick's tablets from his survival kit. As Wednesday drew to a close, he resumed his journey. Based on the setting sun, he calculated that his compass was no longer jammed, and he headed southwest.

Coming to another village, Bruzewski decided to sneak though an alley rather than take the more prudent course of circling around the town. Without warning, a man in tall boots, such as were worn by German troops, stepped into the alley ahead of him, casually smoking a cigarette. Rather than confronting him, Bruzewski just turned and walked back the way he had come. As he rounded a corner, the American glanced back. He was not being followed.

Bruzewski walked all night, and toward Thursday morning, when it was still dark, he turned down a muddy side road. Suddenly, he stumbled into a clearing and saw a group of German soldiers.

"When a man yelled at me in German, I knew something was wrong," Bruzewski recalled with understatement in his escape and evasion report.

"I stopped and looked across the field toward the voice. I saw guns, and realized that I had run into a mobile antiaircraft battery. I froze in my tracks and watched. No one came toward me, so I decided that I had not been seen, and that they must have been yelling at one another. I retraced my steps, and left the area safely."[17]

At last, he found a suitable place, amid some orchards and farm fields, to wait until nightfall. He spent the remaining daylight hours eating plums and apples, and pulling carrots. He picked up a small cabbage, but "it did not taste too good." Compared to some evaders, he was eating well – at least he was getting his fruit and vegetables.

He found a stream to fill his water bottle, but "it tasted disagreeably of rubber," even though he had rinsed it three times. He finally dozed off at the edge of the woods near a corner of a sugar beet field, but awoke a few hours later to the sound of someone working in the field. Bruzewski opened his eyes to see a man standing about 20 feet away looking at him. The man asked by gesturing whether Bruzewski was hungry.

Bruzewski nodded.

"*Moi Belgique… et vous?* the man asked"

Bruzewski explained that he was an "*Americain.*"

For two days, he had run and hid as though he was in Germany, but now he cautiously realized that he was probably in Belgium.

"He told me to wait there until he returned," Bruzewski explained. "I was uncertain as to whether this would be wise or not. I looked at the house to which he was going, and saw that there were no telephone wires [with which to contact the Gestapo]. The field was so long and open, that I decided that if anything suspicious happened, I would have enough time to make a getaway."

His misgivings proved unfounded. A woman came out, bringing him a tray of sandwiches and coffee. She wanted to see his dog tags, and asked whether he had any passport photos. He did. She took one and went away.

As she left, she told him in sign language to stay where he was and that she would be back shortly. When she returned about 20 minutes later, she brought civilian clothes, a pick and shovel – to help him disguise himself as a farmworker – and a note written in English that read:

Dress. Take these tools and follow this woman.

– [signed] a friend

Late on Thursday, August 19, the woman who had disguised him as a farmworker took Otto Bruzewski to a house in Liers, a northern suburb of Liège, where he cleaned up and was served dinner. He then lay down in "the best bed in the house" and fell fast asleep.

It was about 7:00pm that evening when he was awakened and told that a car was waiting for him. He was driven to a Catholic rectory where there was a large group of men and a Belgian woman.

Like a lonely shipwrecked sailor, he was suddenly reunited with at least part of his shipwrecked crew.

In the group, Bruzewski recognized radio operator Staff Sergeant Tom Moore, tail gunner Staff Sergeant Bill Kiniklis, and ball turret gunner Staff Sergeant Joe Walters of *Chug-a-Lug Lulu*.

As with most bomber crews in the Eighth Air Force, this band of shipwrecked brothers from *Chug-a-Lug Lulu* was drawn from widely separated corners of the United States. Bruzewski was from Bay City, Michigan; Walters was from Pittsburgh; Moore was from Martinsville, Virginia; and Kiniklis came from Dorchester, Massachusetts.

As they were reunited, each of them was eager to share his story. Moore explained that he had been jerked so badly when his parachute opened that he blacked out. He awoke to six Fw 190s coming straight at him.

"They apparently split formation in order to miss me," he explained. "Their prop wash caught me and I swung violently back and forth in my parachute."

As later related in his escape and evasion report, Moore told of landing in a sugar beet field, and of how, like Bruzewski, he assumed that he was in Germany.[18] When a group of farmworkers started coming toward him with pitchforks, he saw that there was neither time nor place to hide, so he stayed where he had landed as the group approached and began gathering up his parachute. They were speaking to him in French, but as he later admitted, he could not tell French from German on his first day on continental soil. It was not until they began repeating the words "*Belgique, Belgique*," that he realized that he was not in Germany.

"A number of people came up to me and they all grabbed me and kissed me, a most embarrassing welcome," he recalled.

One man took him to a nearby orchard and offered him some apples, but another civilian approached and demanded that he surrender.

"I refused," Moore said tersely. "I saw that he had no gun and that he was no bigger than I, so I was quite prepared to fix him up in case he wanted to help me surrender."

Moore then left his challenger standing helplessly in the orchard, and went to find the man who'd earlier treated him to the apples. This man found him a place to hide, sent his children to bring waffles and other food, and arranged for him to come to the rectory in Liers.

Joe Walters told of landing in a tree. As later recorded in his escape and evasion report, he found himself about six feet off the ground, dangling above a group of people shouting at him in a language he did not understand.[19] He was sure it was neither French nor German and guessed it was Flemish. One man pulled him close to the ground, while another unbuckled his harness.

When Walters announced that he was an American, the people crowded around and began kissing him. A boy began climbing the tree to untangle his parachute, while two of the men grabbed Walters and escorted him away at a hurried pace. He was taken to a nearby tavern, where his new friends poured him a glass of cognac and showed him some local maps indicating that he was in the village of Boirs. He pointed to the line in his phrasebook that translated the words "Please help me."

Their conversation was rudely interrupted when someone rushed in to say that the Germans were coming. Walters, still dressed in his flying gear, was hustled back out the rear entrance. The two men, identified as Delbert and Lambert Tilkin, "spirited Joe to a barn loft where he squeezed into a small space beneath floorboards."[20] He remained hidden there until nearly midnight.

With a teenager named Janine Dardenne, and nicknamed "Sweetpea," serving as his interpreter, "Joe switched into workman's clothing. Outfitted with a pick and shovel he joined Sergeant Kenneth Fahncke the next day in a foundry. Fahnke had been shot down on the same day and the same area as Joe. The underground kept the two men together for much of the time they evaded."

Fahncke, of Celina, Ohio, had been the tail gunner of an unnamed Flying Fortress, tail number 42-3227, of the 327th Bomb Squadron, and was also part of the Schweinfurt mission. Fahncke had been brought to Liège by the same civilians who had aided Walters, and the two Americans would go on to travel together for the remainder of their time on the continent.

By coincidence, Fahncke's aircraft and *Chug-a-Lug Lulu* had come off the assembly line in Long Beach, California within an hour of one another on April 1, 1943. Both were Block 35 B-17Fs that were part of the 605 B-17Fs built by Douglas Aircraft Company as part of the pool of manufacturers which produced the Boeing-designed Flying Fortress.

On Friday, August 20, the shipwrecked Black Tuesday Boys who had gathered at the rectory – Bruzewski, Kiniklis, Moore, Walters, and Fahncke – were driven to the home of Dr Charles Kramer in Liège by a Belgian who claimed to be a former New York City cab driver. In his professional career, Kramer was a podiatrist, but under the German occupation, he led a double life as a member of the Belgian underground, operating a revolving door safe house through which downed Allied flyers passed.

While they were staying with Kramer, the Americans had contact with a number of civilians who had much to say about the general mood in occupied Europe. "The Germans' morale, according to the Belgians, is getting low and they are much worried about the bombing in Germany," Walters wrote in his escape and evasion report. "The German [occupation] soldiers seemed to be stationed in just the most conspicuous places, very few in the country[side]."[21]

Allied airmen came and went continuously at Kramer's "hostel." Some stayed for just a few days, others for much longer. For example, Walters and Fahncke left for Brussels with another man on September 3, but Bruzewski and Moore would remain in the city until October.

Chapter 19

Not an Easy Road

By the third weekend of August 1943, as the four evaders from *Chug-a-Lug Lulu* were being welcomed into the sheltering embrace of the Belgian underground, Robert Nelson and Raymond Genz of *King Malfunction II* were still dangerously alone inside Hitler's Germany.

Traveling by night through a forbidding world where snapping branches often interrupted heartbeats, one can imagine their horror when two *gunshots* rang out in the inky darkness of Saturday night, August 21.

After four days in the forests and fields of who-knows-where rural Germany, had their freedom – or even their *lives* – reached final moments?

Suddenly, there was an explosion of activity close by.

Three deer came bounding out of the night, nearly trampling the two men. As this boisterous tumult receded into the distance, and no further shots came, the men resumed breathing and moved as quickly as one can move in a darkened meadow, heading in the opposite direction from the deer hunter.

They found refuge in the dark woods and went to sleep, only to awake on Sunday morning in the midst of a heavy rainstorm that showed no sign of abating as the day wore on. Moving deeper into the forest, they began gathering spruce boughs to build a lean-to. They paused as a group of children herding cattle passed by, but then completed their shelter, deeming it "excellent overhead cover" even in a heavy rain.

In the course of their project, they discovered an old iron kettle and decided they would try to use it to boil water. They had not built a fire since arriving in Germany, but they now reasoned that it would be safe because the dense, low fog would obscure the smoke. There were signs that others had built fires in this area before, so they were unconcerned about leaving traces of their presence. Using matches from their survival kit and Genz's cigarette lighter, they finally had a fire going.

They fell asleep contented, but awoke in distress. In the wee hours of Monday morning, the fire spread to their lean-to, and they had to tear it apart to extinguish the flames.

To complicate matters, Genz had come down with severe stomach cramps, and had begun suffering from swollen gums. Nelson, as noted in his escape and evasion report, diagnosed the latter as "trench mouth" (ulcerative gingivitis). They had been subsisting mainly on apples and root vegetables that they had collected, and Nelson decided that for Genz's sake, they needed to vary their diet.

At first light, when the rain finally stopped, they struck out cross country beneath a dense overcast. They passed through a carrot field, and found more blackberries, which Genz ate despite his upset stomach.

Coming across a road that led in a southwesterly direction, they decided to take it. Because it was long and straight, they figured that they would see oncoming traffic with plenty of time to take cover. An hour or so later, they crested a hill and could see about a quarter of mile down the slope. Their road crossed a railway line here, and intersected a main highway being used mainly by bicycles and trucks hauling construction materials.

As they descended this hill, they noticed a man with a suitcase standing near the crossroads. When they got closer, they realized with great alarm that he was a German soldier. This was the first man in uniform they had seen in five days – and he saw them.

"We thought he would move on, but soon it was obvious that he meant to wait for us," Nelson recalled. Still watching them, he put down his bag. Nelson and Genz stopped.

"We couldn't tell whether he was armed. He was just standing, looking at us," Nelson continued. "We saw him pull back his blouse [as though reaching for a pistol] and we were about to run when we saw him light a cigarette. We decided he wasn't armed and that since we were two, he wouldn't do anything. He looked at his watch and we heard a railroad train."

As the locomotive slowed to make its whistle stop, the man picked up his bag and turned toward the train. The two Americans waited until he had boarded, then "tore into the woods" on a run.

After a two-mile detour through gullies, thick brush, and trees, Genz was about 30 feet in the lead. He emerged onto another narrow road, where a girl on a bicycle gave him a puzzled glance as she rode by. She continued to look back until she rounded the next bend and was out of sight.

They spent the rest of Tuesday walking from woods to pasture land to woods, napping occasionally when a well-concealed opportunity presented itself. As they walked, they continued trying to avoid the few people they saw, though at one point they stumbled into a group picking blackberries. They had not seen them because of the thick brush.

Nelson later admitted that he and Genz were "probably getting careless."

The next morning, with their strength ebbing for lack of a balanced diet, they decided to alter their course. Instead of Switzerland, they set their sights westward toward Belgium.

Near a village, they passed within a few feet of a girl emerging from a house. She looked at them askance, probably more because they were two scruffy fellows with a week's growth of whiskers on their chins than because they looked like American airmen on the run.

On the evening of Wednesday, August 25, as they were crossing a bridge, they were passed by kids on bicycles, who completely ignored them. When a woman whom they passed on the other side of the bridge looked them over carefully, they simply ignored her.

"Many people saw us and glanced in our direction, but no unusual attention was paid us," Nelson wrote in his E&E No.170. "We were getting more bold and didn't care if civilians saw us. [Although] our clothes were not as dirty as they should have been and our uniforms were easily recognizable." Of course, most civilians in rural Germany had yet to see American uniforms up close.

The following day, as they continued what Nelson called "our hide-and-seek travel," they started to see heavy fences and unmanned concrete bunkers, which led them to believe that they were nearing the border. As they surmised, these were part of the Siegfried Line, the chain of fortifications which Germany had constructed to defend its western frontier. A year and a half later, German troops would be here in force, defending this very swath of land against the US Army.

Toward dusk on Thursday, Nelson and Genz reached a place in steep terrain where a main road and a rail line followed the course of a river. Following the river downstream, they reached what Nelson described as "an old stone bridge with a building similar to a guard hut at our end."

"We walked slowly and cautiously until we were sure there was no one in the hut," Nelson continued. "Having crossed the bridge, we had no choice but to walk through the village. We saw a woman watching us from a window, but we encountered no real danger. Two miles from the village, we crawled into a hay barn... It was too dark and rainy to go further."

Continuing their trek at dawn on Friday, August 27, they found themselves in a village called Grundhof, the first town that Nelson named in his escape and evasion report. The letters "LUX" on the license plate of a parked motorcycle confirmed that they were finally out of Germany. After ten days on their own, at large inside Nazi Germany, they could relax – but only just a little. They still had a long way to go.

Still a tiny place with fewer than 100 residents, Grundhof is situated in the German-speaking part of Luxembourg overlooking the Sauer River, which forms the border between Luxembourg and Germany. The bridge with the guardhouse that they had crossed the night before had been an unmanned border crossing. With this entire region occupied by the German army, international borders were all but irrelevant.

"In Luxembourg, the Germans have taken all automobiles from the people and are using them for their army," Genz observed. The majority of what is known about the adventures of these two Americans is thanks to Robert Nelson's extensive escape and evasion report, E&E No.170. In marked contrast, Genz's E&E No.171, compiled on the same day in October 1943, and probably in the same room at the same time, relates less than a page of narrative about their travels.

Nelson and Genz were now roughly 80 road miles south by southwest from where they had started, though with all of their meanderings they had probably traveled many more miles.

They continued westward on the road for another three miles to the town of Beaufort, the second town specifically named by Nelson. The few people whom they passed on the street here greeted them cheerfully, to which Nelson and Genz simply replied "*Morgen*" ("good morning").

Having passed several houses on a country lane west of Beaufort, the two hungry Americans started imagining the people inside eating breakfast. "We had traveled about as far as we could without substantial food," Nelson recalled. "We decided to go back and ask for food as beggars. If we got food, we were just that much better off, and if we didn't we would run for cover if the people were hostile. Our plan was to convince the people we were Italian [laborers] who couldn't speak German."

As they walked up to the nearest house, a boy of about 12 came out to meet them, while his mother leaned out an upstairs window with a friendly expression. Indicating that they were looking for food, the two men pointed to their mouths and bellies and used such German words as "*brot*" and "*essen*," meaning "bread" and "eat."

The boy looked at his mother, who told him to fetch some food.

At this moment an old man appeared, who began questioning Nelson and Genz. He had figured out that they were airmen, but not their nationality.

"*Amerikaner? Deutscher? Engländer?*"

At first, they pretended not to understand, but eventually admitted to being Americans. They showed their map to the man, who confirmed their location and told them to keep moving. He was clearly afraid that his family would be in big trouble if Americans were caught here. Munching jam sandwiches given to them by the boy, Nelson and Genz continued walking westward toward Belgium.

Later in the day, they got hungry again and decided to approach two men working at the edge of a field. They simply walked up to the younger man and indicated by sign language that they wanted food. He replied in French and gave them cigarettes. Seeing this, the other man came over to see what was happening.

"As soon as he learned that we were American aviators, he shook hands with us," Nelson recalled. "Our morale went up when this happened, but we were still hungry… He could give us nothing but apples, cigarettes, and directions. We left them feeling happier than at any time since parachuting."

When a suspicious girl in the next village offered them a bite of plum cake, they enjoyed it, but decided to leave the road and head cross country – just in case she alerted the authorities.

Three miles into the hills, they met an old man with a scythe, who took them to see his brother, who spoke English. The brother gave them some bread, but the woman of his house became furious with the man for bringing Americans there.

As they walked westward, Nelson and Genz continued to interact with civilians, finding them to be guardedly sympathetic. People were always willing to share cigarettes, but earnest in urging them to move on. Twice they were warned of specific concentrations of German occupation troops along the road ahead.

On Friday, they stopped to ask for food at a house where a woman and several men eyed them with the usual suspicion – but there was a boy here who spoke English. He asked them about their aircraft and about their travels. They showed him their dog tags and told him their story, which he related to the adults.

After about five minutes, an English-speaking woman arrived and escorted the Americans to a hiding place deep in the nearby woods. One of the men met them here with food and coffee, as well as a shaving kit. Especially welcome were dry civilian clothes because Nelson and Genz had been making their way through wet brush for days, and their uniforms had never completely dried out.

When the two Americans were fed and clothed, their new friends bundled them into a vehicle and drove them about 15 winding country miles due west to the tiny hamlet of Berg, Luxembourg and the home of an English-speaking man who went by the name "Mr King." He greeted them cheerfully with a smile and a carton of Chesterfields, telling them that he had been planning to present these cigarettes to the first Americans he met.

For the next ten days, from August 28 through September 7, 1943, Nelson and Genz were guests of Mr King. He was part of an underground organization calling itself the Lëtzeburger Volleks-Legion (LVL), or Luxembourg Popular Legion, which among other things promised to help them make contact with those who ran the clandestine escape lines.

On September 7, now with a new plan and a new direction, the Americans moved on. Accompanied by English-speaking teenage boys, they bicycled a few miles south to the town of Mersch. The mood was generally upbeat as they connected with an English-speaking LVL man who had been a Luxembourg postal inspector before the war. Plans were made to travel to the Belgian border by truck the next day.

Just as they were starting to congratulate one another for having slipped through Germany and Luxembourg with what seemed like relative ease, the world of Robert Nelson and Raymond Genz imploded.

Suddenly, word came that an American bomber had come down in the area. As with their own *Chug-A-Lug Lulu* three weeks earlier, parachutes had been seen. Panic spread as the Luxembourgers learned that the Gestapo was out in force, scouring the area, looking for the survivors and setting up roadblocks.

It now seemed that there could be no relaxed ride to the border. Instead, Nelson and Genz were hustled beneath the floorboards into a cramped cellar. Their circumstances, like the cellar walls, were beginning to close in upon them.

Chapter 20

Riding the Comet

On the night of September 7, 1943, as Robert Nelson and Raymond Genz faced an uncertain immediate future from beneath creaking floorboards, Joe Walters of *Chug-a-Lug Lulu* had been in Brussels for four days.

The first of his crew to reach the Belgian capital, he had arrived from Liège with Ken Fahncke, and was met by a young woman who introduced herself as "Lily." She was, of course, 21-year-old Micheline Dumon, the dynamic helper of evaders who was then energetically rebuilding Comet Line activities after the arrest of Dédée de Jongh eight months before.

Over the course of the next couple of weeks, they were among many airmen whom Micheline was deftly shuffling, separately and in groups, through safe houses across Brussels. As was the case with Nelson and Genz, where their narrative was contained almost entirely in Nelson's escape and evasion report, the same was true for the other pair. Walters's recollections in his report were extensive, while Fahncke's were minimal.[22]

For Walters and Fahncke, their Brussels safe house was the home of a man whom Walters identified as René Pirate, a sculptor associated with the University of Brussels. On September 25, Micheline dispatched Walters and Fahncke on to Paris, where they joined other airmen being hosted at the home of Germaine Bajpai. She explained that she was the sister-in-law of the Indian commissioner in Washington, DC.

In turn, Walters and Fahncke were introduced to a lively 50-year-old Comet operative named Daisy Benoit, whose husband owned a business in Liverpool. On the first of October, she took them aboard a train and escorted them to Bordeaux. Instead of taking them deep into the Pyrenees, she planned to cross through the less mountainous terrain nearer the northeastern border of Spain on the Bay of Biscay.

Though the topography was less challenging, there were other hurdles. Because the major highways and rail line from western France into northern Spain pass through this area, it was heavily guarded by German troops on the French side, and by unpredictable Spanish border guards on the other.

As they detrained in the town of Dax, they were joined by other airmen who had been shot down on August 17 on the Schweinfurt mission. Among these were crewmen from the Flying Fortress *Stupntakit* of the 323rd Bomb Squadron, 91st Bomb Group. They included the pilot, 1st Lieutenant Charles Bennett, and Tech Sergeant Ford "Chuck" Cowherd, the flight engineer. Together, the airmen and their guides reached a remote stretch of the Spanish border around 5:00am on Sunday, October 3.

Anything could happen now, but tonight, the stars aligned for Daisy Benoit's boys. With some advance information, she had picked perhaps the best time of all to cross the Spanish border.

As it turned out, the Spanish border guards, and indeed everyone in and around the Spanish border town of Irun, were preoccupied with the arrival of Spain's División Azul (Blue Division). This organization had been fighting against the Soviet Red Army, alongside the Germans, on the Eastern Front since July 1941. Spanish dictator Francisco Franco had sent manpower to aid in Hitler's war against the Soviets in appreciation for Hitler's having sent German troops to support Franco's efforts in the Spanish Civil War of 1936–39. Now, considering his debt repaid, Franco was bringing his men home.

As Walters, Fahncke, Bennett, and Cowherd made their way through Irun that Sunday morning, they watched four trainloads of troops pass. Walters overheard someone saying that there were 40,000 men coming home. He recalled that they looked to be in good spirits – not surprising for people arriving in Spain after two horrific Russian winters.

On Monday evening, the American consul from Bilbao arrived with money for Fahncke and Walters and put them into a hotel, where they remained until November 6 when they began their trek back to England by way of Madrid and Gibraltar.

By this time, the other members of the *Chug-a-Lug Lulu* crew were scattered far and wide across France, each one of them still weeks away from getting into Spain.

As Robert Nelson and Raymond Genz lay low on the night of Wednesday, September 8 to elude the Gestapo dragnet in western Luxembourg, they could not have imagined how soon the storm of storm troopers would pass. The Gestapo wrapped up their operation by midnight. Perhaps all members of the bomber crew for which they were searching had been caught. In any case, Nelson and Genz were taken to a workyard where a truck was waiting, and were on the road shortly after the last Gestapo vehicle had driven away.

A few hours later, they reached a town near the border with both Belgium and France. Here, a counterfeiting operation was in place to create new French passports for them – but there was a hitch. Nelson recalled that when they handed over the passport-sized photos from their survival gear, the forgers fussed. They "thought they were unsatisfactory as they showed a well-lighted background which they thought was too Americanized."

The Americans breathed again when the counterfeiters reluctantly shrugged their shoulders and agreed to work with what they had.

At about 5:00am on Thursday, with a LVL man walking ahead of them as a scout, Nelson and Genz stepped across the French border with identity papers identifying them as French workmen. They walked about four miles to a prearranged safe house and rested until noon, when Comet Line handlers took them to the small French town of Longuyon and put them on a train for Paris at around 9:00pm Thursday evening.

They reached the Gare de l'Est in Paris after midnight and spent a few fitful hours in a hotel, after which their escorts put them on another train headed south. Nelson wrote that they wound up at the home of an English steel plant engineer named George Hartung near Saint-Georges-de-Mons, about 200 miles from Paris.

In marked contrast to his meticulously detailed explanation of their exodus from Germany and their adventures in Luxembourg, Nelson's description of the last four weeks in occupied Europe for Genz and himself is extremely brief. His few hasty handwritten lines beg the question of what fascinating specifics could have been written between those lines. Genz's own recollections of the entire adventure add little to the narrative.

Nelson did say that after eight days at Hartung's house, they "moved to the country because the British dropped arms to the French." While it is true that the British SOE did drop weapons to the French Résistance, Nelson did not explain how the air drops might have precipitated their move. During late September and early October, they moved often, passing through "different places" in and around Clermont and Toulouse, the latter being an important crossroads in the escape and evasion networks.

Another anecdote told of their meeting two German SS officers on the train, an obviously tense moment. However, Nelson offered no details, aside from mentioning that their forged identity cards and ration books were examined. Nelson did say that the SS men were with a young French woman, who "talked for us." Apparently, their papers were in order – or at least convincing.

———

It was around the middle of the third week of October 1943 that Nelson and Genz were introduced to a Comet Line operative named Margarite. In turn, she took them to Lourdes, about 100 miles closer to the Spanish border. After six days here at the Hôtel Londres, Margarite moved them and several others by truck to Auzat, by way of Foix. Here, they joined a group of 15 Allied airmen and several French people for the trek across the Pyrenees into Spain.

In this group was Staff Sergeant George Monser of Wenona, Illinois. Flying with the 368th Bomb Squadron, 306th Bomb Group, he had been the left waist gunner on a B-17 that went down south of Beauvais on September 6 during a mission to Stuttgart. Monser's narrative of the crossing into Spain in his escape and evasion report, E&E No.169, makes up for the lack of detail in this part of Nelson's otherwise extensive escape and evasion report.

Local Résistance handlers hid the group in a barn in the hills near Auzat, but the promised mountain guide failed to appear, so they had to wait four anxious days for his replacement. The Pyrenees trek on the snowy cusp of winter took nearly a week, but they finally reached Andorra, where they rested for a couple of days before hiking on to Spain.

Both Nelson and Genz wrote that they entered Spain on October 9, though Monser put that date as October 14. Perhaps the latter date was the day of their arrival in Barcelona. Monser recalled that they walked for four days from Andorra, then boarded a train for a 90-minute trip to Barcelona. After a few days at the British Consulate in that city, they were driven by car to the American Embassy in Madrid, and finally reached Gibraltar on October 27. They were all back at their Eighth Air Force bases by October 30.

Chapter 21

False Starts, and Meeting the Fox Hunter

When he and Ken Fahncke passed though the city of Irun on Sunday, October 3, 1943, Joe Walters was the first member of his *Chug-a-Lug Lulu* crew to reach Spain. The others would not arrive for months.

For Bill Kiniklis, Otto Bruzewski, and Tom Moore, the journey started as smoothly as could be expected, albeit with a bit of cloak and dagger, but they soon became ensnarled in long and unexplained delays, false starts, and the frustration of taking a step backward for each step forward.

As Kiniklis recalled in his escape and evasion report, E&E No.508, he was taken to Brussels on September 4, and was moved to Ghent several days later. His Comet Line handlers took him to a place near the French border around September 16, where he was met by a man with horn-rimmed glasses, who was dressed entirely in black. This guide took him on a four-hour nighttime hike which deposited Kiniklis at the home of a French police officer who was a Comet confidant.

From here, Kiniklis was moved on to Paris, where he spent six weeks at the home of a man named Pirnaud in a six-story red brick apartment house at 27 Avenue Gambetta, across the street from the famous Père Lachaise cemetery in the 20th Arrondissement.

Bruzewski and Moore finally left the home of Dr Charles Kramer in Liège on Friday, October 22, and boarded a train for Brussels. Escorted by a handler known only as Pierre, they detrained in the Belgian capital and took a tram to a church, where they spent the night. They, along with others, were given a security talk by a "middle aged man who worked for the British" and were told they were headed for Madrid.

On Sunday morning, after one night in Ghent, Bruzewski, Moore, and several others were taken to the Belgian border town of Mouscron, probably the same place where Kiniklis had been a month earlier. With their guide leading the way, they walked into the French city of Tourcoing, crossing the border with no questions asked. As Bruzewski observed, "they knew we were coming."

From here, they were taken to the home of a policeman, probably the same one mentioned by Kiniklis, where the Belgian identity cards they had been using were efficiently exchanged for French papers. After dinner, a young woman took them by train to Paris.

They arrived in the French capital after the Metro had stopped running, so, as Bruzewski wrote, "we had to spend the night in the railway station with lots of Germans, but were never questioned." On Monday morning, things seemed to be back on track. They took the Metro to the Odeon station in the 6th Arrondissement and walked to a nearby apartment.

At this point, the whole affair, as it was described by Bruzewski, became very mysterious. The handlers whom they met at the apartment, members of a student organization, were far more paranoid and strict than anyone whom they had met in Belgium. The Americans were kept under lock and key for three days with no visitors except those bringing food.

On Thursday, October 28, they were again in motion, but not toward Spain as they had expected. Instead they boarded a train to Quimper on the Atlantic coast of Brittany, 350 miles west of Paris. Here they were told that a boat would pick them up within a week.

Naturally, Brittany's proximity to Cornwall in England – about 120 miles by sea – made this appear practical, but at the same time the Germans had made the northern swath of France the most heavily fortified part of the country. The initial attempt by Britain's MI9 to use this escape route had succumbed to German disruption earlier in 1943, although the replacement Shelburne escape line, involving clandestine crossings by high-speed motor gunboats of the Royal Navy, would begin operation later in the year.

Bruzewski and the others waited in a safe house until November 6, when plans apparently fell through. They were put on a train back to Paris, escorted by the same man who'd brought them to Quimper. When they arrived, Otto Bruzewski and Tom Moore parted company. Moore's journey would eventually take him *back* to Brittany, from where he would escape by sea, but not until January 1944.

As he noted in his E&E No.320, Bruzewski was sent to the home of a French language professor, where he remained for over three weeks. Finally, on November 20, he was taken to the Gare Montparnasse and put on a southbound train. He was joined by other evaders, including an especially jittery unnamed airman, whose behavior put everyone on edge.

After a four-hour layover in Toulouse to change trains, they continued south to Carcassonne, where they climbed into a diesel road-rail truck that took them deep into the mountains. Contact was made with the guides who would get them across the Pyrenees, and everyone assumed they would start out right away. However, the Comet operatives were still waiting for another group of Americans who were overdue from Paris.

For several days of nail-biting uncertainty, they waited. So as not to attract attention to their large herd of anxious men milling around impatiently in one place, the Comet operatives shuffled the men back and forth between hotels and safe houses in the mountains, using the local bus line running between Quillan and Rouge.

As they watched the snow piling up, and heard stories of the difficulties of crossing mountain passes in winter, Bruzewski and his fellow evaders naturally grew impatient. Finally, they decided that enough was enough. The wait was over. Two of the guides were agreeable, so plans were made to start over the mountains on the morning of November 26.

However, they had barely begun the trip when their plan started to fall apart. As Bruzewski wrote in E&E No.320, the nervous man who had been with their party since Paris "gave up and the guides said he couldn't get through [so] I dragged [him] back to Rouge. He was completely out. [I] tried to get a hotel room and did. Got doctor for [him] and got him to bed."

The next day, they were all returning to Quillan when suddenly the Gestapo descended upon the area and began checking all the busses. Fortunately, Bruzewski and his companions were prepared and managed to bluff their way through a road block with their counterfeit identity cards.

After this narrow escape from the Germans, Bruzewski and his group got out of the mountains. Then, on November 28, for some reason, the Comet people decided to backtrack all the way to Paris!

After more than a week of anxiety and false starts, they were back where they had started – just as they had been after the Quimper debacle more than a month earlier.

Bruzewski and his companions spent the next six days in their familiar world of 6th Arrondissement safe houses, during which time they were finally united with the other group of Americans for whom their handlers had been waiting in the Pyrenees foothills since early November.

Among these men was a badly injured 21-year-old named Billy Howell, whose body was an ugly tapestry of scars and partially healed wounds. For four months, well-meaning Résistance people and back-alley Paris medical professionals had been trying with pliers and forceps to remove shrapnel imbedded in his arms, legs, and head.

Assigned to the 533rd Bomb Squadron, 381st Bomb Group, Staff Sergeant William Claxton Howell had been the tail gunner aboard an unnamed B-17F (tail number 42-29928), piloted by 2nd Lieutenant Olof Ballinger. On July 4, 1943 they were returning from a mission against the Gnome-Rhône aircraft engine plant in Le Mans, southwest of Paris, when they were shot down near La Ferté-Macé in Normandy.

As he and Bruzewski compared stories, Howell recalled his bomber being set upon by a swarm of Luftwaffe interceptors over the target. As he later recalled in his escape and evasion report, Howell told of returning fire with his twin .50-caliber guns, noting that "I think I got one, and I saw another go down in smoke."[23]

He heard the loud explosion of a 20mm cannon round behind him in the center fuselage and felt himself slammed against the bulkhead.

"After the explosion, the radio operator and the waist gunners failed to report," Howell explained. "My oxygen system was shot out... I started to black out and changed my connection to the other side, but it was gone too. I was pretty punch drunk [from lack of oxygen]. We were out of formation and German fighters came after us."

"Let's get out of here!" Howell heard someone shout.

As Howell was kicking his way through the escape hatch, a German 20mm shell exploded in an ammunition can next to him, showering him with shrapnel.

Hanging in his parachute watching his aircraft crash just a half mile away, he took stock of his injuries. He could feel the blood pouring from his head wound and the severe pain from injuries to his arm and both legs. He kicked off his heavy flying boots as he descended, but regretted it as soon as he landed because he was in thick brush with no shoes.

He finally located his boots and started walking. Feeling dizzy from lack of blood, Howell staggered though the woods until he found a stream where he could wash his wounds, and sat down to rest. It was not long before he heard someone crashing through brush in his direction, and he figured it was time to move on.

"Fox hunting used to be my favorite sport back home in North Carolina, so I borrowed a couple of the fox's ideas and started back-tracking and reversing," he explained. "I learned later that several of my crew were also walking in the woods, but I didn't see any of them. I came to the edge of the woods and suddenly saw two German soldiers on a path with another German 400 yards away. I hit the ground immediately, rested, then crawled away."

As Howell continued through the woods, he heard numerous gunshots, which he interrupted as an effort by the Germans to frighten the Americans.

As he emerged from the other side of the woods, it was Howell's turn to be frightened. Staring at him from about 100 yards away was a German soldier guarding a gate.

"For some reason, this German did not fire," Howell recalled. "Perhaps he did not recognize my long underwear and khaki trousers [as an American uniform]. I started back to the woods and this German began to get suspicious, but for some reason, he did not give the alarm or run after me. Perhaps he had been ordered to guard that particular gate and was afraid to leave it."

As Howell continued through woods and meadows, walking and crawling for several hours, he saw more German troops and was seen by a few of them, but luckily, they seemed to take him for a French civilian.

By about 7:00pm, Howell was starting to feel poorly. Earlier, he had been moving on adrenaline, but now the pain of his wounds was starting to catch up to him. He drank some water and found a hiding place to rest. "I must have slept. Everything went black. When I woke up, I felt pretty sick and realized that I needed some medical attention."

As he continued his hike, he met an old French civilian, who took Howell to his "awfully dirty shack" and offered him some dirty fish. The airman declined the fish, but he accepted about two liters of the man's cider, which made him very sick. The man and his wife put the American to bed, but when he awoke the following day, Howell was "so stiff I could hardly move." They put him in their hayloft, where he slept all day and all night.

When he woke up on July 6, Howell still felt dreadful. The flesh around where shrapnel was imbedded in his arm, his legs, and his head was getting infected and it hurt terribly. Nevertheless, he decided that he had to keep going. Though the Spanish border was nearly 500 road miles away, off he went, like a migrating bird.

Caught in a rainstorm, Howell hid in another hayloft, but was awakened by a boy pitching hay – who was scared to death to find a man sleeping there. When it was finally confirmed that Howell was not a German, the boy's family brought him bread and cider and let him spend the night.

Trying to travel south the following day, Howell discovered that he had lost his compass, and that he was wandering in circles. Hungry, tired, and sick, he probably presented a pretty sad appearance as he stopped at farmhouses to beg for food. At one of these, he was having a hard time convincing people that he was an American until he thought to show them an American penny.

Late on July 8, Howell finally got the first aid that he desperately needed, as well as his first hot meal in four days. He met a French army veteran, who took him to a doctor in La Ferté-Macé. This man gave Howell a couple of large shots of cognac and proceeded to extract shrapnel from his wounds and clean them.

After a night's sleep at the doctor's house, he was given a sleeping bag and taken to a concealed hiding place in the nearby woods. He spent a few days listening to wild boars rooting nearby until the Résistance moved him about 15 miles west to Domfront, where he stayed for several weeks, and where he was given forged identity papers.

By September, Billy Howell was in Paris, leading an incongruously normal life under the noses of the Gestapo, a life that even included going to the movies. In his escape and evasion report, he noted seeing newsreels that showed "an American plane toggling out bombs, apparently on non-military targets."

Of course, Howell's wounds from the fourth of July shrapnel were a reminder that despite the theater visits, life was far from normal. He spent his time sneaking surreptitiously into dimly lit medical offices, where doctors anesthetized him and prodded at his partially healed wounds, continuing to remove shrapnel.

From dueling with Focke-Wulfs, to mimicking foxes, to dodging feral pigs, to lounging in a Paris movie theater, it was a trip unlike anything the tail gunner from North Carolina could ever have imagined when he climbed into his Flying Fortress on that fateful day. But now, that strange trip of Billy Howell was about to enter a new chapter.

On December 6, Howell and Otto Bruzewski, along with the groups with whom they had traveled previously, were alerted to be ready to move the next day.

Chapter 22

Homeward Bound

On the morning of December 7, 1943, Otto Bruzewski of *Chug-a-Lug Lulu* left Paris for the third and last time. He, Billy Howell, and their companions boarded a train to Perpignan on the Mediterranean coast, 525 miles south of Paris and only 20 miles from the Spanish frontier.

It was not to be an easy journey. Avoiding the direct – but heavily guarded – coastal route, their handlers dragged them up the winding roads into the exaggerated steepness of the Pyrenees. Bruzewski was back where he had been in November, impatiently waiting for a trip that never materialized.

For him, December was the nightmare of déjà vu, the nightmare of earlier false starts, and of tackling this journey through deepening snow.

"I think we had an especially difficult Pyrenees crossing," Howell recalled in an understatement in his E&E No.328 narrative. "We made three separate and exhausting starts. The first time, the guide got so tired we had to carry him back. The second time, our guides were taking us north instead of south and would not pay any attention to us when we told them they were going in the wrong direction."

Their handlers insisted on withdrawing down to Perpignan between attempts, and this added unnecessary days to the whole process. A not-so-merry Christmas came and went. So too did New Year's Day. The party welcomed 1944 still on the French side of the border – with the Gestapo lurking everywhere.

Finally, on the January 5 third attempt, the evaders refused to turn back. They paused only to catch their breath and scrutinize the darkening sky before plunging forward. Some of the men were in bad shape, but still they pushed onward and upward despite the icy rain. Battered Billy Howell, with his injured leg and shoes that were too small, fell a couple of times, but picked himself up and carried on.

After hours and hours, the word was passed down the straggling line from the guides in the lead – the Spanish border was just 20 minutes away. With this, one man just sat down. As Howell remembered, "he absolutely could not go any further. A German outpost was not far away, and we were a little worried about leaving him in such a dangerous position, but there was no chance of carrying him with us."

At 10:30pm on January 5, they crossed the frontier and staggered into Spain. Howell recalled that "once we got into Spain we somehow felt better, and we hobbled along less painfully. When we had some food at last, things looked decidedly better. I had some bananas, the first I had had since I left the United States."

When he was subsequently debriefed in England, and a questionnaire asked how survival equipment could be improved, Howell answered "Wear a good pair of GI shoes."

Bruzewski was the second of the four evaders from *Chug-a-Lug Lulu* to get out of occupied Europe. They had become so widely separated that their exits were spread over months. Joe Walters had walked across the Spanish border at Irun on October 3, 1943, while Tom Moore returned from Paris to Brittany to escape via the Shelburne Line on January 23, 1944. He was extracted from Douarnenez, a small port town on the coast of Brittany 15 miles from Quimper, and taken to Falmouth in Cornwall.

Four days later, on January 27, Bill Kiniklis crossed the Spanish border by way of the Pyrenees, 600 miles to the south of Douarnenez, making him the last *Chug-a-Lug Lulu* man out of France. Kiniklis had spent Christmas in Valmondois, north of Paris, and traveled to the French city of Pau, 30 miles from the Spanish border in the new year. Once in Spain, he passed through Alhama, where he was debriefed by American personnel before reporting to the US Embassy in Madrid. Unlike most evaders, he was in Spain for almost two months. While Otto Bruzewski had managed to get from the Spanish border to Gibraltar in nine days, and to England on January 18, it took Kiniklis until March 20 to reach Gibraltar. He was back in England by March 24.

Much had happened in the months that followed August 17, Black Tuesday, over Schweinfurt. The Eighth Air Force launched a second mission to

Schweinfurt on October 14, 1943. Again, the losses were steep, earning that day the painful appellation "Black Thursday." In this mission, 229 Flying Fortresses reached the target and 60 were shot down, for a loss rate of 26 percent. On Black Tuesday, the Schweinfurt component of the mission had lost 36 out of 230 bombers.

What had been accomplished on Black Tuesday by the Eighth Air Force and the brave aircrews who flew those missions?

As historian Thomas Coffey later wrote in his book *Decision over Schweinfurt*, the two largest factory complexes in Schweinfurt, Kugelfischer and Vereinigte Kugellagerfabriken, had taken 80 direct hits, and 380,000 square feet of factory structures were destroyed.

Perhaps the greatest praise for the Eighth on this mission came from Albert Speer, Germany's own armaments minister. In his 1969 memoirs, *Inside the Third Reich*, he admitted that production dropped from 140 tons in July to 69 in August, and 50 in September.

"After this attack, the production of ball bearings dropped by 38 percent," Speer recalled. "We were forced back on the ball bearing stocks stored by the armed forces for use as repair parts. We soon consumed these, as well as whatever had been accumulated in the factories for current production."

The Black Tuesday Boys of 1943 returned home to join what much later came to be known as the "Greatest Generation," who defined postwar America. Otto Bruzewski remained in the service, and retired from the US Air Force in 1965. Raymond Genz went back to Minnesota, where he worked as a mechanic in Brainerd, and Tom Moore made it home to Virginia, where he worked in the textile industry in Henry County. Ken Fahncke ended up in Pleasanton, Nebraska, while Robert Nelson resided in Kansas and Alabama before returning to his native Oregon, where he lived in Brookings, overlooking the Pacific.

It was well past the turn of the century when *Taps* was heard for the last of the Black Tuesday survivors from this narrative. Bill Kiniklis returned to Massachusetts, where he died in 2007. Billy Howell passed two years later in Wayne County, North Carolina, where he had long worked as a carpenter. Joe Walters went on to a career in the US Air Force, retiring as a lieutenant colonel after 22 years to take a second career as vice president of the Georgia Loan & Trust Company. He died in Gainesville, Georgia in 2015 at the age of 92.

Through the years, Walters stayed in touch with many of the civilians who had aided him and his band of brothers during the war. In 1998, he went back to Belgium to meet some of them face to face. He found that Janine Dardenne, who had been his "interpreter" when she was a teenager nicknamed "Sweetpea" back in 1943, was married to an American, and they visited Walters in Georgia.

In the article about him in the American Air Forces Escape and Evasion Society (AFEES) newsletter, Walters was quoted as saying that the Belgian underground "never got the credit they justly deserved... They were wonderful, wonderful people."[24]

PART FIVE

LONG ROADS FROM REGENSBURG

Chapter 23

A Rough Start to a Long Day

The ambitious dual mission launched by the Eighth Air Force against heavily defended Schweinfurt and Regensburg on Tuesday, August 17, 1943 was, as noted in Part Four, a milestone in the strategic air campaign against the Third Reich.

Losses on that Bloody Tuesday were steep against both targets. The Eighth Air Force 1st Bomb Wing, the Schweinfurt component of the mission, lost 36 out of 230 bombers, while the 4th Bomb Wing sent 146 B-17s to Regensburg and lost two dozen.

Schweinfurt was all about ball bearings. Regensburg was a target one might call "personal" for a crewman of an Allied bomber. The sprawling Messerschmitt factory complex in Regensburg was the largest production source of Bf 109 fighters, one of the Luftwaffe's most widely deployed interceptors – an aircraft that harassed and dealt fatal blows to the men of the Eighth day after day, month after bloody month.

An element of complexity in the day's mission was that, unlike the bombers that visited Schweinfurt, the Regensburg strike force was *not* going to turn around and return to its bases in England. Regensburg was 100 miles deeper inside Germany than Schweinfurt, so it was decided that the bombers of Regensburg would continue south, across the Alps and on to Allied air bases in Algeria. The idea was that they would refuel, reload, and return to England the following day. The ambitious plan even had them bombing German targets in occupied France on the way back!

From Regensburg, it was around 1,000 miles to the Algerian airfields, compared to about 600 back to British bases, but this route *did not* take the bombers back though the most heavily defended air space in the world.

The commander of the Eighth Air Force 4th Bomb Wing, Colonel Curtis LeMay, led the Regensburg mission personally, flying in the right seat of the lead Flying Fortress piloted by Captain Thomas Kenny of the 96th Bomb Group.

On the morning of August 17, as the crews prepared to climb into their bombers, a heavy overcast darkened the south of England and descended in the form of pea-soup ground fog. The crews had all been briefed that the takeoff roll would begin at 5:45am, but they were delayed by the fog. LeMay worried that the holdup meant that his crews would have to land on semi-improved Algerian airfields in the dark.

LeMay contacted his boss, Brigadier General Ira Eaker, at Eighth Air Force headquarters, and received a "go" for takeoff, but was asked to circle in the blue skies above the fog and wait for Brigadier General Robert Williams and the 1st Bomb Wing.

When LeMay had circled for half an hour, and Williams had not appeared, he decided to wait no longer. LeMay began leading his force across the English Channel. A short time later, the Eighth Air Force command center discovered that the radio link between them and LeMay was down.

"I might have done the same thing myself," Eaker remembered, as quoted by his biographer, James Parton, as he assumed that LeMay purposely shut off his radio to avoid being told to turn back. "It's such a job to get the bombers assembled, it's destructive of morale to cancel because then you've got to do it again the next day."

Of this, LeMay wrote in his memoirs, co-authored with MacKinlay Kantor, that if the 1st Wing crews "had been concentrating on the same sort of bad-weather-instrument-takeoff procedure which we had been developing for a solid month, they might have been able to get off the ground. A few minutes late, perhaps, but still part of the originally planned show. And we couldn't horse around about this – return to our bases, sit on the ground, take off once more."

As it was, Williams was delayed for another three hours, and the 1st Bomb Wing was not on its way to Schweinfurt until LeMay was practically over Regensburg.

Among the 146 bombers in the strike force were *Our Bay-Bee* of the 335th Bomb Squadron, 95th Bomb Group, piloted by 1st Lieutenant Walter Baker, and *Old Shillelagh II* of the 551st Bomb Squadron, 385th Bomb Group, piloted by 1st Lieutenant Wilmont "Bill" Grodi of Toledo, Ohio.

When LeMay's strike force arrived over the Belgian coast at around 10:00am, the Germans were ready almost immediately with a wall of antiaircraft fire. The 335th Bomb Squadron was flying as the high squadron of the 95th Bomb Group, and even at 18,000 feet, they were not immune. In fact, the fuses of these 88mm shells seemed to be set just for them.

Baker's B-17 was one of six ships of the 335th that took off from Horham in Suffolk that morning with a bomb bay filled with 18 250-pound incendiaries of the type used by the RAF Bomber Command. This translated as more than two tons of *fire* that could engulf Baker's bomber in an instant if one of the flak gunners was lucky.

In the right seat opposite Baker, copilot Martin Minnich looked out the window at the black puffs of flak that seemed to have swallowed the Flying Fortress. He wondered whether they could make it through another two hours of this.

The dreaded answer came more quickly for *Our Bay-Bee*'s crew than for most of the Regensburg force that day. As Minnich recalled in his escape and evasion report, E&E No.229, he then watched as an 88mm antiaircraft round sliced straight though the wing between the number three and number four engines, just a few feet from where he sat.

Amazingly, it did not detonate.

Had it exploded, *Our Bay-Bee* would have been a cartwheeling fireball in the Belgian skies.

But things were not good. Oil was literally pouring from ruptured lines and streaming off the trailing edge of the wing like nothing Minnich had ever seen. He reached down to feather the propeller on number three, but this proved impossible. Meanwhile, the supercharger on number four, the outboard engine, was about as controllable as a runaway train.

With two engines in such a state, the Flying Fortress started to fall behind the rest of the formation and to lose altitude. Baker and Minnich turned the big aircraft around, pointing it back toward England while the bombardier, 2nd Lieutenant Henry "Hank" Sarnow, jettisoned the bombs.

Just then, the sound of an explosion erupted in the mid-fuselage. The waist gunners, Roscoe Alderman and William Binnebose, reported that they had been wounded by a flak burst.

As the Flying Fortress dropped out of the formation, the Luftwaffe's Jagdgeschwader 26 (JG 26) pounced. The interceptors loved to pick on stragglers without the supporting defensive fire of other bombers in their formation.

The interceptor wing responsible for this segment of the Eighth Air Force route into Germany, JG 26 flew Regensburg-made Bf 109s that were based at Schiphol Airport outside Amsterdam. On this day, JG 26 was supported by Nachtjagdgeschwader 1 (NJG 1), whose twin-engine Messerschmitt Bf 110 night fighters were normally active against the Royal Air Force at night.

Minnich, among others in his crew, later made note of a trio of Bf 110s that raked *Our Bay-Bee* from nose to tail. The rudder controls and the horizontal stabilizers were badly damaged. Minnich saw cannon shells ripping into the right wing and fired three green flares as a distress call, but no one responded. The P-47 escort fighters that were supposed to have supported the bombers were unable to provide complete coverage because of the size of the bomber force, and because one of the P-47 groups had been behind schedule in the fog.

In the absence of friendly fighters, *Our Bay-Bee*'s gunners stepped up. Minnich watched as two interceptors went down.

Over the intercom, Minnich heard Alderman and Binnebose call back to say that they were out of ammunition and ready to abandon ship. Minnich suggested that they wait until the aircraft was over the English Channel where there were rescue boats, but received no reply. In his later escape and evasion report, he wrote "whether they jumped at this time or later, I never knew."

While the Bf 110s were chronicled in Minnich's and several other American after-action reports for the day, Luftwaffe records indicate that the pilot who delivered the grim *coup de grace* that finally sent *Our Bay-Bee* plummeting was Oberstleutnant Erich Burkert of JG 26, who recorded his "kill" as having been made at 11:42am.[25]

This was Burkert's first aerial victory against American bombers, though he had earlier scored six to become an ace while flying with JG 54 against the Soviets on the Eastern Front. He was killed in action five months later on January 21, 1944 when he was shot down by Eighth Air Force fighter ace Major Walter Beckham of the 353th Fighter Group.

Knowing that the aircraft was uncontrollable and headed down, Baker issued the order for everyone to bail out. He engaged the Automatic Flight Control Equipment (AFCE), but because of all the damage to the control surfaces, he and Minnich had to push the control yokes with their feet to keep the erratically pitching bomber level enough for men to escape.

As they were fighting the controls, one of the oxygen bottles on the flight deck exploded from the heat. Minnich later noted that it "covered me with a sheet of flame, and I jumped back to [navigator 2nd Lieutenant Cedric Nussbaum's] position. Finding that [Nussbaum had] not jumped, I went back to my seat in order to leave him enough room. He had not [yet] put his chute on."

In the bombardier's compartment, Sarnow was thrown down by the explosion. He recalled that "the plush insulator curtains were in flames and part of the compartment caught fire. With my leather jacket, I pushed the curtain to one side."

"I opened the right cockpit window to blow out the flames," Minnich continued, describing this madhouse of an inferno, and of a second oxygen bottle going off. "The oxygen explosion blew the navigator [Nussbaum] out of the aircraft. Flames swept round my seat. I got to the nose hatch, but could not get clear out. The bombardier [Sarnow] pushed me out. When I left the cockpit, the pilot still had his feet against the controls."

Sarnow thought Minnich was stuck, so he pushed him through the hatch and then followed him out. In his escape and evasion report, E&E No.230, Sarnow recalled watching a large piece of aluminum come hurtling through the air, narrowly missing the two men. He looked around, trying to get his bearings. He looked for the North Sea coastline, but he did not see it. In fact, he and his fellow crewmembers were coming down near the Belgian village of Dessel, near the Netherlands border, about 100 miles inland.

They lost sight of Walter Baker, and only much later did they learn that the pilot had escaped with his life only to be captured by the Germans.

Minnich blacked out as he fell from *Our Bay-Bee*, but came to in time to yank his ripcord. As he pulled off his oxygen mask, he saw two parachutes near him and a forest rushing up toward him. He jerked the shroud lines to barely miss a pond, crossed his legs, and crashed into the trees.

Fortunately, the ensuing broken limbs belonged to the trees, not to Minnich, and they eased his fall to the ground. The conflagration in the cockpit had taken its toll. Minnich was "half blinded," his flight suit was still burning, and he had serious burns all over his exposed skin.

He found that he had an audience. As three young boys "collected" his helmet, parachute harness, and Mae West lifejacket, Minnich took off walking through the woods in the direction of where he had seen the other parachutes. As he went, he practically ran into a man on a bicycle. This man, who introduced himself as "Gus," spoke English and took the injured airman into his care. He proceeded to cut Minnich's smoldering flight suit and heavy gloves off his body. Gus convinced Minnich to give up his pistol, which they shoved into a rabbit hole. It was explained that in a confrontation with a well-armed German patrol, his having a gun was certain to get him killed.

In later years, researcher Co de Swart, who investigated the aftermath of the *Our Bay-Bee* downing, confirmed that Gus, the man who came to Minnich's aid on Black Tuesday, was August Fruythof.

Fruythof told the story from his perspective in his own memoirs, published in 1980. He wrote that he saw the Flying Fortress falling from the sky, flames pouring from its engines, about two and a half miles from his house. Grabbing his bicycle, he headed toward the place where he saw parachutes descending. He recalled it as being a hot summer day, and sweat was streaming from his body as he pedaled as fast as he could.

He recalled helping Minnich extinguish the smoldering flames licking at his flight suit, and directing the airman to run north toward the Kempen Canal. The two of them continued through the woods and located both Hank Sarnow and Staff Sergeant John White, *Our Bay-Bee*'s ball turret gunner.

In his own escape and evasion report, Sarnow remembered falling through tree limbs like a "shot out of hell," and how, though his parachute was hung up, his feet touched the ground.[26] He recalled meeting Gus, and how the Belgian cautiously talked him out of his pistol, as he had with Minnich. Sarnow wrote that Fruythof hurried him through the woods to the edge of the canal, explaining as they walked that the Germans were near, and that "it would be best to get right into the water."

"I started to take this advice when a boy ran up," Sarnow recalled. "He told me in sign language, and with the aid of a box of matches, that a burned 'camarade' was nearby. I followed him to Lieutenant Minnich."

As the two Americans were comparing notes, another boy ran up with the Mae West lifejacket with John White's name on it. White himself was a few steps behind the boy, walking with an English civilian named Frank, who apparently lived in that part of Belgium and was part of the underground that aided downed flyers.

Soon, the three Americans were the center of a crowd of excited Belgian civilians who were anxious to shake their hands and kiss them. As this effusive exchange calmed down, Sarnow started attending to Minnich's burns.

"A crowd of boys held his chute, while I cut it up into bandages," Sarnow recalled. "I opened my parachute first aid kit [but] there was nothing in it for burns. [I began] removing his crash-bracelet from his burn-deformed wrist."

As he was doing this, another man arrived to warn the Americans and their new friends that German search parties were closing in. Fruythof, who had earlier advised Sarnow to swim to the other side of the canal, now insisted that they all do this immediately.

As Sarnow gathered up their survival kits and parachute silk, Minnich began pulling off his heavy flying clothes to make the swim. According to Minnich, White just stood there. Telling them that he did not know how to swim, he began arguing with Sarnow who urged him at least to *try*. He did have his life vest.

"I got him into his Mae West and told him to get started," Sarnow later explained. "I had just started to strip [off my flying gear] when White began to shout. Our helper [Fruythof] warned him to be quiet, but he thought he was drowning and kept on shouting. I dove in after him, and applying cross-chest carry, tried to swim with him. He had taken some water and kept struggling. I tried the under-chin carry but he would not cooperate. Our helper said to bring him back to the bank and he would care for him. So back he was brought and we pulled him out."

"The Germans, on motorcycles, and on foot with barking dogs, were now only 150 yards away," Sarnow wrote. "I had to dive back and swim hard, leaving our escape kits behind. I joined Lieutenant Minnich who was hiding behind a rise of ground. [Fruythof] took Minnich, disguised him in fishing coveralls, and carrying a fishing rod, [and put him] further down the canal [to distract the search parties]. He came back then and took me, in the same disguise, to join Minnich."

By placing them in the marsh, Fruythof prevented the German search dogs from following their scent. He told the Americans to wait patiently until the Germans were finished with their search of the area. During the time that they spent among the rushes, the Germans never came close. Minnich recalled that "we sat so quietly, and for so long, in six inches of water, that the rats played all around us with assurance."

Two of the *Our Bay-Bee* men had now made it through the first challenging hours of life as evaders in occupied Europe. A 24-year-old from Piqua, Ohio, Martin Minnich had enlisted in January 1941. Two years younger, Hank Sarnow, from West Division Street in Chicago, had enlisted in March 1942. Having found themselves together as part of a crew of ten, they had now been thrown together in an entirely new and different adventure.

Chapter 24

Tales of a Shillelagh and a Double Agent

At 11:48am on August 17, while Martin Minnich and Hank Sarnow were swimming the Kempen Canal, 131 Flying Fortresses from the Regensburg strike force – out of 146 that started out that morning – were over the Messerschmitt factory in that city.

The 4th Bomb Wing found the skies over Regensburg sparkling clear – a textbook example of the ideal weather for precision bombardment. Indeed, it was one of the Eighth's most precise attacks to date. The lead bombardier, manning his Norden bombsight a few feet ahead of where Curtis LeMay sat, put his bombs directly on the target and the rest of the bomber stream followed.

For the 4th Bomb Wing, this was the good news and the *only* good news. Luftwaffe attacks, which were typically furious but brief, today went on for hours as the stream of Flying Fortresses lumbered across Germany. Among these bombers was *Old Shillelagh II* of the 385th Bomb Group, with 1st Lieutenant Bill Grodi at the controls as it unleashed nearly 300 tons of high explosives on the makers of the very aircraft that had downed *Our Bay-Bee*.

A tale lay in that "*II*" after the name of Grodi's bomber. An Irish-American, he had named his previous Flying Fortress "*Old Shillelagh*."[27] Grodi and his current crew had flown this aircraft into the base at Great Ashfield in Suffolk on June 19, 1943, and were flying their third mission on July 29, when they ran into some bad luck.

As they passed over the islands of Helgoland off the northwest coast of Germany on their way to Warnemunde, antiaircraft fire caught their number three engine and turned it into a fireball. Grodi couldn't feather the prop, so as *Old Shillelagh* dropped out of formation, he decided that the most prudent course was to return to Great Ashfield. Heading for home, Grodi and his copilot, Jack Hughes, watched the flames consume the R-1820 Wright Cyclone. As those flames began burning into the wing, and came closer to the fuel tanks, Grodi made the decision to ditch the aircraft into the choppy waters of the North Sea.

It was only moments before they hit the waves that they managed to contact British air-sea rescue to advise their location. Fortunately, the ditching went well, both life rafts deployed, and all the crewmen were out when *Old Shillelagh* sank seven minutes later. That was the good news.

The bad news was that the crew was still 150 miles short of England, and it was not unknown for the Germans to pick up downed Allied flyers in these waters. The next ten hours in the heaving seas were not the best of times by any account.

But Grodi and his crew had survived the ordeal that day. They'd soon gotten a new B-17F, named her *Old Shillelagh II*, and were back in action. And now, three weeks later, they had survived the air defenses of Regensburg.

In the late afternoon of August 17, while Minnich and Sarnow of *Our Bay-Bee* were hiding in a Belgian swamp, Bill Grodi and *Old Shillelagh II* crossed the Alps and northern Italy, and were over the Mediterranean headed for North Africa. They encountered some antiaircraft fire above Sardinia, but the main focus of concern for Grodi was the fuel gauges.

Behind him, for navigator 2nd Lieutenant Adelbert "Dell" Kneale, the biggest concern was locating the airfield where they were supposed to land. As they neared the Algerian coast, they started to see Flying Fortresses in the water where they had ditched after running out of fuel. The trip had become a nail-biter. Grodi's crew had already had their fill of ditching!

At last, Kneale was able to give Grodi the proper heading to an airfield near the coastal city of Bône. They touched down with all the fuel gauges in the red – but they had survived Black Tuesday.

Also coming into North Africa that evening was author and former Eighth Air Force staffer Major Beirne Lay, now at the controls of a 100th Bomb Group Flying Fortress.*

"The prospect of ditching out of gasoline," wrote Lay in a November 1943 article in *The Saturday Evening Post*, "and the sight of other B-17s falling into the drink seemed trivial matters after the vicious nightmare of the long trial across Southern Germany. We had walked through a high

*See Part 7.

valley of the shadow of death, not expecting to see another sunset, and now I could fear no evil."

It was a classic desert landing strip, one of those dust-blown bases that the Allies had thrown together to support operations in the Mediterranean. Like Telergma Airfield, the main USAAF base 90 miles away in northeastern Algeria, all the North Africa bases were shoestring operations. This was not England, with its paved runways, state-of-the art facilities and hot meals. These were bug-infested tent cities with no amenities and marginal maintenance facilities.

The idea was now to get the Regensburg force ready to fly back to England, but it would take time to patch up the Flying Fortresses and get them ready. Until then, in blistering August heat, there was plenty of work for skeleton maintenance crews, but for the flight crews, it was life under the time-honored standing military order, "hurry up and wait."

As they waited in the Belgian swamp, trying to blend in to the scene on the afternoon of Black Tuesday, Hank Sarnow drained Martin Minnich's blisters and bandaged his wounds. August Fruythof, meanwhile, went home, where his wife, Ida, had prepared sandwiches and a thermos of tea for the downed airmen. He then returned to the marsh with a fishing pole and went through the motions of trying to catch fish before he took the food to the Americans. He had also brought some Purol salve to apply to Minnich's burned skin, and told them that he would move them out after dark.

At about 10:30pm that night, Fruythof took the Americans about two miles across a road and through some woods to his house, where Ida was waiting with a hot meal and a fresh change of bandages for Minnich's burns. Fruythof and his wife also provided clean pajamas, a place to sleep and civilian clothes. By now, the two Americans had learned that the Fruythofs belonged to the Belgian resistance group known as the "White Brigade," an organization with an extensive network across the country.

When he awoke on Wednesday morning, Minnich's eyes were swollen shut and he was running a temperature of around 104 degrees Fahrenheit. To aid him, the Fruythofs had brought in a nurse, a 19-year-old woman named Gerardine. In a twist of irony, she had also been pressed into service the day before by the Germans to care for five members of the *Our Bay-Bee* crew who had been captured and hospitalized.

Publicly, Gerardine was ardently pro-German, but like so many in wartime Europe, she lived a double life. Of urgency at the moment, she had learned by speaking with the Germans that they were under orders not to even take a meal break until they had run down all the fugitives from the bomber crew. With this in mind, she and the Fruythofs concocted a scheme whereby Gerardine would sneak food to the hungry search party, gain their confidence, and stay abreast of their search plans.

Among the useful tidbits she learned from a German officer was that they had decided not to search the houses near that of the Fruythofs because they lay to the east of where the parachutes came down, and the Germans "knew" that enemy airmen *always* escaped westward. Besides that, no Belgian civilian would be so foolish as to hide American flyers!

It was touch and go for Minnich through the next few days. His temperature spiked, and Gerardine did her best. She brought in a topical solution of silver nitrate to treat his burns, and to help battle the infection. Finally, on Friday, August 20, the worst was over and Minnich's fever broke. The most obvious scabs on his face were cleaned up, and he felt up to moving on.

With the Americans dressed in good suits, a small bicycle caravan formed. Two White Brigade people took the lead, with Sarnow and Gerardine following at some distance. Minnich and Fruythof came next, with another man bringing up the rear.

They traveled about five miles south to the village of Mol, where they were safely stashed at the home of Fruythof's uncle, Jos Verbruggen. It was arranged that Fruythof and Gerardine would stop by the next day to check on Minnich's wounds. However, when they did return on Saturday, the Belgians were stunned to find the Americans preparing to step out to the café at the Belle Vue Hôtel for dinner!

After all that had been done to hide them, such a thing struck Fruythof as unthinkable. The scars and injuries on Minnich's face would attract needless attention. A night on the town in a tiny village, where there were no secrets, and where Gestapo agents lurked everywhere, was the height of folly. In his memoirs, Fruythof recalled that in his conversation with the Americans, he had told them that they were "insane."

Chapter 25

A Milk Run Turns Sour

While Gerardine was caring for Martin Minnich of *Our Bay-Bee* through his feverish nightmares, and placing salve on his painful burns in that Belgian farmhouse, Bill Grodi was a thousand miles due south in Algeria, waiting for the 4th Bomb Wing aircraft to be ready to make the long return flight home.

On Tuesday, August 24, it was finally time to leave Africa for England. The mission plan had always been for the Regensberg force bombers to make themselves useful on the way back and to attack German facilities in the south of France. Bombs had been stockpiled in Algeria for just this purpose, and the target picked. It was a Luftwaffe base near Bordeaux from which long-range Fw 200 maritime strike aircraft harassed Allied convoys in the Atlantic.

The flight plan, according to Eighth Air Force strategic planner Colonel Richard D'Oyly Hughes, was for the force to "fly over the Mediterranean Sea, cut across the narrow neck of southwest France just east of the Pyrenees, bomb the airfield, and then fly sufficiently far out over the Bay of Biscay to be safe from German fighter interference all the way back to England."

Hughes predicted an easy mission, a milk run. As he wrote in his unpublished memoirs, now at the Air Force Historical Research Agency, he had information that "there were few German fighters based in the Bordeaux area." He added, in words he would come to regret, that "I chose the easiest target in France which I could possibly select — and yet have some semblance of a military target."

Of the 131 Flying Fortresses that had reached Regensburg on Black Tuesday, one week earlier, only 84 had been patched up sufficiently in their week in North Africa to be deemed mission ready on August 24. One of them was Grodi's *Old Shillelagh II*. Aboard, along with Grodi's crew, was Claude Sharpless, listed on the roster as an "extra gunner." He was a crewman of a 348th Bomb Squadron aircraft that was not yet ready to fly north, and he asked to hitch a ride.

With fuel hand-pumped from 55-gallon drums, the force took off, crossed the Mediterranean, and headed toward Bordeaux at 23,000 feet. With the Pyrenees under their left wings, they passed through minimal antiaircraft fire, but noticed the contrails of German fighters high above. As the bombers neared Toulouse, the Luftwaffe struck the rear of the formation.

Old Shillelagh II took the worst of it. Grodi recalled in escape and evasion report E&E No.156 that he had been having trouble with the number three engine, and was slipping behind. The oil pressure had dropped to zero, and efforts to feather the propeller had failed.

The Luftwaffe defenders loved a straggler. Attacking from behind, from six o'clock high and from six o'clock low, three Bf 109s shot up the tail and destroyed the ball turret oxygen system. Grodi ordered the ball turret gunner, 22-year-old Staff Sergeant Melvin Frazier of Niobrara, Nebraska, to get out of his cramped sphere and into the mid-fuselage.

According to E&E No.156, the oxygen system for the whole aircraft was then knocked out. With a windmilling prop and no oxygen, Grodi finally gave the order to abandon ship while *Old Shillelagh II* was at 19,000 feet and about 35 miles east of Toulouse.

It should be pointed out that while E&E No.156 bears Bill Grodi's name and includes his story, it was compiled as an after-action report for the whole crew and contains their detailed narratives as well. Numbered escape and evasion reports in their names do exist for some of the men and are named in parentheses below, but these each contain a scant few pages. Their full stories are in E&E No.156. Obviously, escape and evasion reports exist only for men who successfully escaped and evaded.

In the center of the aircraft, waist gunner Staff Sergeant Robert Really of New York had been badly wounded in his shoulder and thigh, and was lying in his own blood, conscious, but in shock and unable to move. As Grodi later recalled in his 2006 oral history interview, Really's fellow waist gunner, 20-year-old Staff Sergeant Denver Canaday of New Castle, Indiana, came to his aid.

Canaday (E&E No.160) clipped Really's chest pack parachute into place, and prepared to push him out the escape hatch. Knowing that Really would be unable to pull his ripcord, Canaday attached a length of rope to the aircraft and tied the other end to Really's ripcord handle.

Canaday jumped as soon as he pushed Really through the hatch, recalling that he blacked out briefly, but that he regained consciousness just in time to see *Old Shillelagh II*, with two fighters attacking it, as it went into a dive.

In his 2006 interview, Bill Grodi remembered Canaday telling of a Messerschmitt that made a slow pass as he was hanging in his parachute. Canaday expected to be shot out of the sky, but instead, the German pilot lowered his flaps, opened his canopy and saluted.

The two waist gunners landed near one another, but Really was still unable to move. A Frenchman came from a nearby farmhouse with water. He and Canaday tried to help Really, but he was in terrible shape, drifting in and out of consciousness.

When it was his turn to jump, Bill Grodi delayed pulling the ripcord when he saw enemy fighters beneath him. During a 14,000-foot freefall, Grodi recalled feeling "no sensation of falling," but "when the ground looked as though it were coming up fast, I pulled the ripcord."

After hitting the ground hard in a farm field near the village of Marsan, Grodi was knocked out for a moment, and came to feeling the pain of his difficult landing. There were many civilians in the field where he found himself, but a woman and a boy reached him first. He struggled to his feet and they helped carry him to the shade of a nearby tree.

As Grodi was getting his bearings, "a crowd of peasants came running to help me out of my chute. I got out my French language cards and pointed to the question that asked about Germans. They shook their heads to tell me that the Germans were not near."

The woman and two young boys gathered up his parachute and led him to the nearby home of Henri Marambat, a postman turned Résistance man who is still remembered in the lore of the wartime underground. At Marambat's house, Grodi was given something to eat and a change of clothes to replace his heavy flying gear. Only then did he discover that he was covered with blood from his hard landing.

Twenty minutes later, some other people arrived at the house with Grodi's copilot, 2nd Lieutenant Jack Hughes (E&E No.157). No relation to British-born Richard D'Oyly Hughes, Jack was from Evanston, Illinois and had enlisted in December 1941. At age 28, he was three years older than Grodi, who was just ten days shy of his twenty-fifth birthday.

Like Grodi, Hughes had delayed pulling his ripcord, but his had not been an effortless descent. As related among the interviews in Bill Grodi's E&E

No.156, Hughes had found himself in a violent spin for most of the way down. Weighing more than 200 pounds, he'd hit hard, but had recovered and was shedding his gear when a crowd of civilians came running up. Hughes asked them, in halting high school French, whether there were Germans nearby. They told him that there were some in Auch, 11 miles to the northwest, and in Toulouse. The people brought him food, along with some civilian coveralls. They asked Hughes for his gun. He was not carrying one, but he gave them his keys and some Algerian money that he had in his pocket.

As the swarms of friendly people descended upon them, busily gathering up their parachutes, shoving their flight gear into gunny sacks, and providing them with clothes, it became evident that these people were not all ordinary civilians. They were people who knew what was necessary to protect Allied airmen from the Germans.

Among the group was Henri Marambat, who told Jack Hughes that he would be taken to join another American airman – who turned out to be Bill Grodi. Marambat told the two Americans that he'd be back at midnight to take them to another safe house, and so he was. After a three-hour walk in the rain, they arrived at a *château*, where they would be reunited with other members of their crew several days later.

Meanwhile, Dell Kneale (E&E No.158), the 26-year-old navigator from Tulsa, Oklahoma, had opened his parachute at 5,000 feet and "had plenty of time to watch the ground." With a navigator's eye for geography, he tried to pick out landmarks, "so that later I would know the area in which I was landing. I could see Auch and the line of the highway between Auch and Toulouse."

Kneale came down on a hillside and broke his left leg. In trying to soften his fall, he became entangled in his parachute and was, in his estimation, "helpless."

A man arrived almost immediately to aid him, and within a couple of minutes, there were around 15 people on the scene. As Kneale recalled, "I motioned that I wanted my chute hidden, and they seemed to know what to do." Indeed, they did. As with his fellow crewmen, he was in the good hands.

When they saw that he could not stand, two men picked him up and carried him to a nearby farmhouse, where they immediately provided a change of clothes and took his flying gear away to be hidden. Before he knew what was happening, Kneale had been given some food and someone had gone for medical assistance. One of these men, who introduced himself as René Dubois, was actually Résistance man René Derbaize. He was in communication with Henri Marambat, then sheltering Grodi and Hughes.

Several miles away, Denver Canaday had by now removed Robert Really's gear and, with the help of some French civilians, had carried the injured man to the shade of a nearby tree. When he was sure the French people understood that Really needed a doctor, Canaday checked his compass and set off through the woods, walking south, in the general direction of Spain.

Canaday came to a house, where the people recognized him as an American, and were very friendly. They took him about six miles to another house, where the man who lived there produced a French-English dictionary. This man then took him by bicycle to the home of Ramon Muroel, where he was promptly given a change of clothes.

At around midnight on the very long day of Tuesday, August 24, Canaday and Muroel cycled to a church, where Canaday was pleased to be reunited with ball turret gunner Melvin Frazier (E&E No.159) and two other *Old Shillelagh II* men – Staff Sergeant George Elliot of Elmhurst, New York, the tail gunner, and hitchhiking "extra gunner" Claude Sharpless of Vindex, Maryland (E&E No.162).

As the four sergeants were eating a meal brought to them by their French hosts, a man arrived with news that no doctor had yet reached Really. Elliot, who had some minor injuries, said he had a morphine syringe from the first aid kit aboard the aircraft that he did not need. He volunteered to go with the man and give Really an injection to at least alleviate some of his pain. When Elliot reached Really, the doctor had now arrived and had already given him a painkiller, but Elliot made sure that he got some water and was made comfortable. The Eighth Air Force later received word that he had reached a hospital in Auch – courtesy of the Germans.

The doctor, knowing that the Germans were coming, warned Elliot to put some distance between himself and Really. As he was making his way back to rejoin the other sergeants, Elliot and his French companion learned that the others had been moved.

Elliot was taken to a barn to spend the night. On Wednesday morning, he was visited by a young boy who understood written English and who "kept advising me to give myself up."

"I countered by asking for directions to the Pyrenees, and he insisted that I would not get there," Elliot recalled. "While we were talking, another French boy came in and called me outside to tell me that the boy to whom I was talking was pro-German. I went back in the house and told the young boy that I would think over what he was telling me and he left."

The second boy then told the American that he knew a man who could help him, and after a 15-minute walk through the woods, Elliot was introduced to a man named Henri Daubney, who took Elliot to his home in Marsan and called for a doctor to treat Elliot's minor wounds. On Friday night, Elliot was reconnected with Denver Canaday.

On Saturday, August 28, Elliot and Canaday were startled to find themselves being picked up in a French police van by a man who identified himself as "Capitaine Ricardo." This man, whom they called "the Little Captain," was actually Marcel Taillandier, the leader of Groupe Morhange, or Réseau Morhange. This was a Résistance organization based in Toulouse, and active throughout the Haute-Garonne Department and the broader Occitania Region.

Taillandier had been with the Deuxième Bureau, France's prewar foreign intelligence agency, and had gone underground to form Morhange as a sabotage and assassination group targeting the occupiers, especially the Gestapo and their French collaborators. Taillandier was also known as "Agent X-1," one of at least 16 known Morhange agents who took an "X" designation.

Taillandier drove the men about an hour to the *château* where Henri Marambat had taken Grodi and Hughes on their first night. By now, they had also been joined by Frazier and Sharpless. The Little Captain picked up this foursome and took all six Americans to the town of Brax, about six miles west of Toulouse, where they were lodged at another *château*.

In the crew's joint after-action report, E&E No.156, this place was referred to as Château Colonie, "an armed fortress, the center of the organization which operated in and around Toulouse." This description actually applies to the Château de Brax, a sixteenth-century medieval castle, which was the headquarters – and torture chamber – for the Groupe Morhange during the war.

Incapacitated by his broken leg, *Old Shillelagh II* navigator Dell Kneale had barely missed being swept up by German search parties during his early days on the ground, but his French benefactors had worked overtime to safeguard him. He was moved a couple of times, staying one step ahead of the Gestapo. He finally had his leg set on Saturday by Emmanuel Magnouac, a pharmacist in l'Isle-Jourdain, a town halfway between Auch and Toulouse, and just eight miles from Brax.

On Wednesday, September 3, proudly sporting a beret that he had been given to help him fit in among French civilians, Kneale was driven to Château de Brax to rejoin the other members of his crew.

Chapter 26

To Brussels and Beyond

It was on August 30, the same Saturday that Dell Kneale of *Old Shillelagh II* was having his leg set in southwestern France, that Martin Minnich of *Our Bay-Bee* was in northwestern Belgium and feeling so good about his recovery from his burns that he was ready for a night on the town. He and Hank Sarnow were preparing to expose themselves to the world – and likely the Gestapo – by dining at the Hôtel Belle Vue in Mol.

Their benefactor, August "Gus" Fruythof, who had gone to great lengths to protect them, had told the Americans to their faces that they were "insane" for even considering such a plan. Though he talked the Americans out of this heedless frolic, the incident really rattled those who had been putting their own lives on the line for the two men.

Fruythof and the young nurse, Gerardine, washed their hands of Minnich and Sarnow, passing them off to a man named Edouard, who had operated a nearby Ford Motor Company dealership before the war. While they were at his home, Minnich and Sarnow were given passwords and addresses of safe houses from Liège to Paris where they could stay as they continued their trip. Minnich was also visited by a doctor, who deemed the healing of his wounds to be "coming along okay."

On September 1, the Americans and a White Brigade handler stepped into a third class car and traveled 60 miles south by train to the Liège suburb of Bressoux. When they met the woman who was supposed to be their contact, they found her to be unusually and unexpectedly suspicious.

"What is cinema?" she asked, using a coded security question for which the Americans were unfortunately unprepared. Perhaps they should have been briefed for this exchange, or perhaps Edouard *had* briefed them and they forgot what to say. We'll never know.

The woman stared skeptically, told them that her "life was broken," and slammed the safe house door in their faces.

Equally put off by this turn of events, their handler took the Americans to Hasselt, about 30 miles north of Liège, for a change of Minnich's bandages at a dentist's office, and a change of plans.

On September 2, Martin Minnich and Hank Sarnow were introduced to Anne Brusselmans. Neither American mentioned her by name in his escape and evasion report, but both Anne and her daughter, Yvonne Daley-Brusselmans, named both men in their own recollections, and in Yvonne's memoir of these years.

Anne Brusselmans, an unassuming 38-year-old Brussels housewife and mother of two young children, was on her way to becoming a legend in the annals of the wartime Belgian underground. She had begun helping British soldiers stranded in Belgium in 1940, and by 1943, she was one of the most important figures in the enterprise of aiding downed airmen. She hosted them in her apartment at 127 Chaussée d'Ixelles, while coordinating their movements through numerous other safe houses throughout the city and beyond.

As Minnich recalled in his escape and evasion report, she took them into Brussels, where she brought in "the best doctor in town" to care for him.[28] The doctor provided "special preparations" and clean bandages, as well a black scarf to cover the bandages on Minnich's neck. With him thus disguised, he and Sarnow made their way to 45 Rue des Fraises in the suburb of Anderlecht, the home of a banker named François Delen, who helped begin the process of forging identity cards for the two Americans.

On Monday, September 6, according to Minnich, they "moved to another part of Brussels by tram. Sarnow was elsewhere and I stayed with a nurse in a children's hospital. While I was here, my picture was taken and a young girl [possibly Yvonne Brusselmans] brought me an ID card."

Anne Brusselmans then decided to take Sarnow back to her apartment while Minnich convalesced at the hospital. It was a most memorable cross-town journey. In her memoirs, Yvonne recalled that by the time they left, "it was dark in the streets and Hank was having trouble walking on the cobblestones... One also has to remember that all young [Belgian] men

18 years and older had been deported to Germany to work in ammunition factories… In other words, not looking European, being tall and well fed, Hank might as well have been strolling down the streets waving the Stars and Stripes."[29]

A tram was approaching and Anne decided that they should take it the rest of the way. Yvonne wrote that as it slowed to a stop, "the doors opened and Mother was faced with a group of noisy Germans. There was no backing out now; they would have to board the tram in order to not look suspicious. She did, and, after the briefest moment of hesitation, Hank followed, probably very reluctant to place himself amid the enemy. He did not hesitate to get off the tram, however, when Mother signaled to him. They both heaved a sigh of relief when they finally reached the apartment."

On another occasion, when Sarnow needed to be taken out to get a headshot for his fake identification papers, Anne took her daughter along. As Yvonne observed, "it looked a lot less conspicuous for me to walk hand-in-hand between Mother and Hank. His photo was taken at one of the automatic booths, and we returned home without any problems."

While Minnich and Sarnow had been taken under the wing of Anne Brusselmans in Brussels, what had happened to their fellow crewman, John White?

Back on August 17, when faced with having to swim the Kempen Canal, the ball turret gunner from *Our Bay-Bee* had panicked. He could not swim, and he was afraid of the water. We all have our fears. The 21-year-old from Dorchester, Massachusetts had his. White could handle the extreme claustrophobia of being squeezed into a ball turret, and peering at the earth from three miles in the air through a thin piece of Plexiglas, but he simply didn't like the water.

Frank, the Englishman who had found White dangling from his parachute and then guided him to the canal, also tried to cajole him into swimming. When this proved impossible, he hid White in the woods and told him that he would send help after nightfall.

As White told it in his own escape and evasion report, E&E No.95, a priest and another man arrived about two hours later in a rowboat and tried to convince White to give himself up to the Germans. As White told it, for the second time that day, he replied with an emphatic "*no!*"

White wrote that he then turned the conversation around. Pointing to their rowboat, he insisted that they row him across the canal, which they finally did.

In August Fruythof's recollection, however, the boat belonged to his friend, Marcel Coppins, who happened by immediately after Minnich and Sarnow had swum across, and it was Fruythof who arranged for White to make the crossing. After pushing White into the boat, Fruythof lost track of him when he returned to Minnich and Sarnow.

About an hour after his canal crossing, White was overtaken by two young women almost certainly associated with the White Brigade. They were carrying a change of clothes and some Belgian money for him. They also gave him a bicycle and handed him off to a boy who led him north on a 20-mile ride to the city of Turnhout. With this, he was now heading in the direction opposite from that taken by Minnich and Sarnow.

On the morning of Wednesday, August 18, after spending the night with the boy's English-speaking aunt and her husband, White was taken to the train station. By the end of the day, he was in Brussels, two weeks ahead of Minnich and Sarnow.

Still escorted by the English-speaking aunt, White was taken to a safe house where he remained until Saturday. A man named René then took him to be photographed for his forged identity papers. After the papers arrived that night, René's wife took White by train to an unnamed small town near the French border. At 5:00am on Sunday morning, they walked, with a wink and a nod to cooperative border guards, into France and boarded another train to Paris. Luckily, White's papers, thoroughly examined by the Gestapo on the train, passed scrutiny.

Sergeant John White, the man who'd elected not to swim the canal that he crossed later in the day by boat, was now six weeks *ahead* of Martin Minnich and Hank Sarnow, who would not reach Paris until early November.

After a couple of nights in the home of an English-speaking former French air force pilot, White was picked up by Comet Line handlers and taken by train to Bordeaux, and then to Bayonne. Traveling by bicycle, and guided at least part of the way by a former French army tank officer, White crossed into Spain and made his way to Gibraltar. He reached England on September 16, 1943, while Minnich and Sarnow were still in Brussels.

Chapter 27

Unexpected Threats

On September 20, about 500 miles south of Brussels, a man named André Fontes, but who introduced himself as "André Blanc," drove up the gravel driveway of Château de Brax. Within this grim medieval castle near Toulouse, seven crewmembers from *Old Shillelagh II* had been hiding out for more than two weeks.

In the melodramatic nomenclature of Groupe Morhange, where the "Little Captain," Marcel Taillandier, called himself Agent X-1, Fontes was designated as Agent X-4. He announced that he was ready to start moving the *Old Shillelagh II* men to the Pyrenees for their walk across the mountains into Spain.

He began with Bill Grodi, Jack Hughes, Denver Canaday, and Melvin Frazier. Taillandier and Fontes promised the men that the American Consulate in Barcelona had been alerted, and that someone would meet them when they had crossed the border. Everything was arranged. What could possibly go wrong?

At first, everything *did* go according to plan. Squeezing the four Americans into his vehicle, Fontes drove about 100 miles southwest through Perpignan on the Mediterranean coast, depositing them 20 road miles from the Spanish border. In the coming hours, the four Americans were passed through a series of handlers, ending with a 19-year-old man called Pepito, who led them on an uneventful four-day hike through the Pyrenees.

By September 24, one month after they were shot down, Grodi, Hughes, Canaday, and Frazier were camped in the woods outside the Spanish city of Figueres waiting with Pepito for someone from the American Consulate in Barcelona to come get them. If their passage from occupied France into neutral Spain was supposed to have been cause for a collective sigh of relief, the foursome from *Old Shillelagh II* soon discovered that it wasn't. The plan was starting to unravel.

For three days, they waited, growing increasingly frustrated. Grodi and Frazier were sneaking into gardens to steal vegetables, but other than that, they hadn't had anything to eat since they arrived in Spain, and they were anxious to move on. If the consulate in Barcelona wasn't coming to them, they would go to Barcelona.

Pepito argued that they should continue waiting, but they insisted, so he bought them train tickets for the 80-mile journey and sent them on their way.

Grodi, Hughes, Canaday, and Frazier managed to reach Barcelona without incident, but when they detrained, they made it only as far as the first encounter with Spanish police checking identification papers. They had gotten rid of their American identification, which had been a liability in occupied France, but undocumented travelers in Spain were assumed to be smugglers. They should have listened to Pepito.

After a month of successfully staying one step ahead of the Gestapo, they were now thrown into what they described in their joint escape and evasion report as a "dungeon" in the city of Medla.[30] According to Bill Grodi in a 2006 oral history interview, they were kept for most of the next month in an eight-by-ten-foot concrete cell with a metal door. Mealtime came once a day when a metal portal in the door opened and a ladle of soup for each inmate was poked through. If a man did not have a bowl, he was out of luck. Grodi traded his wristwatch for one.

The narrative mentions that they were eventually visited by Thomas J. Corey, the American vice consul in Barcelona, but according to Grodi's later account, this did not happen until well into their confinement. Grodi explained that a fellow inmate, an Englishman jailed for an unspecified minor crime, had served his sentence and was being released, so they asked him to phone the American Consulate to report them, which he did. Had it not been for him, who knows how long they would have rotted in jail.

The fate of Grodi, Hughes, Canaday, and Frazier was completely unknown to their fellow *Old Shillelagh II* crewmembers as they made their way south on an alternate route. To mislead any prying eyes that might have been looking for a pattern in his movements, Fontes took Claude Sharpless and

George Elliot in the opposite direction, driving west to Tarbes. Dell Kneale would follow later.

Sharpless and Elliot were placed in the care of a one-armed former French army officer name Jean. A graduate of the French military academy at Saint-Cyr, Jean was an intrepid individual who promised to escort Sharpless and Elliot all the way to Barcelona. He had the confident air of someone who knew what he was doing. This was not, he assured them, his first clandestine mission into Spain.

They started out on September 29, driving about 100 miles eastward to the town of Foix in the Pyrenees, where they met a mountain guide who would escort them about 50 miles south to Andorra.

On October 3, after several days on steep mountain trails, when they were within sight of Andorra, the guide wished them well and headed back. With Jean leading the way, the two Americans crossed the border without incident.

In contrast to the way the plan had unraveled for Grodi, Hughes, Canaday, and Frazier nine days earlier at Figueres, things worked perfectly. Jean made contact with a taxi driver who had been expecting them, and soon they were headed south on winding mountain roads for the town of Sant Julià de Lòria on the Spanish border. Knowing both the route, and those who guarded it in Andorra and Spain, Jean was able to prevent his two Americans from being confused with smugglers.

After three nights at the Hotel Nationale in Sant Julià, Jean took Sharpless and Elliot into Spain on October 6, using one of those ubiquitous mountain trails to which they had become accustomed. For the next few days they traveled south, staying at safe houses with which Jean was familiar.

On their last night in the Pyrenees, they stopped at a hotel where they were met by one of Jean's British diplomatic contacts. He had a car, and by the evening of October 13, they were enjoying a meal at the British Consulate in Barcelona.

Meanwhile, as his fellow crewmembers departed for points along the Pyrenees frontier, Dell Kneale, *Old Shillelagh II*'s navigator, had been moved from the Château de Brax back to l'Isle-Jourdain, where his broken leg had been set a month earlier. On October 7, Emmanuel Magnouac, the pharmacist who had set the leg, deemed Kneale good to go, and he was taken to Foix, where Sharpless and Elliot had been on September 29.

In Foix, Kneale was met by a man named Pierre Cornet, who had arrived a few days earlier from Paris, escorting two other Eighth Air Force airmen from the 524th Bomb Squadron, 379th Bomb Group. Tech Sergeant Albert Tyler and 2nd Lieutenant John Boyle were the top turret gunner and bombardier respectively of a Flying Fortress that had been shot down by antiaircraft fire over Méry-sur-Oise near Paris on a raid against Le Bourget airport on August 16, one day before the Schweinfurt-Regensburg mission.

As Jean had done with Sharpless and Elliot about a week before, Pierre chose to take Kneale, Tyler, and Boyle into Spain by way of Andorra. The trip was, however, nowhere near as smooth. They ran into a blizzard in the Pyrenees that forced them to turn back to Foix, where their mountain guides promptly abandoned them.

Pierre knew a bicycle shop owner, who knew somebody who might know a guide. Eventually, they were connected to three guides who were about to embark with a group of 32 people. The mountain trails were now covered with drifted snow and their progress was slow. A couple of days into the climb, Tyler could go no further, but most of the group pressed on. Kneale and Boyle, as well as Pierre and Antonio, one of the guides, elected to stay with Tyler until he felt he was able to travel. So too did a husband and wife named Fouger and a Belgian named Paul Ferrari.

This group of eight managed to reach Andorra on October 11, where Fouger arranged for bus tickets to Seo de Urgel, the Spanish city about five miles south of the Andorra border. Antonio had a car waiting here, and he was able to drive Kneale, Tyler, and Boyle to the British Consulate in Barcelona. They arrived on October 13, just ahead of Sharpless and Elliot.

The consulate alerted Major Clark at the American Embassy in Madrid, who brought them to the embassy. Clark, who had recently freed Grodi, Hughes, Canaday, and Frazier, then moved all of the *Old Shillelagh II* crewmen on to Gibraltar. Kneale and Elliot reached the "Rock" on October 22, while Sharpless arrived on October 27. The others followed the next day. By October 29, all of the members of the *Old Shillelagh II* crew who had evaded capture were back in England.

Chapter 28

The Belgian Waiting Game

During the first two weeks of September 1943, as John White of *Our Bay-Bee* was back in England, and all the evaders from *Old Shillelagh II* were in or within sight of the Pyrenees, Martin Minnich and Hank Sarnow of *Our Bay-Bee* remained in Brussels.

These were tense times on the Comet Line. With the increase in Eighth Air Force operations, the increasing number of airmen being shot down, saved, and needing to escape put a strain on the network. Momentum slowed. At the same time, efforts by the Gestapo to infiltrate and undermine the Comet organization were in full swing.

Around the middle of September, Minnich, who had been lodged at a children's hospital, was taken "to meet a little girl on the street named Lily [who] looks 16 and dresses like a schoolgirl." She was actually 21-year-old Micheline Dumon, the experienced Comet Line operative who was taking care of Joe Walters of *Chug-a-Lug Lulu* around the same time.* Very youthful in appearance, she carried identification showing her to be still just a teenager, and she often dressed to appear even younger. This apparent innocence was an effective disguise.

Sarnow, meanwhile, was still staying with Anne Brusselmans at her apartment on Chaussée d'Ixelles. As they aided evaders, she and Micheline Dumon continued to look for opportunities to safely move them on the Paris and beyond.

*See Chapter 20.

Andrée de Jongh, known as Dédée, was only 24 when she became one of the founders of the Comet escape line. (© IWM HU 55451)

The navigator aboard *Wulfe Hound*, 2nd Lieutenant Gilbert Schowalter, was shot down in October 1942. He spent most of January 1943 interned at the British Embassy in Madrid before finally reaching England. (USAAF)

William Whitman and Lee Fegette lived here at the Château de Breuil in the commune of Rozay-en-Brie for two months from December 1942 to February 1943. (Author's collection)

Tech Sergeant William Whitman remained in northern France with fellow crewman Lee Fegette until April 1943, but they were back in England via Gibraltar by May. (USAAF)

Sergeant William Claxton "Billy" Howell was shot down over France on July 4, 1943. He later walked across the Pyrenees in the company of Sergeant Otto Bruzewski of the B-17 *Chug-a-Lug Lulu*. (USAAF)

Like many fellow evaders, Fred Hartung and Norman Therrien passed through the village of El Serrat in neutral Andorra as they made their way toward Spain and Gibraltar. (Nisse57, Wikimedia Commons, CC BY-SA 4.0)

20 (THERRIEN, Eno.)

X 041.2 EVE #

14

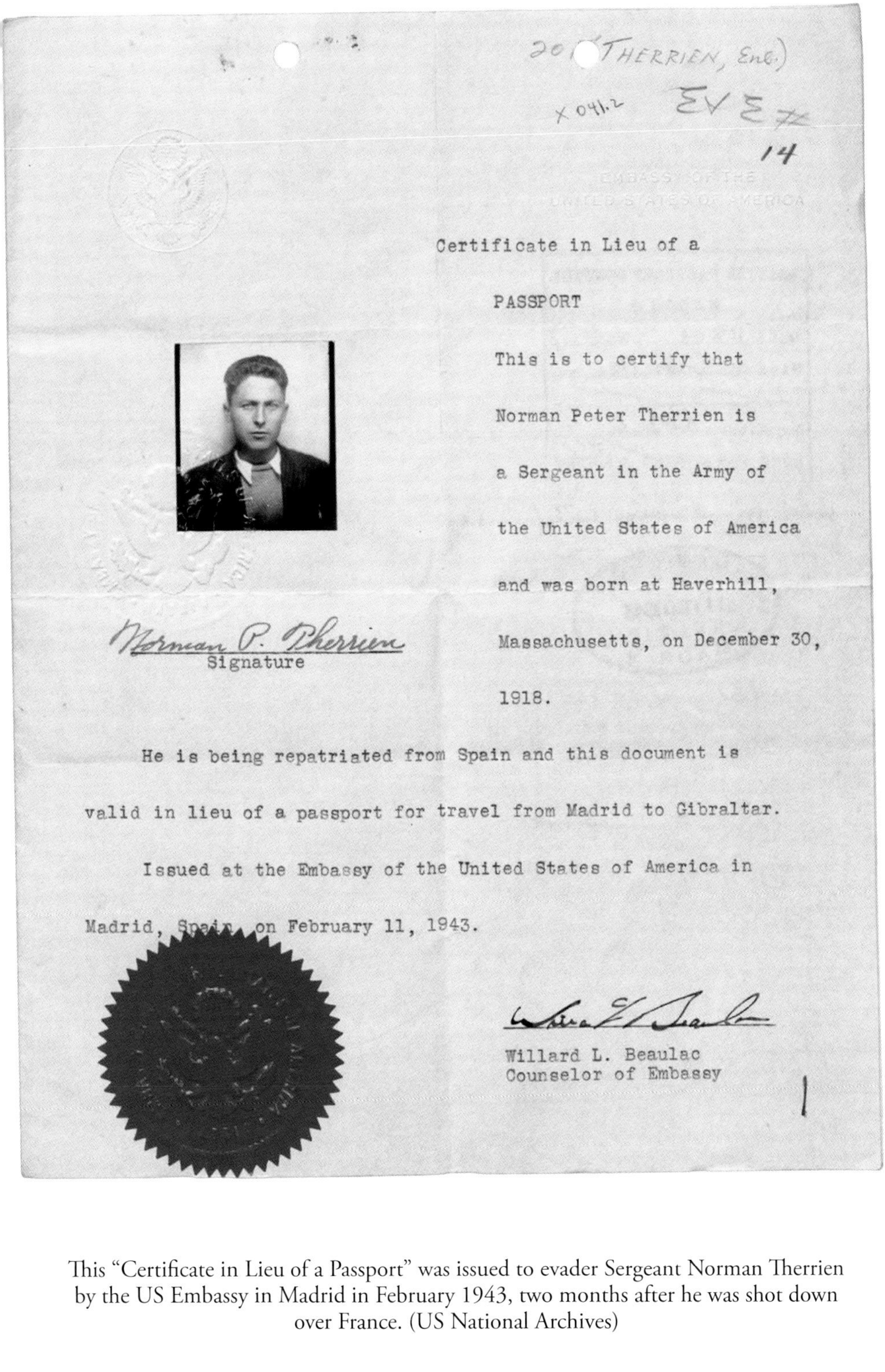

Certificate in Lieu of a

PASSPORT

This is to certify that

Norman Peter Therrien is

a Sergeant in the Army of

the United States of America

and was born at Haverhill,

Massachusetts, on December 30,

1918.

Norman P. Therrien
Signature

He is being repatriated from Spain and this document is valid in lieu of a passport for travel from Madrid to Gibraltar.

Issued at the Embassy of the United States of America in Madrid, Spain, on February 11, 1943.

Willard L. Beaulac
Counselor of Embassy

This "Certificate in Lieu of a Passport" was issued to evader Sergeant Norman Therrien by the US Embassy in Madrid in February 1943, two months after he was shot down over France. (US National Archives)

Wulfe Hound was the first B-17 captured by the Luftwaffe and restored to flyable condition. She was operated by the Luftwaffe from March 1943 until April 1944 when she was ditched in the Mediterranean. (Author's collection)

Shot down on August 17, 1943 during the "Black Tuesday" mission, and badly burned, 2nd Lieutenant Martin Minnich was cared for by the Belgian underground and taken under the wing of the Comet Line. (USAAF)

2nd Lieutenant Hank Sarnow hooked up with crewmate Martin Minnich shortly after their aircraft was shot down on "Black Tuesday." Thanks to the Comet Line, they were back in the UK by November 23, 1944. (USAAF)

Anne Brusselmans (left) opened her Brussels home to fugitive Allied airmen and coordinated many safe houses. In November 1957, she had a surprise reunion with Major Hank Sarnow (center) on the reality TV show *This is Your Life*, hosted by Eamon Andrews (right). (USAAF)

The Château de Brax near Toulouse was used during the occupation by the underground Groupe Morhange as a fortress, torture chamber, and safe house for evading airmen. (Didier Descouens, Wikimedia Commons, CC BY-SA 4.0)

Shot down in January 1944, P-47 pilot 1st Lieutenant Joel McPherson spent most of five months on the run with the Maquis in southwestern France. His harrowing adventures culminated in his stint as a getaway driver for a gang of Maquisard bank robbers. (USAAF)

After his B-24 Liberator was shot down in May 1944, Lieutenant Colonel Beirne Lay Jr evaded in northern France until August, when he was able to link up with elements of General Patton's Third Army. He later co-wrote the novel *Twelve O'Clock High*. (USAAF)

On June 18, 1944, high on the crest of the rugged Pyrenees, evading airmen Lieutenant Joel McPherson and Lieutenant Gilbert Stonebarger crossed the border into the Spanish village of Canéjan. (Père Igor, Wikimedia Commons, CC BY-SA 3.0)

Flying with the 56th Fighter Group, Major Walker "Bud" Mahurin was the highest-scoring American ace in the European Theater through early 1944. He had 19.75 confirmed victories when he was shot down in March 1944. (USAAF)

Seen here as a US Air Force major in 1950, Jack Terzian was shot down over Belgium on May 22, 1944. He managed to evade capture until July, but he escaped in a mass break-out of Allied airmen from a German freight car on September 3. (USAF)

The crew of the 801st Bomb Group B-24 known as *C for Charlie*, piloted by 1st Lieutenant Henry W. "Hank" Wolcott (top row, second from left). The aircraft went down in Belgium in May 1944 while on a secret Operation *Carpetbagger* mission. All but tail gunner Richard Hawkins (front row, second from left) escaped and evaded. (USAAF)

2nd Lieutenant Alfred Sanders was shot down over Belgium on May 28, 1944. He met 1st Lieutenant Hank Wolcott four days later and they evaded together until they were betrayed in mid-August. (USAAF)

Prosper DeZitter was an infamous Belgian criminal and Nazi collaborator. He set up a faux safe house in Brussels, into which he and his confederates lured dozens of Allied airmen before turning them over to the Germans – for a price. (Author's collection)

The dreaded Saint-Gilles Prison in Brussels was deliberately designed to have a foreboding, medieval appearance. Taken over by the Nazis in 1940, it was used mainly to house political prisoners pending transfer to concentration camps in Germany, but Allied airmen were also imprisoned here. (Author's collection)

"Inactivity weighed heavily on the airmen," Yvonne Brusselmans later wrote. "The men became restless at times. Once in a while, we would venture to the park with our house guests to keep them in shape for the long walk across the mountains. Surely days must have felt like weeks for them with so little to do and so much free time to brood over their fate… Hank [Sarnow] showed a lot of patience and became a member of the family. I remember him sitting in the living room reading *Scaramouche* [Rafael Sabatini's 1921 novel about the 'little skirmisher' of sixteenth-century folklore], which became our nickname for him. We played endless games of cards, just to pass the time away."

During this waiting time, Sarnow had ample time to speak with many Belgians and to get a sense for how they were holding up during the occupation.

"The Belgians hate the Germans and pro-Germans," he wrote in his escape and evasion report, speaking from both what he observed and what he learned talking to people whom he met.[31] "Those who helped the Nazis in the early days are mending their ways and doing everything they can to fabricate proof that they never collaborated. Some have gone so far as to get themselves arrested."

In 1940, there seemed no doubt that the occupation would last indefinitely, but by 1943, it was becoming clear that German rule would be going away – if not soon, *eventually*.

Minnich and Sarnow saw how noticeably frustrated the Germans had become with the growing wave of sabotage by organizations such as the White Brigade. Sarnow pointed out that "large numbers of hostages are taken in reprisal [to underground sabotage]. The hostages are taken at random. [I heard that] one night the Germans took everyone at a tram car stop."

Yvonne Brusselmans later wrote that on October 20, her mother got a call telling her that 11 members of the Comet organization had been executed early that morning.

At the same time, Sarnow was doing some soul-searching about the damage being done in and around Brussels by Allied air strikes against German facilities in the area. He later wrote of a conversation in which he asked Belgians "how they felt when their relatives, who were prisoners of war in Germany, were bombed in the destruction of German cities. [They] had but one reply: 'If they are killed by English or American bombs, it is the same as if they gave their life for their country, for if they were with the Allied forces it would be the same.' When civilians are killed during a raid, the attitude is that 'it is unfortunate that they lived near a military objective of which the destruction was necessary!'"

Yvonne recalled a time when her mother and father supplied Sarnow with an Air Raid Patrol armband so that they could take him out to view the aftermath of an Allied air strike on a pro-German militia barracks.

"Hank was obviously distraught," she wrote. "He realized the difference between being in a bomber thousands of feet above ground dropping bombs, and being at the receiving end on land. Although proud of the accuracy with which the bombs had reached the target, the desolation in the adjacent neighborhood had a devastating effect on him."

At 6:00am on Friday, November 5, 1943, the long-stalled momentum changed for Sarnow and Minnich as Anne Brusselmans and her daughter took them to the train station. Yvonne wrote that "mother bought a heavy coat for each of the men for the crossing of the mountains and directed a final rehearsal of answers in French to questions they were bound to be asked at one time or another. They went over how to produce their documents if requested to do so by a German patrol, and what to do in case they were asked how much currency they had on them. With sandwiches stuffed in their pockets, they left us after a fond goodbye."

Anne put them aboard in the care of a handler named François who got them to the French border by nightfall. They spent that night in the home of a friendly Belgian border guard who got them tickets on the train into the Gare de l'Est in Paris. The next day, properly ticketed and with their convincing forged identity papers in order, they were off.

As they traveled across France, it was easy to feel the mood of a country at war – the crowding and the continual parade of people in uniform going through the motions of checking identity papers. Outside their passenger car, they noticed that the freight trains all had a pair of cars with antiaircraft guns.

In contrast to their confusing and seemingly endless time in Brussels, Minnich and Sarnow were in and out of Paris in a few days. They reached the City of Lights on Saturday night, and boarded a southbound train late Wednesday. Escorted by a woman whom Minnich described as "a very little lady in her thirties," they traveled to Bordeaux, where they spent about six hours before being passed off to a man named Max for the 125-mile train trip to Biarritz.

Minnich and Sarnow spent Thursday night at a safe house in the countryside, then hiked for about ten hours to a safe house near the border. After an unusually uneventful crossing on Friday, they boarded a train to the Spanish city of San Sebastian, about 30 miles from the frontier, where they arrived on Saturday afternoon, November 13.

On Tuesday, they were taken to the British Embassy and Madrid, and then on to Gibraltar.

Both Minnich and Sarnow of *Our Bay-Bee* were back in the UK on November 23, more than two months after their fellow crewman, John White, and nearly a month after the evaders from *Old Shillelagh II.*

Chapter 29

This is Your Life

In his postwar life, Martin Minnich, the evading copilot of *Our Bay-Bee*, returned to Piqua, Ohio, where he later served as a city commissioner and as president of the chamber of commerce. Hank Sarnow remained in the service after the war. In November 1957, while a major stationed in Spain with the US Air Force, he had a remarkable reunion with Anne Brusselmans.

Sarnow was invited into BBC's London television studios by the producers of the documentary/reality program called *This Is Your Life*, which was based on a similar, contemporary program of the same name aired on the American NBC–TV network. The premise of the show was to invite unsuspecting guests onto the show and then surprise them with colleagues and friends whom they had not seen in many years.

Anne Brusselmans was chosen to be the person to be surprised, and with the help of her daughter, Yvonne, a brief documentary of her life was made, and she was brought to London under the pretense of watching some friends who were to be featured on another program. When the surprise was sprung, she was greeted by numerous people from the war years, including a grinning Hank Sarnow in his blue major's uniform.

Along with Anne Brusselmans, Micheline "Lily" Dumon had been among the fortunate helpers of wartime airmen who themselves evaded capture. Lily was extracted to England in June 1944 after her cover was compromised. She was preparing to go back when Belgium was liberated three months later. Anne became active in the Royal Air Force Escaping Society (RAFES) and later in the American Air Forces Escape and Evasion Society (AFEES). Yvonne went to work for the US Air Force in Europe, and married RAF officer Ian Daley. After his death in 1980, mother and daughter emigrated to the United States, where President Ronald Reagan intervened personally to grant Anne permanent resident status.

August "Gus" Fruythof, who aided Minnich and Sarnow on Black Tuesday in 1943, was not so lucky. He was arrested by the Gestapo and incarcerated in the Flossenburg concentration camp in Bavaria. When he was liberated in 1945, he came home weighing 85 pounds. His book about his wartime experiences, *From Purgatory to Hell*, was published in 1980. In later years, Martin Minnich and his family came to Belgium to call on the Fruythof family, who returned the visit, coming to see the Minnichs in Ohio.

Marcel Taillandier, the leader of Groupe Morhange, the man who helped save the crew of *Old Shillelagh II*, and the man whom Bill Grodi called the "Little Captain," lived a fast life and died young. He and his Morhange colleagues continued their covert and overt war on the Gestapo and their Vichy cohorts. They even captured the files of the collaborationist Parti Populaire Français, thus preventing an attack on the Maquis in the Grésigne forest, north of Toulouse. Betrayed by a traitor, though, Taillandier was gunned down by the Gestapo in Saint-Martin-du-Touch in 1944.

In 1944, after Wilmont "Bill" Grodi, *Old Shillelagh II*'s pilot, returned to the States, he was assigned as a Flying Fortress fight instructor, and had just been transferred to flight training for the B-29 Superfortress when the war ended. By this time, he was beginning to have serious residual effects from the blow he had taken when he bailed out of *Old Shillelagh II*. According to his 2006 oral history interview, he went through a series of hospitalizations, including a stay at the Fitzsimmons Army Hospital in Aurora, Colorado.

Grodi recalled that he had wanted to try for a career as an airline pilot, but "my health failed me." Instead, he went to work in banking. He was a loan officer with Security Pacific Bank, and later presided over his own commercial and residential appraisal business before retiring to Lawrence, Kansas.

In August 1993, on the fiftieth anniversary of his first visit to Toulouse and France's Haute-Garonne, Grodi went back. He was joined by some of his *Old Shillelagh II* mates – Jack Hughes, Dell Kneale, and Denver

Canaday – as well as members of their families. Celebrated as dignitaries in 1993, they visited many of the towns through which they had passed as fugitives a half century before. The city of Toulouse hosted an elaborate reception at which each man received the Diplôme d'Honneur de la Ville, and a representative of the US Embassy in Paris flew down to join them for a commemoration at the crash site.

"Grodi recovered his cigarette case, lost in the debris 50 years earlier," the Toulouse newspaper *La Dépêche du Midi* reported in a 2010 article about the 1993 visit. "Kneale bought himself a beret like the one that had turned him into a Gascon when he came out of rehabilitation, his leg fractured; finally, Canaday's wife offered her necklace to the woman who had rescued her husband."

PART SIX

BANDITS OF THE DORDOGNE

Chapter 30

A Journey *Formidable*

Early on the afternoon of Saturday, January 29, 1944, the Eighth Air Force bomber stream that had come calling at industrial sites around Frankfurt was now streaming home. This was the first day that the Mighty Eighth had launched more than 700 bombers on a single mission, but 29 had been lost.

Among the American fighter aircraft escorting the big bombers that day were the P-47 Thunderbolts of the 352nd Fighter Group. One of these Thunderbolts was piloted by 1st Lieutenant Joel McPherson of the 487th Fighter Squadron. He had made it through the gauntlet of flak and fighters, but one of the German bullets had caused an electrical short circuit in his aircraft, causing him to lose the use of his radio and his instruments. To make matters worse, McPherson had become separated from the rest of the squadron in the thick overcast.

McPherson thought he could see the English Channel through breaks in the clouds, but he flew over water for 40 minutes without spotting land. He had no idea where he was.

His flight leader, Captain George Preddy, later one of the leading Eighth Air Force aces of the war, reported losing sight of McPherson near Hody, Belgium, south of Liège. That was the last anyone had seen of Joel McPherson. Coincidentally, Preddy himself ditched his flak-damaged fighter over the Channel that same day, but he was promptly rescued by a British seaplane.

Though McPherson's fuel gauge didn't work, it didn't take much of a stretch of the imagination to guess that the Thunderbolt's tanks were running toward empty. Not wanting to bail out over water, he turned around. High above the clouds, he could see the sun, and he knew which way was south, so he decided to head for Spain and to get as close as possible.

Flying over western France, he was about 100 miles north of Bordeaux when the P-47's Pratt & Whitney R-2800 Double Wasp engine finally began to cough and sputter for lack of fuel.

Hanging beneath his parachute canopy that day, the boyish former railroad office worker from Lakewood, Ohio contemplated his next move. He'd been briefed in methods of escape and evasion, but he needed no encouragement in his determination to stay out of the hands of the Germans for as long as it took to get out of France.

McPherson landed in a field near the small town of Rouillac in the Department of Charente. He hurt his leg landing, but was able to walk on it without too much difficulty.

As he was pulling his parachute from a tree so that he could hide it from German search parties, he noticed that he was being watched curiously by an elderly woman and her grandson. They took him to their nearby farmhouse, but the woman's husband insisted that McPherson should leave immediately. There were Germans in the area, and it was certain that they too had seen McPherson as he came down. The grandfather wanted no part of the trouble that would descend upon him for harboring a fugitive American.

Outside the farmhouse, the small, curious crowd that had gathered shared the old farmer's sentiments.

"*Partez, partez*," they shouted, giving McPherson dirty looks and making obscene gestures. "Go away, go away."

McPherson got the message.

"I decided this was good advice," he recalled in his thoroughly detailed escape and evasion report.[32] "After kicking off my heavy flying boots and locating myself on the map, I set off south, down the road toward Spain." The border was 200 miles away.

As he walked along in the rubber-soled GI shoes that he had worn beneath his flying boots, he didn't expect that his journey would be easy, but at first it did seem reasonably straightforward. He had no idea what lay ahead over the next six months.

About a mile from the farmhouse, he spotted his crashed P-47. There was a crowd of civilians swarming around it, and since he had been warned to avoid crowds, he gave it a wide berth. He then took off cross country for about four miles, running most of the way to put as much distance as possible between himself and his aircraft.

Finally, he found some thick woods and paused there to catch his breath. A short time later a man herding cattle passed by. McPherson decided to take a chance that he was friendly. Luckily, he was. Using hand gestures and the card with "useful phrases" from McPherson's survival kit, they were able to communicate. The farmer told him to stay hidden, and that he would be back after dark with some food.

However, the man returned a half hour later, breathlessly explaining that the Germans were searching houses all over the area looking for McPherson. As if to underscore the perilous situation, they could now hear the continuous rumble of motorcycles in the distance.

The man then led McPherson to a culvert under a road and told him to hide there until he returned. Hiding in this place proved especially unnerving, as the German BMWs were now passing back and forth on the road a few feet above his head.

Finally, late into the night, the farmer returned with a friend, bringing McPherson some bread and wine, as well as an overcoat and a blanket. As the three of them began walking down the road, there was an attempt at conversation, but this suddenly led to an unexpected turn.

"I was asked a question and answered 'Yeah,'" McPherson recalled. "Suddenly they stopped dead in their tracks."

"*Allemand*," they said in unison.

"*Non, non, non*," McPherson replied, insisting that he was *not* a German.

Later, when he made the mistake of saying "Yeah" again, an argument between the two men ensued, and the first man stomped off, leaving

McPherson trying to explain to the second man the difference between the American "yeah," and the German "*ja*."

Though the first man wanted nothing more to do with McPherson, the second man seemed convinced that he really was an American, and took him to a hayloft where he spent the rest of the night, and hid out through the next day.

By late Sunday, McPherson had been in occupied France for 24 hours and had managed to scare off several of the locals, but at least he had not been captured. His second benefactor gave him some civilian clothes and a hot meal, as well as a loaf of bread and a bottle of wine. However, the man charged him 500 francs, the equivalent of about ten dollars, which McPherson paid out of the cash in his survival kit.

On Monday morning, McPherson arose without being seen, sneaked out of the hayloft, and continued south using the compass from his survival kit to guide him. He hiked along the back roads, chilled by a cold drizzle. Late in the day, he took refuge in a barn to rest. Two days of running and walking had put a strain on his injured leg.

At nightfall, McPherson was discovered by some curious French civilians. When one of them asked where he was headed, he replied "Spain."

"*Formidable!*" the man replied, astonished at the idea of someone walking across the Pyrenees in the winter.

In fact, McPherson had set an initial goal of reaching Bordeaux. Having been briefed that the French underground would be able and willing to facilitate his escape into Spain, he assumed that a large city such as Bordeaux would present a more likely place to contact them than the small villages that he had seen so far.

By the end of the day, McPherson had reached Barbezieux-Saint-Hilaire, about 20 miles from where he had started. Here, he was befriended by an old man who had been in the French Army during World War I, and whose son had joined in the second. The son had been captured during the Battle of France in 1940, and he was among those French prisoners of war who had been impressed into enforced labor in Germany.

On Tuesday, the first day of February, after spending the night in the man's hayloft, McPherson decided to continue his "*formidable*" trek with a different mode of transportation. He would start hitchhiking!

This decision was partly because of his sore leg, partly because he was getting accustomed to his surroundings, and probably because he was emboldened by having so far eluded the Germans. He had heard no motorcycles for two days.

During the day, McPherson "hitched three rides on French trucks without mishap," and grew complacent. He flagged another vehicle, which he realized "to my horror" was a German ambulance. He breathed more easily as the driver passed him by with hardly a glance.

That night, McPherson reached the small town of Montlieu-la-Garde, about 50 miles from Rouillac. Here, he asked around discreetly, and found a man who spoke English. He introduced McPherson to an old man who turned out to be a former French Army intelligence officer. McPherson explained his situation, and told this man of his plan to go to Bordeaux and why. The man insisted that he should "keep clear of the city by all means," and told McPherson that he could not help him, but "if I would be patient, he would find help for me."

After three nights, the man finally connected the American with people from the Maquis, who gave him a bicycle and another change of civilian clothes. On Saturday, February 5, McPherson and a carpenter friend of the English-speaking man biked south through Montguyon and Saint-Aigulin, and into the Dordogne region of France, where McPherson would spend two very eventful months.

Chapter 31

Hollywood Maquisards

As they rode south from Saint-Aigulin through the town of La Roche-Chalais, Joel McPherson and the carpenter began to see large numbers of German troops. In his escape and evasion report, McPherson noted that the city square in La Roche was filled with tanks and artillery, but that the German troops, mostly very young, paid little attention to the pair of cyclists.

In Le Fenage, the local Maquis contact was another elderly former French intelligence officer, though McPherson later noted that "in those days almost the whole village was Maquis." They were told to continue on to Échourgnac, where the man had arranged for them to make contact with "Marcel the baker."

McPherson waited in the woods while the carpenter went to meet Marcel, and they arrived back at McPherson's hiding place an hour later in a Citroen sedan, with several men armed with submachine guns. It seemed to McPherson like "a Hollywood act."

As McPherson recalled, Marcel and his "Hollywood" Maquisards drove him to a *château* near Saint-André-de-Doublé that looked like a "deserted castle," but when the car stopped, "armed men swarmed out of all the doors and windows."

In charge at the *château* was a man named Achille, "who looked like a prizefighter and was not too bright [though he was] well organized and informed and [he] maintained discipline."

Two days later, "the Gestapo got hot," and everyone at the *château* packed up to leave. They all moved twelve miles to a "hideout" in the woods near Les Mignots, where they would remain for three weeks. During this time,

McPherson was accepted into the band and given the dark blue shirt and trousers that were the *de facto* "uniform" of the Maquis.

By now, McPherson had begun to figure out that the main business of these Maquisards was not that of freedom fighters battling the German occupation, but that of gangsters.

As McPherson recalled, "gangsterism started, and sabotage was carried on only as a sideline to the senseless looting of *châteaux* on the pretext the owners were collaborators [and] blowing up railroad tracks and trains with plastic explosives."

By the end of February, McPherson had become "thoroughly fed up with this life and could not see how it was going to take me to Spain."

Around this time, when another "Maquis chief" named Georges paid a visit to Achille's hideout, McPherson approached him with his eagerness to get out of the gangster life and be on his way to Spain. Georges said he "could help me [and] promised to come back on March 3 and did. He is the only Maquis chief I ever met who kept his word."

McPherson climbed on the back of Georges' motorcycle, and they were off, headed for another hideout near Beauregard-et-Bessac, 40 miles to the southeast.

When they arrived at the small farmhouse that served as a headquarters and safe house, McPherson found himself being interrogated by Georges' "intelligence chief," an English-speaking man known as André Doublemètre.

When McPherson explained that his primary interest was in getting to Spain, Doublemètre told him that the snow was then too deep in the Pyrenees for him to cross. It was March, after all.

McPherson seemed satisfied with Doublemètre's explanation, whereas he had been impatient with Achille, but the intelligence chief was a persuasive and charismatic brigand. He had lived many lives. Born in Serbia as Andrij Urbanovich in 1910, he had become a fixture in Paris society in the 1930s, and had been married twice to well-connected ladies. He had enlisted in a foreign volunteer regiment to fight the Germans in 1940, was captured, and escaped. He was back in Paris in 1941, where he barely eluded the Gestapo and wound up in the Dordogne by way of the Alsace.

His postwar biographer, Jean-Jacques Gillot, described Doublemètre as being as "opportunistic as he was endowed with intellectual and physical faculties well above the average." He was one of those men who had a certain star quality to him that inspired a following. Indeed, Joel McPherson himself seems to have been swept up in the mystique of this colorful character.

But Doublemètre had a dark side, having developed a reputation as a ruthless guerilla fighter. In his book, *Purification in the Dordogne According to Doublemètre*, Gillot called him a "mercenary of purification." When it was fashionable, he had dabbled in Marxism, and still found it to be a motivator for the Maquisards. McPherson described him as "a rabid communist."

On McPherson's second night with his new Maquis gang, Georges ordered everyone – except Doublemètre, who had left during the day – to load up their trucks with the goods they had looted in their raids and prepare for a move to another hideout.

With their job only partly completed, the men, 18 in all, fell asleep exhausted in the farmhouse. It was still dark when they were rudely awakened.

"*Debout! Debout!*" Someone shouted. "*Get up! Get up!*"

"I had been through so many false alarms," McPherson recalled. "But when I heard machine guns, I knew we had really been surprised."

McPherson and several other men were inside a room with one window and a door to the adjoining room where Georges was sleeping. The man known as Albéric dashed through the doorway toward this room, but turned around, slamming the door shut after himself.

Machine-gun bullets ripped through the door as another man, François, slipped out the window.

McPherson recalled that "as a second man reached the sill, he was shot dead from the doorway and I dashed back to a corner. A grenade was tossed in and the lights went out. I came out and gave up before they had a chance to toss in another."

As the dust settled, they discovered that their attackers were not Germans, but French – members of the pro-Vichy, paramilitary Groupe Mobile de Réserve (GMR). It was also discovered that, in the darkness, nearly half of the Maquis had gotten away, leaving McPherson, seven others, and the body of the man killed escaping through the window.

The GMR had figured out that Georges was the leader and were "working on him." As they beat and cajoled Georges, they ordered the other men to resume loading the trucks.

They were taken to nearby Bergerac and turned over to the local gendarmerie. When the gendarmes discovered that McPherson was an American, they treated him well. He was let out of his cell and allowed to walk around the grounds with an English-speaking guard. The sergeant of the guard befriended him, and let him dine in the officers' mess. The sergeant even hid him when the jail was visited by officers from the regular Vichy police, who were known to cooperate with the Germans.

Later on in McPherson's first day in jail, the sergeant told him that he could sleep in a room with a bed. McPherson was already sizing up the possibility of escaping through a window in this room when the sergeant came back to say that he had been overruled by his captain. The captain, like the sergeant, actually did take a liking to his American "guest." Like most Frenchmen, he had no particular animosity toward Americans.

The captain sat down with McPherson and promised him that he "would find some way out" for him, but at the same time, he could not let him escape. As they talked, the captain at one point told McPherson that he might send McPherson to Switzerland in care of the Red Cross, but they soon decided that this scheme was impossible.

Chapter 32

We Thought He Was a Madman

On Wednesday, March 8, when Georges and his crew were all transferred to the jail in the larger city of Périgueux, McPherson was also sent there, but the captain delivered him personally, inviting him to ride with him in his Citroen, rather than in the back of a van with the Maquisards.

Once in Périgueux, the captain may well have sat in on McPherson's interrogation, as the American convinced the police that his only time with the Maquis had been his three days at Georges' safe house. They seemed satisfied with this and never learned of his three weeks with Achille's gang.

McPherson was handcuffed to his cot on his first night in Périgueux, but, as an American, his treatment was benign by comparison to that meted out to his Maquis friends. Georges was badly beaten and jabbed with a bayonet, while Maurice, his second in command, received rougher treatment because he was Jewish. McPherson later learned that these men, as well as another man who "talked too much," were turned over to the Gestapo and shot.

Others in the group were luckier. A benevolent booking officer charged them as "boxcar thieves." This meant that they'd be imprisoned, but at least it probably saved them from being summarily executed by the Gestapo.

Luck also smiled on McPherson, who came down on the favorable side of the rivalry between the French police and the Gestapo. His captors had decided that he was *their* prisoner, and they were not going to give him to the Germans. They kept him apart from the others and told him that he would be sent to a French "concentration camp."

The next morning, McPherson was approached by a friendly gendarme and "warned to be absolutely silent." By now, he had deduced that "something was obviously afoot." Only later did he learn that the Gestapo was in the building looking for him at that moment, but the French police were looking the other way.

A short time later, a guard slipped him a small package containing tobacco and aspirin. With this was a message which began, "Friends await you in the hospital."

Intrigued but confused, McPherson read on. The message told him that he should fake appendicitis in order to be sent to the hospital, from which he would be rescued.

The note explained that he was to roll crushed aspirin into cigarettes and smoke them; this would give him a fever. In turn, he should stick his finger down his throat and force himself to vomit, then feign the cramps associated with an appendicitis.

McPherson's cellmate, a Frenchman named Max Paulius, convinced him that if this worked, it would be a lot easier for him to be rescued from a hospital than from the Périgueux jailhouse – or from a concentration camp. As McPherson recalled, Paulius rolled the cigarettes for him. He wanted to help because he "knew that he could never escape, but hoped that I would."

As incredible as it is, this story related by Joel McPherson in his E&E No.849 report is corroborated by historian Guy Penaud in his 1985 book, *Histoire de la Résistance en Périgord*. He wrote that "agents working for the Allies had heard about [McPherson's] capture and approached a doctor by the name of Jean Gaussen who was working at the hospital at Périgueux and involved with the Résistance. He was told to help McPherson escape, whatever the cost."

According to Penaud, it was Dr Gaussen who had dictated a note explaining "the old recipe that would bring on vomiting, a crushed aspirin mixed with tobacco."

McPherson did as instructed, and smoking about ten of the aspirin-laced cigarettes made him truly miserable. By the time the prison doctor was called in, McPherson was running a high fever. Nothing could be done short of a trip to the hospital, so an ambulance was called.

With a last nod to Max Paulius, the American was off. The first part of the plan had worked as advertised. By 2:30pm that Saturday afternoon, McPherson was at the local civilian hospital, where he was taken straight to the operating room. It was now time for him to feign a recovery. After some fast talking, they relented, and took him upstairs to the prison ward

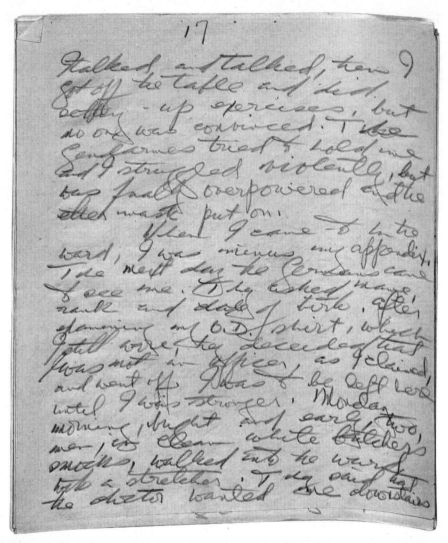

Joel McPherson's handwritten description of having his perfectly good appendix removed the day before his twenty-sixth birthday in March 1944. In the custody of French police, he faked an appendicitis attack to get into a hospital from which escape was easier than from jail, but the scheme backfired. (US National Archives)

for observation. It was here that someone whispered in his ear. He would be rescued on Monday.

According to Guy Penaud, an elaborate plan had been devised, in which "a 'commando' dressed as a hospital worker would enter the hospital discreetly, pass the concierge who would think he was from a nearby hospital, get to the ward where McPherson would be awaiting surgery, knock out the guard and with the aid of a wheelchair, wheel him out of the hospital."

All the pieces were coming together. The young aviator had a smile on his face as he relaxed on clean sheets and a soft pillow.

What could possibly go wrong?

After a few hours of contentment, this question was answered. That evening, the hospital apparently decided to clear the schedule. The patient upstairs awaiting an appendectomy? Let's get it done! At around 8:00pm, McPherson found himself being wheeled back to the operating room. Panicked, he tried to convince the doctor that the operation was unnecessary. He was feeling *much* better.

"The gendarmes tried to hold me," the pilot recalled. "I struggled violently but was finally overpowered and the ether mask [was] put on."

What had gone wrong?

As Penaud was able to piece it together, McPherson had misunderstood the directions in Gaussen's note, and had made a dreadful mistake! He acted a day too early. Gaussen was not on duty until Sunday. The plan had been for Gaussen "to examine him, confirm the diagnosis and inform the surgeon that the problem was not extremely urgent, and that surgery could wait until the following day or the day after."

This would have allowed plenty of time for him to be smuggled to safety.

As it was, when Gaussen arrived for his shift on Sunday afternoon, one of his colleagues told him, "You should have been here yesterday evening! A prisoner arrived suffering from appendicitis, an American or Englishman we presume. You should have seen the circus; he certainly didn't want to be operated on. When the surgeon came in wearing his mask the prisoner jumped off the operating table, shouting 'I'm not ill.' We thought he was a madman!"

Joel McPherson awakened in the hospital's prison ward on the morning of Sunday, March 12, 1944 – his twenty-sixth birthday – without an appendix. But this was only the beginning of his troubles.

Chapter 33

Over the Wall

On Monday, Joel McPherson lay in the prison ward of the Périgueux hospital with a terrific pain in his gut and the gloomy memory of his worst birthday ever.

To add insult to injury, two men in clean, white smocks walked into the ward with a stretcher and announced that they were there to take McPherson "downstairs for an examination."

These were the men from the Résistance who were supposed to break him out and take him away.

The nurse on duty told them that the patient was too sick to be moved.

"Why is he sick?" asked one of the men.

"He's had his appendix removed," came the answer.

They had not been briefed on Sunday's mix-up. They didn't know that McPherson had actually had a *real* appendectomy.

With a sinking heart, McPherson saw their startled glances, and watched as they turned and beat a hasty retreat.

The nurses checked into what they said, trying to figure out which doctor had ordered McPherson to be taken "downstairs for an examination." The answer, of course, was that nobody had issued such an order.

Very quickly, the hospital put two and two together and correctly ascertained that an escape attempt had just been foiled.

Before the end of the day, the Gestapo had been alerted and an ambulance arrived to transport the American to a German military hospital.

Aside from this facility being in the middle of a secure compound, conditions were not too bad. The young American was not on a prison ward, but in a large room with two German soldiers. The guards were Georgian, and therefore not nearly as strict as German guards might have been. They were part of the German Infanterie-Bataillon 799, a unit composed mainly of Georgians who had been captured by the Germans while serving with the Soviet Army on the Eastern Front, and who considered life in the German Army preferable to life in a German POW camp.

However, the Georgians with whom he communicated "refused to believe anything but German propaganda, for they feel they personally are lost if Germany should lose now. The Georgians believed that England would be wiped out by aircraft in May or June [1943]. When the German lack of aircraft was pointed out, they said this did not matter because Hitler [had a plan]."

While the Georgians were friendly to their American guest, McPherson recalled them being "harsh and cruel" to Romanian prisoners who were being held at the same compound.

As for the Germans who ran the place, they could afford to be lax with McPherson. He was in bad shape physically after the operation, and he was clearly not a flight risk. It took eight days of convalescence before he was able to walk, and even then he was "so weak that no one paid much attention to me."

This is not to say that he had not been *thinking* about an escape since he had first been brought in. From the window he could see a tree on the opposite side of the exterior wall surrounding the compound. On the near side of the wall, across the courtyard, there was a latrine with a slanted roof, and around that, some scaffolding. As the days passed, he formulated an escape plan using the scaffolding and the tree. If he could climb the scaffolding, he could get over the wall and climb down the tree. But if he couldn't even walk, all he could do was imagine.

The second part of his dilemma was what to do if he actually got across the wall. This conundrum was resolved when he was approached by a young woman named Jacqueline Braillard, who worked in the prison kitchen's forced-labor detail. He learned that outside the wall, the Résistance had not forgotten McPherson. They had asked Jacqueline to get word to him of a safe house in Coursac, a village about eight miles south of Périgueux where he could hide if he could escape.

As he finally began to get around, moving with more of a shuffle than a walk, he was permitted to exercise outside in the grounds of the compound.

It was about ten days after the operation when he finally visited his scaffolding, and took a close look at his tree. He placed his foot on one of the lower rungs of the scaffolding and timidly tried to hoist himself up – just to try it out. But his incision was too painful, and the strain on his stitches so severe that he was forced to give up.

It was only a minor setback. Time was on his side, time that he spent finding a rickety old folding table that he hid near the latrine to use to get up onto the scaffolding.

He could afford to wait. The doctors, who like the guards were Georgians, had told him that they would not bother taking out the stitches until he had recovered his strength. The tree and the scaffolding weren't going anywhere.

But once again, Joel McPherson's fortunes were about to go sideways.

On Sunday, March 24, there was a great clamor at the German base. A battalion of troops was being pulled out for action against the Maquis as part of a bloody offensive undertaken under the command of Generalmajor Walter Brehmer that involved a division-strength command centered on elements of the 325. Sicherungs-Division. Operations throughout the Dordogne were to begin on March 26 with an encirclement of the town of Ribérac, about 25 miles west of Périgueux, and continue until the third week of April.

As part of this mobilization, the German surgeons from the hospital were being pulled out to go into the field with the troops. Before leaving, they were ordered to clean up their roster at the hospital, and this included removing the stitches in the American. This done, they pronounced him ready to be sent to be imprisoned at a Stalag Luft.

As he observed, "I realized that it was now or never."

That evening he drank a lot of lemonade to guarantee that he would wake up during the night, and this worked. At 4:30am, he climbed out of bed, dressed quietly, and slipped on his shoes. Just in case, he grabbed a bed sheet to use as a rope if necessary.

He descended carefully through the building, but just as he reached the main floor, so too did the kitchen staff arriving for work. He hid himself and waited breathlessly for them to pass.

At last, the coast was clear and he made his way to the courtyard. With the German troops having all departed during the day, the courtyard was quiet and McPherson reached the wall without being seen. He set up his folding table and climbed on top. He tried to get onto the scaffolding – but he found he could not reach it without wrenching his side.

Trying not to panic or to make any noise that would alert the guards, he considered his options. What could he do?

At last, in the dark, he spotted a metal can about 18 inches tall that had been discarded near the corner of the scaffolding. He climbed down, got the can, put it on top of the table, and climbed back. Fortunately, it gave him the extra height that he needed to get onto the scaffolding without tearing open the painful incision. From the scaffolding, he was able to crawl onto the latrine roof and slide down to a point where he could reach a telegraph pole near the tree. He slid down the pole, and at last his feet were on the ground outside the German compound.

Free at last, but not yet out of the woods.

Chapter 34

A Bandit's Life for Me

Joel McPherson dashed across the street and took cover in a darkened doorway while he caught his breath. He knew that the curfew patrols ended around 6:00am. By then it would be getting light, so he had to take care with his next move.

As he sneaked through the streets, walking quietly in his rubber-soled shoes, the American fugitive could hear the German patrols marching in their hobnail boots at some distance, so he was able to stay hidden.

Eventually, he reached the southern edge of Périgueux and was back on country roads, just as he had been in early February, albeit without a compass. At least he knew which way led south toward Spain.

Early that morning, McPherson met a family who, though obviously poor, shared some potatoes and onions with him. They also gave him a small calendar map that would be vital in navigating the back roads of the Dordogne.

At first, he was limping with great difficulty because of his still-painful incision, but he gradually gained strength and momentum. By the end of the day, he had managed to hike about six miles when he met some people who took him to their small house between La Jarthe and Coursac.

"I looked very badly," he recalled, "and when I told them my story, they said I must hide there and recuperate." Which he did.

He was still hoping to make contact with the people whom Jacqueline Braillard had mentioned, so he explained this to the man at the house. He sent word to the Maquis to come and get McPherson.

At the time, McPherson was unaware of the rampage wrought by Walter Brehmer's troops that was ongoing in the region. "I did not know," he wrote, "that [the] Dordogne was now a *zone interdite*, and that two German divisions had been sent in to wipe out the Maquis [nor] that the group I was heading for was attacked two days [after I escaped]."

After hiding out for several days with no word from the Maquis, McPherson was starting to figure out that they had been attacked by German troops, almost certainly part of Brehmer's offensive.

"There were Germans everywhere and I was afraid of endangering this kind family, so on March 29, I set out on my own."

He hiked about six miles and spent the night hiding just outside Grignols. The following morning, he met a woman who said she could probably put him in contact with another Maquis group.

At about 2:00pm that afternoon when she returned, McPherson found himself looking into two familiar faces. Here was the man he recognized as Alfred, who had been the intelligence man with Achille's group – and none other than the mercurial André Doublemètre!

They took him to their hideout near Saint-Jean-d'Estissac, where McPherson was introduced to the leader of the gang with whom they were now operating. He was a Spaniard named Alejandro, a tough veteran of the Spanish Civil War, who also went by the French name Gérard.

On his second day, as he was helping his new colleagues pack up to relocate to a new safe house, as the Maquis frequently did, McPherson recalled the previous time that he'd done this.

"I had had a funny feeling the day before Georges was caught," McPherson recalled. "And I had it again now."

When he shared this with one of the Maquis, the man took it seriously – much to McPherson's surprise – and hurried back to camp to tell Alejandro.

"This group was mostly Spanish and highly superstitious," McPherson observed. "So we packed up and left immediately."

His intuition had been right. The following day, 400 Germans descended upon this corner of the Dordogne with a vengeance, blocking roads and rounding up pro-Maquis suspects. McPherson later found out that they had killed the man who sheltered him near Coursac, and had brutally tortured his wife.

Thanks to McPherson's prescience, Alejandro and company had managed to get away in the nick of time, dashing south about a dozen miles to Saint-Georges-Blancaneix as the Gestapo closed in. Coincidently, their new safe house was back near Bergerac, where the GMR had turned McPherson, Georges, and that group over to the French police nearly a month earlier.

Frustrated with having come full circle, and with his lack of progress toward his goal of getting to Spain, McPherson once again approached Doublemètre for help. Just as he had before, the wily brigand *still* maintained that the snow was too deep in the Pyrenees mountain passes. He insisted that McPherson would just have to be patient. McPherson had believed this story in early March – but it was now the first of April! Nevertheless, he again succumbed to the charisma of this man who exuded both confidence and competence. McPherson accepted his word.

Perhaps to get the nagging American out of their hair, Alejandro and Doublemètre "transferred" McPherson to another Maquis group in early April. They operated farther south, down around Saint-Aubin-de-Cadeleh, so at least McPherson was inching closer toward his goal.

These Maquisards, led by a man named Rolland, were a busy bunch. As McPherson recalled, they "had recently been driven from their headquarters and were robbing right and left to get set up again."

Over the next two weeks, McPherson was with Rolland as his gang was on the move, bouncing back from several near misses with German patrols and roadblocks. At one point, they spent two days living with a Swiss family from Paris named Doxat, whose young son was an aviation enthusiast who enjoyed the company of the American pilot.

By the middle of April, Rolland's group was operating out of a safe house near in Sérignac, nearly a hundred road miles southeast of Périgueux. McPherson sat down with one of the Maquisards, a man named "Jimmy," who was the group's driver, and asked him about getting into Spain. He cautioned McPherson that it might cost as much as 50,000 francs, the equivalent of a thousand dollars in 1944, or around $16,000 today. McPherson told Jimmy that he did not have that kind of money, but Jimmy said he'd look into it and see if he could find somebody else who could arrange to get him out.

McPherson was cautiously optimistic. Unfortunately, as so often had happened since he landed in France, he watched a promising plan go up in smoke before his eyes. The very next day, Jimmy was killed in a car wreck.

While this left McPherson without a contact for his Spanish escape, the loss of Jimmy placed Rolland and his gang in a difficult dilemma of their own. Jimmy had been their wheel man, not so much because he was a skilled driver, but because he *could drive*. In rural France at that time, it was uncommon for people to know how to drive. In America in the 1940s, on the other hand, everybody under 30 knew how to drive.

All eyes fell upon McPherson.

"I became a chauffeur for the Maquis," he recalled succinctly, adding that for two weeks, "I lived a bandit's life."

This gang of about 40 Maquisards, armed with British Sten submachine guns air dropped by the British SOE, went on a crime spree with McPherson at the wheel.

During this time, they were occasionally in contact with and joined on a "job" by Doublemètre and Alejandro's crew. Doublemètre seemed especially pleased at how well his old American friend was fitting in with the Maquis mischief. And yes, the snow was still *very* deep in those mountains.

As McPherson remembered, the Maquisards engaged in "an awful lot of plain thievery of *châteaux*. [I] drove on several raids [as we] robbed post offices, banks, etc… These groups [Rolland's and Alejandro's] were all communists and used the slightest pretext to brand a man a collaborator, particularly if he owned a *château*."

Chapter 35

Danger All Around

As Joel McPherson was robbing banks and *châteaux* with Rolland, Alejandro, and Doublemètre in the Dordogne, the air war over the Third Reich continued. The great Eighth Air Force strategic air campaign against German industry during "Big Week" at the end of February had come and gone and with it a tipping point in the air war.

Though the going was still rough in the missions over Germany, and the losses still undesirably high, the Eighth Air Force was growing stronger with each passing week. New bombardment groups, such as the 453rd, which arrived in February and had three dozen missions under its belt by April, were coming on line all the time.

On Tuesday April 25, the 733rd Bomb Squadron of the 453rd had been tasked with a strike against Munster in Germany's heavily defended industrial heartland, but was diverted to targets near Paris. It seemed like the crewmen aboard these B-24 Liberators had been handed a break – a much shorter mission against a less well defended target.

In fact, only one bomber was shot down by 88mm antiaircraft fire that day. Out of more than two dozen bombers, this was a loss rate much lower than would have been expected over Germany. Of course, such odds were not the least bit comforting if you happened to have been a crewman aboard that one bomber – a Liberator piloted by 1st Lieutenant Elmer Crockett. One enemy round ignited an uncontrollable fire in the bomb bay, which was an immediate crisis for all aboard. Flames were just inches from the wing roots and the central structure of the aircraft – not to mention that the fuel tanks were nearby.

As the aircraft descended through 18,000 feet, the copilot, 2nd Lieutenant Gilbert Marvin Stonebarger, pressed the alarm bell that told the crew that it was time to abandon ship. The 22-year-old from Los Angeles boosted Tech Sergeant Elmer Lincoln, the radio operator, through the top hatch and followed him out.

Flying only his fifth mission, Stonebarger had not yet even contemplated the long countdown to his twenty-fifth, after which he could go home. Now, his combat career was at an abrupt end.

He contemplated what would come next. Death? Imprisonment as a POW? Or could he get away?

Stonebarger felt himself floating in the silence of the open air as the flaming B-24 plunged away from him. Then it occurred to him that he was falling at a rapidly increasing velocity. Struggling with his ripcord, he plummeted for thousands of feet. Then, just 150 feet from the ground, his parachute snapped open with a tremendous jolt, wrenching his back so severely that it would hinder his movements for months. At the same time, his sheepskin-lined flying boots flew off.

Seconds later, he slammed into the dirt of a field northwest of Le Tillet, a tiny village about 40 miles due north of the French capital, but he had no time to think about geography. His parachute was snagged in a tree, and he needed to pull it down before it provided the enemy with an arrow marking the spot where he'd landed.

This finally done, he looked around, trying to figure out which way to go. In the distance, he saw a woman near a small house. She seemed to be beckoning to him, so he ran toward her. As he ran, he passed a man who waved for him to take cover, so he dived into a nearby ditch to hide.

Welcome to German-occupied France.

After a time, when the coast was clear, the man returned. Introducing himself as Joseph Louis Legrain, he invited Stonebarger to come to his home for a cup of coffee and something to eat – and to see a place in the cellar where the American could spend the night.

A Dutch man named Miller, who lived nearby and who was associated with the Résistance, came to visit during the afternoon. He asked Stonebarger whether he had any instructions about what he should do and where he should go.

"I said that I was trying to get to Spain and asked whether he could help," Stonebarger recalled in his escape and evasion report.[33] "When he said that he could not help but that he would try and find someone who could, I asked whether he was in contact with an organization, explaining that we had been told that they could help aviators. He professed to know nothing whatever about organizations."

In the meantime, Legrain supplied Stonebarger with civilian clothes and suggested that they should go to the only bar in the village for a drink, which they did.

When they returned later on Tuesday evening, Miller was back. Though he had earlier said he had no idea how he might help Stonebarger, Miller now told him that he "could take me to a farm where I might hide out until we could decide what to do."

He added that the Germans were searching hard for Stonebarger and his fellow crewmen from the downed bomber. They were offering 25,000 francs ($500) for information and reminding people that they could be shot if they were caught harboring an American. Stonebarger wished that he'd known this *before* he went to the bar with Legrain.

The following day, a tall man in a leather jacket and goggles arrived on a motorcycle and asked Stonebarger whether he'd met Miller. When this was confirmed, he explained that Miller was actually "in touch with all the organizations in France."

He went on to say that the Germans had rounded up everyone else from Stonebarger's crew. Seven of them had been snatched as they came down under their parachutes, and two had been caught overnight. This left Stonebarger as the lone fugitive from the doomed Liberator still at large. This, and the knowledge of a price on his head, brought the reality of life in occupied France into perspective and made Stonebarger realize how precarious his situation really was.

Meanwhile, he began to truly appreciate that he was surrounded by people trying to figure out what to do with him, despite their own lives being in danger. By Wednesday night, they had come up with a plan. Legrain would take Stonebarger by car to Belgium, where a boat would pick him up. On Thursday, though, the plan changed. He was now to be taken to southern France, and flown back to England from there. Next, as Stonebarger's back injury was causing him a good deal of pain, it was decided that they would take him to a hospital in Bobigney, one of the northeastern suburbs of Paris. The man with the motorcycle returned and off they went.

After outpatient treatment at the hospital, details of which Stonebarger omitted from his escape and evasion report, he was taken by a French gendarme friendly to the Résistance to the home of a woman named Madame Quinot. Here, he met a Canadian airman, Sergeant Jerry O'Shaughnessy, who was also recovering from injuries. He explained that Madame Quinot had helped numerous Allied airmen who passed through Paris.

There was a tension in the air at the safe house. Not only were the Gestapo and pro-German Vichy police lurking about, there were also some among the evaders themselves who endangered the whole operation by their own imprudent actions.

For obvious reasons, evaders were cautioned to stay put and be inconspicuous, but Stonebarger learned of an incident in December when one American had refused to do this. He had decided that he was in Paris, and he was going out on the town, and to pick up some female companionship. His Résistance handlers expressly forbade him to do this, but he ignored them. As Stonebarger later related, "he was so insistent that he went out to get a woman and the organization had to kill him."

The recklessness of one endangered many, and the "organization" was seemingly prepared to do anything to protect its safe houses. Stonebarger swallowed hard, recalling that his comrades had been snapped up by the Gestapo while he was relaxing in a bar.

On Sunday, the last day of April, Stonebarger moved on. He was first taken out to be photographed for his forged identity papers, then handed off to Joseph Darras, a man who worked in the electrical shops of the local police prefecture. In turn, Darras took him to the nearby suburb of Pantin, where a shopkeeper named Joseph Theuier hid him in an unfurnished apartment above the shop.

Eerily, as Stonebarger learned, this place was not far from La Cité de la Muette in Drancy, the "Silent City," a sprawling modernist housing development completed in 1936, which had been turned into an internment facility that now held as many as 7,000 French Jews *en route* to extermination camps.

Also staying with Darras was another Canadian, Flight Officer Hugh Thomas. Later, Jerry O'Shaughnessy also arrived. They were part of an ongoing stream of Allied airmen who were being aided by Eugénie Roby, a French nurse, and Odette Ernest, a language teacher from England who had been working in Paris when the Germans occupied the city in 1940.

Over the next two weeks, this pair of energetic women efficiently supplied them with food and civilian clothes, completed fake IDs, and even provided English-language reading material to take the edge off the anxious boredom.

Chapter 36

Waiting for the Right Moment

In Paris, as the Gestapo was a pervasive presence in daily life, the Résistance operated, but deep in the shadows, and speaking in whispers. Far to the south, in the Dordogne, it was another world. The Maquis may have been hunted by the Germans and the Vichy police, but they fought back, operating brazenly and ruling much of the countryside – like bandit gangs from medieval times. Instead of shadows and whispers, there was the rattle of Sten guns in broad daylight.

Joel McPherson was tired of this world. By early May 1944, whatever passing fascination he may have had for the life of a getaway driver for the Maquis bank robbers had waned. He was "becoming thoroughly fed up" and ready to be on his way to Spain and beyond. The days were hot in the Dordogne, so McPherson reasoned that the mountain passes, or at least most of them, *had to be* open by now.

Because Doublemètre repeatedly declined to help him, and his earlier confidant, Jimmy, was dead, McPherson turned to another Maquisard named Philippe Brigett, who promptly introduced him to a woman named Marie Schieffluer. McPherson was astonished by how quickly Philippe had acted, recalling that "I was furious to discover that the Maquis member I knew best and longest [Doublemètre] was a good friend of all these people [who guided in the mountains] and could have passed me on months ago."

It was now obvious to McPherson that Doublemètre had been lying to him about the deep snow in the Pyrenees: "He had refuted all knowledge of a route because he wanted me to stay with the Maquis."

Good wheel men were not, after all, easy to find in the Dordogne.

It was around May 5, 1944 when Lieutenant Joel McPherson left his career as a getaway driver for Rolland's band of Maquisard bank robbers, but his excitement about finally being on the move was soon dashed. Philippe Brigett and Madame Schieffluer stashed him in a safe house in the tiny commune of Lunas, north of Bergerac, where he found himself cooling his heels for more than three tense weeks, waiting for someone to come and get him.

Alas, his new friends had skidded into a patch of ill fortune. Philippe was supposed to have taken McPherson to Toulouse around the middle of May, but he had been in some sort of "accident." McPherson didn't know exactly what had happened.

Another man named André was then supposed to come, but he had to make a trip to northern France to pick up ten other American airmen. McPherson learned that André had been killed on May 15 during a Ninth Air Force B-26 strike on the railway yard at Creil, near Paris, before he could make his rendezvous.

At last, André's wife came for McPherson on the first day of June and took him by train to Toulouse. They went to the home of Jean Bovis, who owned a flower shop with a safe house upstairs. Among those who had stayed with Bovis was Lieutenant Robert Martin of the 448th Bomb Group. He was the pilot of a B-24 that had been shot down on March 5 during a mission against Luftwaffe facilities around Limoges, and had passed through Toulouse in the first part of April.[*]

On June 3, McPherson was sent south to Boulogne-sur-Gesse, which put him within 50 miles of the Spanish border. Here, he was greeted by Joseph "Joe" Barrère, a Résistance man who went by the name "Frisco." He explained that his parents lived in the United States, presumably in San Francisco.

Frisco helped him check in to the Hôtel Moderne, and took him to the hotel bar. Here they met a short, rotund man named Jean Bazerque, who introduced himself by his *nom de guerre*, "Charbonière." A celebrated Résistance figure, his name appears in numerous accounts of Allied escape and evasion, though with such alternate spellings as Chabonnier, Charbeneri, or Charbonnet.

[*] His story is mentioned in Chapter 37.

Charbonière explained that he was going to be McPherson's guide for the crossing of the Pyrenees, and that they would be joined by a number of others, including three Dutchmen who were also staying at the hotel.

McPherson was then introduced to a Dutch intelligence man named Rudi Scheltema (aka "Schrijnemacher"), a Catholic priest called Lodewyk van de Velde (aka "Bleys"), and a fighter pilot, Lieutenant Bram van der Stok. As McPherson would soon learn, van der Stok had been a POW whose escape from the Germans had been one of the epic tales of World War II.

In 1940, when the Germans invaded his country, van der Stok was flying with the Netherlands Luchtvaartbrigade (Army Aviation Brigade) and had downed a Messerschmitt Bf 109. He had escaped to Britain after its defeat, where he joined the Royal Air Force and flew Spitfires with No.41 Squadron. He had scored six additional aerial victories to become an ace. He was himself shot down in April 1942, and was imprisoned at Stalag Luft III, 100 miles southeast of Berlin.

On the night of March 24–25, 1944, the prisoners in Stalag Luft III staged the mass breakout attempt that would be celebrated in popular culture as "The Great Escape," and made famous by the 1963 film of the same name starring Steve McQueen. Of the 76 men who actually escaped, 73 were recaptured and 50 of these were executed. Bram van der Stok was one of the three who eluded recapture.

Traveling by train and hitchhiking, he made his way across Germany and into France, connecting with Scheltema and van de Velde along the way. Together, they finally reached Toulouse, where they met Frisco and were taken to Boulogne-sur-Gesse.

Over lunch at the hotel cafe on June 3, Charbonière cautioned McPherson, as he had van der Stok and company, that he must be patient and to wait at the Hôtel Moderne until the time was right. With this, Charbonière put down his napkin and excused himself, saying that he'd be back in 20 minutes. He would not be seen again for nine days.

It was a bizarre situation. As McPherson and van der Stok soon discovered, the Gestapo used the Hôtel Moderne as both a billets and a headquarters, so the evaders often found themselves sharing the hotel bar or dining room with uniformed Nazis. As McPherson recalled, "everyone in town except the Gestapo agents… knew we were there."

The situation was equal parts unnerving and farcical. It might have been a scene out of a thriller – improbable if not for the fact that it was really happening. For McPherson, these uneasy waiting games were like Doublemètre all over again.

While Joel McPherson was biding his time 50 miles from Spain, waiting for Charbonière to come back, Gilbert Stonebarger, Hugh Thomas, and Jerry O'Shaughnessy were in Paris, 450 road miles away, also waiting impatiently. They were sitting around in the safe house of Joseph Darras, while Eugénie Roby and Odette Ernest were figuring out how to get them to Spain.

May 18 had been promised as their date of departure from Paris, but the man who was to take them, whom Stonebarger described as "a high ranking organization man," was among several Résistance figures nabbed by the Gestapo.

For the next week or so, the airmen were shuffled through a series of apartments in the fashionable 16th Arrondissement of Paris. Adding to the consternation was that their host at one of these places was a scientist who claimed to have inside information about German stockpiles of poison gas in the city.

During this time, Stonebarger also learned that one of the people arrested had been carrying a suitcase filled with 17 million francs that was meant to be parceled out to the Allied evaders, mainly to pay guides in the Pyrenees. It was typical for each evader to carry 2,000 francs in his survival kit, so it is unclear why so much extra money was needed. In any case, the organization had other resources, and funds were secured, which Mademoiselle Roby herself would carry in a satchel as they went south.

Finally, on June 4, 1944, with Stonebarger escorted by Eugénie Roby, and O'Shaughnessy and Thomas in the care of Odette Ernest, they arrived at Paris's Gare Montparnasse rail station. Here they were met by Yves Ottalie, an organization man who guided them into separate compartments in a third class coach which they expected to take them to Toulouse.

Stonebarger slumped into his seat and exhaled, staring out the window at the people coming and going – liberally interspersed with men in German uniforms. He waited patiently for the jerk of the train starting to move, but it never came. Finally, Ottalie hustled them off to a first class compartment, where they spent a fitful night on the soft benches.

Unbeknownst to any of them, it was only two days from D-Day, the Allied invasion of Normandy. To thwart German movements, Allied tactical aircraft had brought the rail network in northern France under attack and trains weren't moving.

The train finally got under way, but not until late on June 5. At the city of Nevers, about 150 miles south of Paris, the train ground to a stop and two Germans came aboard to check papers. Stonebarger was pleased that Ottalie had split their party into separate compartments of the train. As he wrote, "at least we would not be bagged as a group."

He recalled that the Gestapo men were questioning everyone in French, and he was sure it was all going to end badly for him.

As he was resigning himself to this fate, one of the Germans entered an adjacent compartment occupied by two of the Allied airmen and a pair of Frenchmen. As everyone handed over his documents, Stonebarger was surprised to see the German merely glance at those of the airmen before handing them back, while he seemed to get angry about those of the Frenchmen. An argument ensued.

A second German approached Stonebarger, who was standing near the door to another compartment. Again, he handed over his fake identification, which the German checked carefully, even measuring the thumb print to be sure it was real.

The suspense was terrifying.

"Just as he started to say something, the other German called to him," Stonebarger recalled. "They talked back and forth while I stood there shaking. The German became so engrossed in his conversation that he handed me my card and went on."

It turned out that two Frenchmen had *expired* identity cards. For their fixation upon this minor transgression, the Germans allowed a group of Allied airmen to slip through their fingers.

The train lumbered south another 150 miles to Villeneuve-d'Aveyron, where it again jerked to a stop at around 3:00am in the early hours of June 6, 1944.

"When it had not moved by 8:00, we knew something was wrong," Stonebarger noted. "Soon we learned that the Allies had invaded France and that the Maquis had blown up the railway tracks on either side of us. All the Frenchmen went around cheering."

This sentiment was not shared by the nearly 250 German troops who were on the train. They responded by ordering everyone off. It was assumed that they were going to commandeer the train, but because the tracks were blocked, they instead decided to commandeer all of the vehicles in the area and go out to find the saboteurs who had disrupted the rail line.

When they had gone, the passengers reboarded the train. Stonebarger and his group made themselves comfortable in the first class compartments where the Germans had been, and waited.

"After 18 hours' delay we finally moved on," Stonebarger wrote. "We arrived in Toulouse after curfew and went to a theater until morning."

Chapter 37

D-Days

On June 6, 1944, news of the long-anticipated Allied invasion of northern France reached the Hôtel Moderne in Boulogne-sur-Gesse, where Joel McPherson and Bram van der Stok were impatiently waiting for Charbonière to come back and take them into Spain.

With news of the invasion, there came a marked change of mood among the French people. Except for those who had chosen to collaborate with the Germans, people now had an optimistic spring in their step and smiles on their faces. The Maquisards, meanwhile, now ratcheted up their sabotage activities and guerilla attacks. The Germans were on edge.

With their Gestapo neighbors at the hotel growing more and more fidgety, McPherson could see that the situation for the airmen was becoming untenable. When he insisted that Frisco move them somewhere a bit farther away, he obliged and relocated them about ten miles south to a farmhouse in the mountains near Saint-Gaudens that was a Maquis arms cache.

It was here that Joel McPherson met Gilbert Stonebarger, the first American airman he had seen in more than four months.

When Stonebarger had arrived in Toulouse on June 7, along with Hugh Thomas, Jerry O'Shaughnessy, and Eugénie Roby, Frisco had first stashed them with an older couple at their *château*, but decided to consolidate everyone at the farmhouse in preparation for an imminent trek across the Pyrenees.

When Charbonière finally showed up again on June 12, McPherson asked where he'd been. He just shrugged and said that he'd been busy driving Maquisards around. In the aftermath of the Allied invasion, the Maquisards were in high gear. McPherson understood, having recently been a Maquis chauffer himself.

Amid making excuses, Charbonière did promise that their own D-Day for departure to the border would be in two days' time. Both McPherson and Stonebarger had heard this sort of promise before.

The next day, they were visited by a young Scottish woman named Nan from nearby Saint-Gaudens, who worked with the Maquisards and who came to bring food for the airmen. She also brought bad news. Both Charbonière and Frisco were dead.

For some reason, they had decided to try to run a German checkpoint in their car. Amazingly, they made it, but unfortunately, there was a second roadblock just beyond the first. Their luck ran out in a hail of bullets.

The Americans found themselves back to square one, but Nan did promise that she'd try to find them another guide. According to McPherson, she returned on June 15 with a man named Jean Duval, who went by the *nom-de-guerre* "Willie."

He and another Maquisard moved them on to a deserted house in the woods closer to the Spanish border, where they joined a group of about two dozen Jews who had escaped from Belgium, Poland, Germany, and elsewhere in France. They too were waiting to make their final escape. Soon the party grew in size to around 40.

It was here that Eugénie Roby dipped into the cash that she had been given by Odette Ernest in Paris, shelling out 10,000 francs each for the two Americans, two Canadians, and three Dutchmen. The price was considerably higher than was being charged in 1943, even as the quality of the guides appeared to have deteriorated.

The trip ahead was not without its complications. Eighth Air Force Lieutenant Robert Martin, who had traveled the same route around the second week of April, reported that the guides had trouble finding the right trails, that they got lost several times and that repeated backtracking consumed several days as food supplies ran low. When a blizzard set in and the terrain became more difficult, Martin's party became widely separated. When the guides had to go back for slower members, Martin and several others decided to continue on their own. In turn, all but Martin himself were picked up by a German patrol before reaching the border.

Unaware of these difficulties, McPherson, Stonebarger, and their Dutch and Canadian companions set out on June 18, hiking through the foothills of the Forêt de Cagire to follow Willie across the Pyrenees. Though Stonebarger was in such pain from his back injury that he had to be carried part of the way, the hike went smoothly. At least blizzard season had passed.

Whereas Martin had needed to sneak past a bridge guarded on one side by German troops and on the other by Spanish soldiers, the crossing on June 18 was an anticlimax for Willie's band. They took their last steps on French soil and crossed uneventfully into the Spanish village of Canejan. As McPherson described it, they "walked into the arms of the [Spanish] police, who were very friendly."

Relieved no longer to have the Gestapo and the Vichy police breathing down their necks, the group nevertheless kept moving as briskly as they could, trekking through the snow-covered mountains on narrow roads and steep mountain trails. They stayed together for the first legs of their Spanish travels, spending their first night in Bossòst, then continuing to Vielha e Mijaran, ten miles from the border, on June 19. According to McPherson, it was here that a truck driver offered to take them south, nearly 80 miles, to Tudeda for five pesetas.

On June 22, they reached Lérida, about 100 miles from the border, where they all reported to the British Consulate. Here, the group parted. Scheltema and van de Velde were turned over to the Spanish police and jailed until Dutch diplomats from the consulate in Barcelona came to bail them out. It turned out that they had been secretly carrying film with photographs they had taken of German activities in the Netherlands.

As their comrades went to jail, all the airmen were taken by a British car to Alhama de Aragón, 150 miles to the west. Here, a British Embassy car took van der Stok and the Canadians to the British Embassy in Madrid. They were flown back to Britain on the night of July 10.

McPherson and Stonebarger, now on their own, continued hitchhiking to Gibraltar, still more than 600 road miles away. It took them more than a month, but they finally reached Gibraltar on July 28. They were both back in Britain on the last day of the month.

Chapter 38

Unsettled Lives

Gilbert Stonebarger went on to work for many years as an electrical engineer in the aerospace industry. He and his wife later retired to Athens, Georgia, where he passed away in 2004. Bram van der Stok, ultimately the most decorated airman in Dutch military history, turned down a commission in the postwar Royal Netherlands Air Force to return to medical school in Utrecht. He, his wife Lucie, and their family later emigrated to the United States, where he practiced medicine in New York, New Mexico, and Hawaii. He passed away in 1993.

In 1950, Joel McPherson was recognized by the French government for aiding the wartime Résistance, and was awarded the Brevet Militaire de Pilote Avion. He remained in the USAAF as it became the US Air Force in 1947, and married Virginia Eva Uher a year later. When he left the service in January 1953, he and Virginia settled in Winter Haven, Florida, where they raised two children and where Joel worked as a building contractor. As reported in obituaries in the *Lakeland* [Florida] *Ledger*, three members of the family died in 1981. Their daughter drowned in Lake Ruby, near the family's Florida home in March, while Virginia and Joel passed three weeks apart in the autumn.

André Urbanovich, aka Doublemètre, the man whom Joel McPherson had described as "a rabid communist," reinvented himself as a member of the same bourgeois class whose *châteaux* he had shot up with a Sten gun. As the war ended, he had already resettled in Paris, where he would open a gallery on Rue du Faubourg-Saint-Honoré and become a wealthy art dealer specializing in contemporary masters.

Jean-Jacques Gillot wrote in *Purification in the Dordogne According to Doublemètre* that as a "beneficiary of the broad amnesty laws, and protected by the code of silence of the time and the support of his accomplices, he got out of trouble" for his wartime mischief. Though Doublemètre was awarded the Légion d'Honneur and the Rosette de la Résistance (Résistance Medal with Rosette), he did not earn the respect of all members of the Résistance.

As Gillot later wrote, in 1948, Christiane Couturoux, a Résistance leader and French Médaille de la Liberté (Medal of Freedom) honoree, personally wrote to McPherson to dissuade him from endorsing Doublemètre, telling him that "Urbanovich is a dangerous man."

Joel McPherson already knew this. He had learned on the job.

PART SEVEN

REFLECTIONS OF SILVER SCREENS

Chapter 39

Leading from the Front

At about 11:00am on the morning of Thursday, May 11, 1944, the ground in the environs of Lavenham in Suffolk shook with the thunder of 72 Consolidated B-24 Liberators of the 487th Bomb Group taking off for a mission over occupied France. Newly arrived a month earlier on April 11, the group's four squadrons had just three missions under their belts since their first on May 7, and had yet to suffer their first combat loss.

Flying with the 487th today was 34-year-old Lieutenant Colonel Beirne Lay, Jr. As group commander, he was assigned to no specific aircraft, so when he accompanied a mission, he took the copilot's right seat on the flight deck of the lead aircraft of the lead squadron. Today, he was aboard *Peg O'My Heart*, leading the 838th Bomb Squadron, an aircraft named for the old Ziegfeld Follies show tune that had become a hit when it was covered by Bunny Berigan and his orchestra in 1939.

In the left seat opposite Lay, *Peg's* pilot was 26-year-old 1st Lieutenant Frank Vratny. As was often the case when the group commander took the right seat, the copilot moved aft to the tail gunner's position, where his perspective as a pilot would be useful in observing the rest of the squadron's formation that was following the lead aircraft. Today, that man was 22-year-old 2nd Lieutenant Walter Armstrong "Walt" Duer from Red Bluff, California, whose six feet three inches and long legs were poorly suited to the cramped tail position.

This was Lay's second mission with the 487th – he'd come home with a battle-damaged Liberator on May 7 – but he had led the group in its Atlantic crossing, and he was already an Eighth Air Force old-timer. In fact, he had been present at its birth. When Brigadier General Ira Eaker had arrived in Britain in January 1942 to set up shop, Lay was at his side. He, like Eaker, was also an old-timer in Army aviation. Born in Berkeley Springs, West Virginia, Lay had graduated from Yale in 1931, enlisted a year later, and earned his wings in 1933. He left active duty as an Army Air Corps first lieutenant in 1936 to pursue a career as a magazine writer, and contributed to leading publications such as *Esquire* and *The Saturday Evening Post*.

Lay's first book, *I Wanted Wings* (1937) was optioned by Hollywood and became a movie in 1941. In the meantime, when he volunteered for active duty in 1939, he found that his book had gotten him noticed by Eaker and by Eaker's boss, Major General Hap Arnold, the Chief of the Army Air Corps – both of whom were published authors themselves. They brought him to headquarters as Arnold's speechwriter. By 1942, the Air Corps was the USAAF and Lay was on Eaker's Eighth Air Force staff in Britain, where his projects included coordinating director William Wyler's efforts to create the well-received film *Memphis Belle*.

In the summer of 1943, as Lay left his desk job to be groomed for operational command, he returned to the cockpit to fly five B-17 missions with the 100th Bomb Group. These included the Regensburg component of the August 17 Schweinfurt-Regensburg mission, about which he wrote an article for the November 6 issue of *The Saturday Evening Post*.* Thereafter, Lay was sent stateside to organize and train one of the many new bomb

*See Chapter 24.

groups that the USAAF was forming. This group was the 487th, and Lay was now back in combat.

Their target for May 11 was to be the railroad marshaling yards at Chaumont, 140 miles southeast of Paris. The countdown to Operation *Overlord*, the Normandy invasion, was in motion, with D-Day less than a month away. Crippling the railway network in northern France to prevent the passage of German reinforcements was high on the Eighth Air Force agenda.

At around 2:00pm, the leading edge of the 838th Bomb Squadron, flying at 12,000 feet, slammed into a wall of German antiaircraft fire over Châteaudun, about 175 miles west of Chaumont. *Peg O'My Heart* took the worst of it. The squadron's Liberators were of the B-24H type, the first Liberator variant to be equipped with both the retractable Sperry ball turret in the belly and the powered Emerson nose turret. The latter was a welcome addition for dealing with head-on attacks by Luftwaffe interceptors, but it did nothing useful in a battle with flak.

In his escape and evasion report, E&E No.1036, the navigator, 22-year-old 1st Lieutenant Alfred Richter, summarized the damage. In the opening salvo, the number one engine was knocked out and a shard of shrapnel that crashed though the nose severely injured the head and the leg of the bombardier, Captain Francis Hodge.

Another burst took out the number two engine. The aircraft slowed and dropped out of the formation, so Lay handed off group command to his deputy in another aircraft and Frank Vratny wheeled *Peg O'My Heart* around, pointing the stricken beast back toward England.

Another barrage of flak ripped into the right wing, and the number three engine was on fire. Cutting off the fuel flow slowed the fire, but then the number four engine was hit. The big aircraft was going down. Lay gave the order to abandon ship, but the interphone was dead. As he sounded the alarm bell, he told Richter, who was standing on the flight deck, to pass the word. Richter went below, where he pushed the wounded Hodge out before jumping himself.

Lay then clipped on his own chest pack parachute, grabbed the controls, and gestured to Vratny to let go of the yoke and get out of the aircraft. Lay glanced back, noting that the radio operator and waist gunners were already gone. With no interphone connection, there was no way of knowing what had happened to Walt Duer in the tail position.

When everyone he could see had jumped, Lay prepared to do the same. Giving the alarm bell one last pull, he hit the emergency bomb release lever, planning to jettison the ordnance and dive through the open bomb bay doors – but the system was jammed.

With *Peg O'My Heart* in a steep, spiraling descent, did he have time for a Plan B?

Did he have time to crawl back underneath the flight deck and into the nose hatch before the bomber hit the ground?

In his memoirs of this installment of his life story, aptly titled *I've Had It*, Lay wrote that it was "like crawling from the ceiling to the floor in an elevator that was falling faster than you can drop."

As he crawled past the retracted nose wheel, his parachute strap caught, and he worked desperately to free himself. "Here I was trapped," he recalled. "It seemed as though I had been crawling for five minutes and that we should have hit the ground long ago."

Anticipating the blinding impact with the ground at any second, Lay freed himself and continued crawling. As he neared the hatch, the suction effect of the 400mph – his estimate – slipstream just outside the hatch grabbed him and sucked him out.

As he pulled his ripcord, the ground seemed to be as close as the floor when rolling out of bed but he had a thousand feet left. Into that thousand fleet hurtled *Peg O'My Heart*, plummeting faster than him. Suddenly there was an enormous explosion as the bomber hit the ground. The five thousand-pound bombs in the bomb bay would detonate as soon as the fire was hot enough.

Lay looked around, saw another descending parachute and recognized Walt Duer. They were coming down in the vicinity of the villages of Bretoncelles and Coulonges-les-Sablons, about 30 miles northwest of Châteaudun and 70 miles southwest of Paris. As the last ones out, they were eight miles or more from their fellow crewmembers.

Alfred Richter, the *Peg O'My Heart* navigator, had pushed Francis Hodge, the injured bombardier, out ahead of him, watched until his parachute opened, then delayed opening his own until he was about 1,000 feet above the ground. Richter could see most of the other parachutes to the north of him, but he landed near none of them.

He noted the time as 4:13pm, and being a navigator, he had a good idea that he was about four miles southwest of the little town of Nogent-le-Rotrou. A girl and a man ran up to him and indicated that he should conceal himself in a nearby hedge when he'd gathered up and hidden his parachute.

After a couple of hours of waiting, Richter had neither seen nor heard any Germans. Having grown impatient, he decided to go look for fellow crewmen. He walked north toward Paris until about 7:00pm, when he changed his mind. As Richter wrote in his escape and evasion report, "I turned south to go to Spain by myself."[34]

About an hour later, he stopped at a farmhouse, where they gave him something to eat as well as civilian clothes and a pair of shoes to replace his heavy, sheepskin-lined flying boots. The farmer then told Richter to go into Nogent and simply take a train to Paris, but when he reached the town, "too many Germans arrived," probably part of the search party trying to round up the *Peg O'My Heart* crew. Richter prudently put his head down and walked straight through the village and out into the countryside. Around midnight, he crawled into a haystack and fell asleep.

On Friday morning, Richter awoke to the continuing generosity of the French people toward Allied airmen. The two French women who discovered him in his haystack fed him, as did a woodcutter whom he passed around noon as he was continuing to walk south.

Around 5:00pm, he met a group of teenaged boys who took him to the edge of some woods, where he was reunited with two other men from his crew – Sergeant Arthur Pelletier and Captain Donald Wilson, the 838th Bomb Squadron's chief navigator. He, like Beirne Lay, had been aboard because it was the lead aircraft of the formation. They told Richter they'd seen Hodge, the bombardier, getting captured. His shattered thigh bone left him unable to walk.

The farmer who owned this plot of land, and who had been hosting Pelletier and Wilson in the woods, brought dinner and bedding for Richter. On Saturday morning, the farmer returned with a French plain clothes police officer. After a moment of apprehension, it was established that he was on their side – part of an underground network that could help them. He then reached into his pocket and took out the picture IDs of three other members of the *Peg O'My Heart* crew.

It was established that the ball turret gunner, Sergeant Lawrence Heimerman, as well as the two waist gunners, Sergeant Robert Peterson and Sergeant John Watson, were safe and that the six men would be reunited soon.

As Richter, Pelletier, and Wilson would later learn, these three men had bailed out together from the center fuselage and rendezvoused shortly after they reached the ground. In Peterson's escape and evasion report, E&E No.1511, he wrote that they walked until they reached a cemetery, where they met a small, red-faced man with a mustache, who turned out to be the caretaker. He took them to a cave in which they hid for three days. While the Americans were there, a half dozen families from the nearby village of Condé contributed food, which the caretaker brought to them.

Chapter 40

Suspicious Characters

Because they bailed out several minutes after the other men from *Peg O'My Heart*, Beirne Lay and Walt Duer landed so far to the north that they would not see them again while in France.

As he stood there, rattled by his narrow escape from the falling aircraft, Lay took in the unfamiliar surroundings, of which he had only a brief glimpse, About a hundred yards away in an adjacent farm field, he saw Duer walking toward him.

The two men were burying their parachutes in a thick hedge when a man and a teenage boy ran up. They were in the midst of introducing themselves as American airmen when a huge explosion rocked the landscape. A tenth of a mile away, the flames that engulfed the wreckage of *Peg O'My Heart* had finally grown hot enough to set off the thousand-pound high explosive bombs in her bomb bay.

The blast and the pyre climbing skyward from the crash site were enough to get anyone's attention, and it was immediately on the mind of all four that the Germans would soon be on the scene.

As French civilians gathered in the surrounding fields to gawk at the burning wreck, the two Americans tried to make themselves inconspicuous – a challenge for men in heavy flight suits, one of whom was over six feet tall. Finally the Frenchman who had first approached them decided to take charge of the situation. Lay knew enough French to understand that they were to wait ten minutes, then crawl through the tall wheat to a distant gate in the wall surrounding the field. Beyond a second gate, the man explained, was a large stone stable where they could hide.

They had just managed to climb into the hayloft of this building when a group of Germans arrived to inspect the place for fugitive Americans. One of the Germans started to climb up into the loft and got so close that the anxious Americans could hear his wheezing as he exerted himself.

Just then, the German in charge decided that there were no Americans in the place and called off his men to go look elsewhere.

As he tried to sleep that night, Lay replayed the day's events in his mind. As he later confided in his memoirs, he realized, "stung with bitter regret," that "I had lost my group [command] just five days after we had started operating [on May 7]. I knew that I was swallowing the bitterest disappointment of my life... I was out of the fight, responsible now for only two people instead of over 2,500 [airmen and ground personnel]."

On Friday, a red-haired girl brought them breakfast and lunch, and the man returned late in the day with more food, cognac, and some civilian clothes, shoes, and berets. Lay found that his fit fine, but Duer's trousers were six inches too short, so matching material had to be sewn on.

"You will leave tonight," the man told them. He pointed out Nogent-le-Rotrou on Lay's map. He explained, as Richter had learned first hand, that the town was crawling with Germans and must be avoided.

At midnight they headed south into the unknown, armed with their luminous dial compasses and a belief that they had a chance.

All night they zigged and zagged, hiking and climbing, through walled fields and orchards. The Frenchman had told them to travel only at night, but when dawn came on Saturday morning, May 13, they decided to keep going. They met the first test of their new clothes, when they passed a German patrol. Lay and Duer just shuffled along, earning hardly a glance from the soldiers.

Late in the day, a Frenchman working in a field noticed them and ran off – to alert the Germans to the presence of two suspicious characters. When Lay and Duer spotted a Gestapo officer approaching, Lay decided to do what a suspicious character would *not* do. He walked up to the German, betting that he recognized French, but did not speak it. He bet right, and was able to use what little French he knew to convince him that this character was a Frenchman. Duer played his part by acting completely bored.

It turned out that the Gestapo man did know two words of French. When he said "*Papiere*," asking for their papers, which they did not have, Lay played dumb. The German bought the story of a pair of country bumpkins. At last he used his other French word, "*allez*," of which Lay later wrote "no invitation to scram has ever been carried out more promptly to the letter."

As the two faux yokels ambled off, the German watched them for a very long time. A few minutes after they were out of his sight, they heard a German armored car coming in their direction so they dived unseen through a hedge and took off running as though their lives depended on it – which, of course, they *did*.

"I wondered what a guy was supposed to do now," Lay later mused. "The whole thing was getting too corny, like a second rate cops and robbers melodrama… Fear was completely absent. Intense anxiety and humiliation was the only conscious feeling."

To make matters worse – or more comedic – they were soon discovered by a barking watchdog, who was followed by his startled owner. Lay quickly explained who they were, and the old man hustled them into his home, where his wife was cooking dinner. After a lengthy, one-sided introduction in French, the man pulled an official German document out of a drawer and handed it to Lay. It was the man's release from a German POW camp. He had been captured when the French were defeated in 1940.

As the foursome was preparing to sit down for a meal, there came a banging at the door. Lay and Duer were shoved into a bedroom and covered with a quilt. They listened as the jovial old couple invited the Germans to sit down for a glass of wine in the kitchen. The Germans declined. They were on a house to house search for two suspicious characters.

When the Gestapo had gone, they finished their dinner, and the suspicious characters slept soundly in the hayloft. On Sunday morning, Lay and Duer were gone before sunrise. The watchdog was not even awake.

They guessed that during the course of that drizzling Sunday, they had covered about nine miles, sticking mainly to the woods and avoiding the roads. By evening, they had slipped into a village church and were kneeling in a rear pew when a woman came in. Lay asked to speak to the priest and after a while, he entered.

"He had a lean, scholarly face and brilliant black eyes," Lay recalled. "I told him we were hungry and thirsty and tired and… American aviators." He might have added that they were both coming down with colds.

It took some pleading, but at last the priest saw the desperation in their eyes and accepted their story. He led them high into the belfry where they waited, listening to the rustling of waking bats, while the priest went away to bring them a tray of soup, bread, cheese, and cider. When it was safely dark outside, he took Lay and Duer to the rectory, where they slept in real beds for two days while they fought their colds and fever.

Unlike their six fellow crewmen near Nogent-le-Rotrou, who had made contact – albeit accidentally – with the Résistance within their first 24 hours on the ground, Lay and Duer had been in France for six days without meeting anyone associated with an escape and evasion network.

Chapter 41

Moving in Circles

On Monday, May 15 while Beirne Lay and Walt Duer were sleeping off their fevers in a rectory less than 50 miles away, fellow *Peg O'My Heart* crewmen Alfred Richter, Arthur Pelletier, and Donald Wilson were hidden in a car and taken to a farm. Here, as Richter described, "we got into a horse and buggy driven by a dapper man who drove us to Nogent-le-Rotrou that afternoon to a tavern next to a railway station." Here, two men arrived to escort them into Paris by train.

With stops and starts, it took all night, but they finally reached the Gare Saint-Lazare and were taken to a jewelry store owned by one of their two handlers. After breakfast, the three Americans were moved to the eastern Paris suburb of Lagny-sur-Marne, where their safe house turned out to be a building behind a school for refugee children. It was here at the school that the trio was reunited with Lawrence Heimerman, Robert Peterson, and John Watson.

Peterson later wrote in his escape and evasion report that they were at the school for six days, so it was around May 22 when the men were taken to a house in a cemetery, split up, and interrogated by the group which was going to smuggle them on to Spain. This step was, of course, consistent with the practices of the Comet Line, which carefully vetted airmen in their care in order to weed out possible German plants.

For the next several days, the Americans were scattered around the city. Richter, for instance, spent two days at the home of a man who had been in the French Navy submarine service during World War I. Next, he was taken across town by a "French detective working with, but not for, the Gestapo."

Richter recalled that after again being reunited with Peterson and Wilson, "the policeman came in and told us we'd go [back to England] by plane. [He] took us to a small house where we met Watson and Heimerman. Plans cancelled. Sergeant Peterson and I [were] then taken to home of English-speaking Frenchman."

The accounts of both Richter and Peterson agree that on May 30, they went to the apartment of a Mademoiselle Christol on the top floor of a six-story nineteenth-century apartment building at 4 Rue Edouard Quenu in the 5th Arrondissement of Paris. Richter would stay until June 27, but Peterson remained there until August 7.

During the third week of May 1944, while six *Peg O'My Heart* crewmen were moving around Paris, Beirne Lay and Walt Duer were also on the move – but they were on foot and still without the benefit of contact with any underground organization. Feeling themselves recovered from their colds, they gave the priest 1,000 francs from the 5,000 they had between them in their survival kits, and headed out on the evening of Wednesday, May 17.

For the next five days, with seriously aching feet, the two men continued their journey, each night sneaking out of the constant rain and into haylofts to sleep. Lay wrote in his memoir, *I've Had It*, that their situation "evolved by increasing degrees into a nightmare of frustration and despair." Though Lay outranked Duer by four consequential levels of command hierarchy, they were now just two guys sharing the same haylofts, the same daily dilemmas, and the same deadly risks. Duer's recollections of this asymmetry, and of their dilemmas and risks, were not officially recorded in his escape and evasion report, E&E No.940. Like many others, it consists of little more than pro forma documents. Lay's escape and evasion report, E&E No.339, and his 1945 memoir of the experience, amply carry the narrative.

At dawn on Thursday, a farmer caught them and was none too pleased – but his wife calmed the man down and served up a hot breakfast for the two shivering Americans. They spent another night with this farm family and departed on Friday evening after one last hot meal. Over the next few days, they had a narrow escape from an angry man and his dog, and spent one uncomfortable night with a scarred veteran of France's 1940 defeat whose father had tried to run them off.

By now, they had practically given up on making contact with any escape network. As Lay noted in his memoirs, they were exchanging "bitter remarks about the French underground. As far as we were concerned it was all a myth, for of the numerous people we had approached, it seemed that on the law of averages at least one must have known to whom to turn."

Indeed, given how quickly the others had been found and taken aboard the escape network, it is amazing that Lay and Duer remained adrift for so long.

Having studied their maps, they had come up with what they called a "final plan." They would make their way to the nearby town of Oucques, about 50 miles south of Nogent-le-Rotrou. Through it ran a railway line.

"From there, we would buy a train ticket to southern France," Lay explained, "although [admitting that] with no forged identification papers, it meant almost certain detection."

On the morning of May 23, the lieutenant and the lieutenant colonel were passing through a village a few miles from Oucques when they decided to stop into a small church to rest. Their joints ached from the cold and damp, and their feet were rubbed raw – literally bleeding – after days of walking in soggy, ill-fitting shoes.

They were kneeling in the last pew when the priest noticed them. Lay told him their story, and he replied with two of his own, one plausible, one preposterous. First, he told them that there was a nearby *château* where an English woman lived, and that she could probably help them. Next, he spoke of a village with an airport that offered regular airline service to England. He said he'd heard the airplanes coming and going at night.

The Americans stifled their incredulity.

Ignoring the absurd airline story, they decided to explore the tale about the *château*. An hour later they were at the end of a winding driveway framed by giant oaks, and knocking on the door.

A blonde woman greeted them in French and asked what they wanted. Lay asked if she was English, she nodded, and he told her they were American airmen who had been on the run for 12 days and were "at the end of our rope."

She told them that she was on their side, but that they had best make themselves scarce before her French husband – obviously a collaborator – returned. She had tears in her eyes as she handed them some British cigarettes and closed the big front door.

Deciding that they had a train to catch, they walked painfully through the night on their worn-out feet and reached Oucques by dawn on Wednesday, May 24. Lay had practiced the phrasing required for a ticket purchase and was ready when they reached the station. It was then that Duer noticed that there were no railway tracks!

It turned out that they had long ago been pulled up – and now existed only on the map that the Americans carried.

As they stood there in despair, they heard a bell tolling from the steeple of the nearby Église Saint-Jacques, People were now swirling around them, headed for church. Lay and Duer decided that they'd go to Mass and approach some of the church-goers for help afterward.

As they walked laboriously across the square, they noticed a man opening the front door of the restaurant at the Hôtel Auberge du Bon Labourer. On a whim, probably born of the dizzy aftergloom of a sleepless night, Lay suggested that they go into the restaurant and order breakfast.

They had the money, so why not?

"*Petit dejéuner?*" Lay asked as he stepped through the door.

The people inside stared at him with a mixture of disbelief and condescension. They were looking not at a prominent, high-ranking military officer and Hollywood screenwriter, but at a disheveled tramp with damp, tattered clothing, straw in his hair and sodden shoes on the verge of disintegration.

"*Non,*" the man in charge replied. "*Non petit dejéuner!*" There would be no breakfast for the shabby vagabonds, certainly not here!

Disappointed, but not surprised, the threadbare pair reverted to their Plan A and ambled over to the church. Mass was over by this time, but the nave was aglow with candles and light streaming through stained glass. When they found the priest praying at one of the side altars, Lay stammered out his usual appeal. The priest became nervous and looked them over suspiciously. Before scurrying away, he said that he would consider their plea for help. At least he did not give them the boot.

They sat down and waited. After a time, they heard a voice speaking to them in English. They turned to see a small, gray-haired woman introducing herself as Jeanne Gilbert. She explained that she had worked in England for over 30 years as a governess for Lord Edmund FitzAlan, the last British Lord Lieutenant of Ireland. Mademoiselle Gilbert said that the priest told her of strange men claiming to be Americans. He feared that someone would get suspicious and call the Gestapo.

Recognizing Lay's American accent, she quickly took charge of the situation, hustling the two men off to the church sacristy. She explained the situation to the priest, who soon reappeared, his apprehension gone, bearing two cartons of cigarettes for the Americans. Lay tried to refuse, knowing that cigarettes were scarce, but the priest insisted. A barber came to give them each a shave, and their feet were treated and bandaged.

Mademoiselle Gilbert returned with food, but not just any food. The hot meal included *filet mignon* trimmed with bacon. She said that she would take them to see the head of the organization with which she was associated. She added that they would soon be taken back to England *by air*. Her organization had already done this for 18 others, and they would bring the total to 20. When she asked how that sounded, they were incredulous.

Had the other priest who told them the unbelievable yarn about *airline service to England* been right?

She returned after the evening services at Église Saint-Jacques, bringing Monsieur Jacques, the small unassuming man who headed the local underground organization. Together, they went out into the night to an undisclosed destination that turned out to be the Hôtel Auberge du Bon Labourer – where Lay and Duer had been refused service that morning.

Inside, behind heavy blackout curtains, was a well-lit bar, where they recognized the restaurant manager who had kicked them out the last time they came through this door. Greeting them, he apologized and explained that they had taken him off guard. At first, he thought they might be disguised German agents, but when he realized they were American, he wanted to get them out before this became evident to any of his patrons – especially an officer of the Vichy police who was dining there.

Parenthetically, the restaurant called Auberge du Bon Labourer remained a fixture in Oucques for decades before closing permanently in 2020.

On Thursday, after a comfortable night in real beds at the hotel, Lay and Duer were taken to a large concrete silo that was part of a grain processing plant on the edge of town. This was supposed to be their safe house for the next two days until it was time for them to meet their "airline connection." However, after 12 days – in which the only excitement was once when their hiding place was almost discovered – they were still lying in the silo, waiting. At least the organization was feeding them well and their ravaged feet were healing. Finally, Mademoiselle Gilbert was back with bad news. The Gestapo was tightening the noose. Monsieur Jacques had been caught using his clandestine radio and had been executed. It was time for them to move – but *not* to an airport.

As they said their last goodbye to Mademoiselle Gilbert, she asked Lay to convey her regards to Lord FitzAlan when they got back to England. In the back of his mind, Lay was probably thinking of the phrase "*if* we get back to England."

For about an hour, a delivery van drove Lay and Duer over a series of narrow country roads to a place where another driver took over and the first rode away on a bicycle. This relay continued for some time until they seemed seriously lost. Each driver knew only his segment of the route, so none would be able to explain it to the Gestapo.

Their destination was the farm of Robert and Georgette Paugoy, located near the village of Mazangé, about 25 miles east of Oucques and 12 miles northwest of the city of Vendôme. The Americans were treated cordially by the Paugoys and the others at the farm, who included their son, Georges, and the farmhands, Denise and Gilbert. Also staying at the farm were several members of the Forces Françaises de l'Intérieur (FFI), the paramilitary wing of the Résistance. They were there because the remote farm had become one of the places where the British airdropped supplies, such as guns and ammunition, for the use of the FFI and the Maquis.

Robert's first question was "*quand viendra le débarquement?*" He wanted to know when the Allies were going to finally launch their long-expected cross-channel invasion of northern France.

"*Bientôt,*" Lay told him, "soon."

Chapter 42

Hollywood on the Seine

While Beirne Lay and Walt Duer were down on the farm in the countryside 100 miles southwest of Paris, Alfred Richter and Robert Peterson were living an entirely different life at Mademoiselle Christol's Left Bank apartment.

Since arriving at 4 Rue Edouard Quenu on May 30, they had traded their flying gear for civilian clothes with a Parisian cut and were beginning to move in the circles of their well-connected hostess. Beirne Lay may have had an earlier Hollywood connection – with his own book having been made into a film and his assignment with William Wyler on the *Memphis Belle* project – but now it was the turn of Richter and Peterson.

Just a few days after their arrival, Hollywood actress Drue Leyton dropped by. Something of a minor celebrity, she had starred in nine Hollywood features during the 1930s, including in the role of Norma Foster in *Alibi for Murder* (1936).

Born Dorothy Blackman, Drue had moved to Paris in 1937, where she met and married French-American actor Jacques Tartière. After Jacques was killed while fighting with the Free French in the Middle East in 1941, she had been interned by the Germans in France, but had been released in 1942 after a sympathetic doctor gave her a fake cancer diagnosis.

"The war seemed to be a ghastly disease from which there was no relief," she wrote in her postwar memoir *The House Near Paris*, but she devoted herself to the Résistance and to providing relief to Allied airmen on the run. She hid them at her Paris apartment, and at her house in suburban Barbazon, where she grew vegetables to help feed her guests.

During the first week of June, Drue Leyton, aka Dorothy Tartière, told Richter and Peterson that they would be moved in just a few days, but soon the wheels that had been in motion to get them out of France were derailed.

Throughout northern France, the rail network was being pounded by a dramatically increasing wave of Allied air strikes. Something big was afoot.

On the morning of Tuesday, June 6, 1944, Paris awoke to the news of the great event for which so many had yearned for so long. The Allied armies had landed in Normandy!

Radios were tuned to the BBC, as they so often were when people wanted news that was unfiltered by the hands of Nazi spin doctors. At Madame Christol's, Richter and Peterson heard the news and felt the same optimism as the French people. Their hostess may even have opened a long-sequestered bottle of champagne. If so, perhaps they all toasted a victory that now seemed tangible, but no mention was made of this in the recollections of the airmen.

Liberation seemed to be at hand, though wishful thinking clouded the reality that this was a battle still far from won. Allied armies would not arrive in Paris for nearly a dozen anxious weeks. Nor did the American evaders realize on June 6 that the invasion would redirect the priorities of the underground operatives who worked for their escape. Within in a day or so, Genevieve, a member of Mademoiselle Christol's circle who appeared often in Richter's descriptions of life in Paris, came with bad news. She told the Americans that they now "probably couldn't get out."

Richter recalled that Genevieve had been making inquiries, and her network "couldn't find the other four of our crew." Richter and Peterson were the lucky ones. Lawrence Heimerman, Arthur Pelletier, John Watson, and Donald Wilson had all been captured by the Germans.

On June 11, there came a sliver of hope for Richter and Peterson. Genevieve came to take them to meet a man who might be able to get their derailed escape back on track.

Having met Dorothy Tartière, Richter and Peterson were about to shake the hand of another figure from the world of cinema, the colorful French documentary filmmaker Albert Malhuzier.

The 37-year-old Malhuzier was an outdoorsman, author, and adventure filmmaker in the mold of the American Lowell Thomas. He had written instructional books about kayaking and canoeing, while his prewar films included *Jeunesse en Liberté* (1936), one of the first professional films about canoeing, and *La Croisière Sauvage* (1939), which he shot while kayaking the Grand Canyon of the Verdon in the French Alps.

Malhuzier had yet to visit Hollywood, but if a casting director had been looking for the ideal candidate to portray a dynamic and resourceful escape facilitator, the flamboyant Albert Malhuzier would have fit the bill. He immediately took the Americans to a photo booth at the Trocadéro for pictures to use in fake identification papers.

But alas, even the boundless energy of Malhuzier felt the weight of the German crackdown on the Résistance. For two weeks, nothing happened. At last, on Tuesday, June 27, Genevieve took Richter to see Malhuzier. The next day, Richter and Malhuzier boarded a train at the Gare du Lyon and headed south. With no explanation given in either man's escape and evasion report, Peterson was left behind.

Richter and the filmmaker spent the night in Tarbes and were in Toulouse by 11:30pm on Thursday. By the weekend, they had reached the French city of Pau, within 100 miles of the routes that the Comet Line used to smuggle Allied airmen across the Pyrenees.

In Pau, a woman named Rosemarie took them to the home of a man named Leon Vanderpool with the assumption that they would soon meet the mountain guide who would escort Richter across the Pyrenees, but it was not to be. As Richter later wrote, Rosemarie came back disappointed, telling him "the guides had joined the Maquis" and gone off to shoot Germans.

The ranks of the Maquis swelled in the weeks after the invasion, in some places fivefold, in others even more. It was not as easy as they expected. As Julian Jackson writes in *France: the Dark Years*, "joining the Maquis in 1944 was more dangerous than ever before. The sudden concentration of men excited German attention, often with tragic consequences."

For three weeks Richter waited. By now, Malhuzier had returned to Paris, thus cheating us of what might have been an exciting tale of the great outdoorsman, an American airman, and their alpine adventures.

At last, on Thursday, July 18, Richter's prospects perked up. He wrote "Rosemarie said I'd leave next Tuesday, but Vanderpool said he'd make arrangements. On Saturday morning, Vanderpool, his son Jack, and I cycled 80 miles to Saint-Palais, where [we] met a Belgian and [his] French wife and a French captain. Then I cycled with them [20 miles south] to Saint-Jean-Pied-de-Port."

In this town, whose name literally means "St John at the Foot of the Pass," Richter and his companions, the Belgian and his French wife, rendezvoused with a Basque guide.

Richter notes that their next move came at 1:00am on Sunday morning. Running on adrenaline after bicycling 100 miles through the mountains on Saturday, they began the last leg of their trek. Hiking all day Sunday, they followed one of the mountain trails that is part of the Camino Francés, the ancient pilgrimage route to Santiago de Compostela in Galicia, Spain. They finally reached the crest of the Pyrenees and the Spanish border around midnight.

At daybreak on July 24, they came to an olive grove where a priest was waiting for them. He took the very weary travelers to the church of Santa María in the village of Roncesvalles, which has been a favorite rest stop for pilgrims since the twelfth century. In the shadow of the ancient Chapel of Sancti Spiritus, they caught their breath and ate a meal, comparing themselves with countless others who had come this way, in search of something – or running *from* something else.

A car met them in Roncesvalles and whisked them back into the twentieth century and off to the American Consulate in San Sebastian. After about a week in the Spanish border town of Irun, overlooking the Bay of Biscay, Alfred Richter was taken to the American Embassy in Madrid, from which Colonel Spellman drove him to Gibraltar on August 14. Richter boarded a night flight on August 16 and was back in Britain the next day.

Robert Peterson of *Peg O'My Heart*, whom Richter and Malhuzier had left behind in Paris on June 27, finally bade *adieu* to Rue Edouard Quenu on August 7. The Allied armies were moving quickly toward Paris, but who knew how soon they would arrive, and what diabolical mischief the Germans would perpetrate as the City of Lights slipped from their grasp? Peterson, the 27-year-old former tile-setter's helper from Chicago, had had his own taste of the City of Lights, and was ready to go.

He boarded a train to Foix, from where he traveled the last 50 miles or so to the French border on foot. Paris was liberated on August 24, just 17 days after Peterson left, and with much less turmoil than many feared. Hitler had ordered General Dietrich von Choltitz, the city's military commander, to destroy Paris, but he did not.

Peterson's E&E No.1511 report gives few details of his journey south, aside from noting that he crossed the Pyrenees on August 22 by way of Andorra, 150 miles east of Richter's crossing. From there, he reached Gibraltar by way of Barcelona on September 2 and was back in England two days later.

Chapter 43

Operation *Overlord*

On Monday, June 5, 1944, when Beirne Lay confidently promised Robert Paugoy that the Allied invasion was coming "soon," he did not realize *how* soon.

The following morning, Robert woke the two Americans to tell them, with great excitement, that it was happening now. He had heard it on the radio. Lay and Duer made their way to the kitchen, where the dial was tuned to the BBC. Only 130 miles to the north, thousands of American, British, and Canadian troops were battling their way ashore on the beaches of Normandy.

General Dwight Eisenhower, the Supreme Commander of the Allied Expeditionary Force, broadcast a statement to the French people, telling them that their liberation was "at hand." Within 24 hours it was clear that Operation *Overlord*, the largest amphibious landing in history, had succeeded. The beachhead had been established and secured. There were around 160,000 Allied troops ashore, and more coming.

General Charles De Gaulle, feeling slighted that his own radio address to his people was postponed until *after* Eisenhower's, ignored the Allies, telling the French people that "it is France's battle and it is the battle for France." He then told the French people, especially the disparate elements of the Résistance, to obey the orders given by the "French government," by which he meant himself. The Comité français de Libération nationale (French Committee of National Liberation; CFLN), which he had chaired since 1943, was renamed the Gouvernement provisoire de la République française (Provisional Government of the French Republic; GPRF). De Gaulle was not just the leader of the Free French Army, but he now asserted himself as the leader of a provisional government. On June 10, with Eisenhower's blessing, De Gaulle formally integrated the FFI into the Free French Army.

The situation was exactly what Lay and Duer's FFI friends had been thirsting for. Martin Blumenson wrote in *Breakout and Pursuit*, the official US Army military history of the campaign, that "the [German] withdrawal from southwest France got under way as approximately 100,000 men moved northeastward, mostly on foot. The great majority had engaged in [support] operations, and very few combat troops were among them. Their movement stimulated the FFI to activity that increased from relatively minor nuisance raids to major harassing action, including intensified FFI operations."

With Allied armies now on French soil, three years of covert operations against the Germans now transformed into overt action. As all of the evaders in occupied Europe now saw, this meant that less emphasis was placed on the ongoing efforts by the underground to aid Allied airmen.

The role of the underground organizations changed. For Beirne Lay and Walt Duer, the invasion and the change of Résistance priorities that came with it meant resigning themselves to being on the Paugoy farm until the Allied troops reached them.

The only thing that Lay and Duer saw of the Allies in the early weeks after *Overlord* was increased air activity overhead. As Lay wrote in his memoir of his time in France, "Thunderbolts or Mustangs came over nearly every evening and beat up rail targets near the farm, close enough so that bombbursts shook the window, sometimes recovering from a dive so low that we could see the pilot's face as he shot past us."

As June became July, a waiting game routine developed. The two Americans pitched in to help out on the farm, working in the fields and bringing in crops. Duer, a trained mechanic, impressed their hosts by repairing broken down farm machinery.

The weeks passed slowly. The Allied armies, bottled up by the Germans at first, finally made their dramatic breakout from Normandy on July 25. As they did so, the US First Army pushed toward Paris. On their right flank, Lieutenant General George Patton's Third Army swept south of Paris to prevent a German escape across the lower Seine River. By early August, Patton's rapidly advancing offensive was coming tantalizingly close to the farm.

Finally, the impatience became intolerable. Lay went to Robert Paugoy and "told him of our resolve to leave that night and head for the advance elements of our forces."

"You do not trust me," Paugoy replied with disappointment. "No confidence. I have protected you day and night and now you would risk it all. The Germans would shoot you on sight and so might your own soldiers. I pledge to you on my honor that I have arranged for the Maquis to come at get you at the earliest safe minute to take you to the Americans."

"We finally gave in," Lay admitted. "How could you argue further with a man who got down and prayed with you to stay, in spite of the knowledge that the minute you left he and his family would be immediately relieved of the danger of being shot?"

A few days later, they at last heard the sound of American artillery in the distance. They celebrated that night, though the electricity went out – they blamed the Germans – and they could not listen to the radio.

For two nights in a row, they caroused, and for two days in a row, they went to work in the fields nursing hangovers. The third month anniversary of their arrival in France came and went on Friday, August 11. The phrase "missing in action for three months" haunted Lay and Duer. What must their families think?

Early Sunday morning, the Paugoys and their lodgers had just finished their breakfast when two carloads of "fierce looking," heavily armed Maquisards wheeled into the farmyard carrying cartons of American cigarettes. Suddenly, the moment had arrived!

The Maquisards insisted that the Americans "must leave immediately."

Meanwhile, not far to the north, the sweep of the Third Army campaign followed routes along the north bank of the Loir River, which runs near the Paugoy farm and through Vendôme, paralleling the larger Loire River. As Blumenson described, "a buffer zone about twenty-five miles wide existed between the Loire and the Loir – a sort of no man's land inhabited by American and German patrols and by the FFI." It was into this "no man's land" that Beirne Lay and Walt Duer were about to plunge.

Handing each American a submachine gun for use if they were interrupted by a German patrol, the two-car Maquisard convoy took off, racing north at top speed on dusty, winding dirt roads.

With the French Résistance having gone on the offensive, there were gun-toting Maquisards and random civilians on the streets of every village. In one town, they were introduced to an English-speaking FFI officer, who regarded them with an ironic grin.

"You are Lieutenant Colonel Lay?" the man asked. "It was you who were shot down May eleventh in a *Libérateur avion* [B-24 Liberator aircraft] near Coulonges-les-Sablons? I received orders from England the same day to take twelve of my men to fetch you. We arrived eight hours after you left the stable and there was no trace of you."

If not for that clean getaway on their second morning, they would have been *flown* back to England three months ago! The "airport" stories they had heard were true.

———

Later that day, Sunday, August 13, 1944, Lay and Duer were barely 20 miles from Paugoy's farm when they first saw American uniforms. The 5th Infantry Division lieutenant to whom Lay introduced himself was suspicious at first, because the two shaggy farmworkers looked like anything *except* American officers.

Finally, they managed to convince the wary GIs that they were really Americans, and a jeep took them to battalion headquarters. Here, Lay and Duer sought out the radio man and dictated messages to be relayed to their families. They then moved up to regimental headquarters, where they were offered coffee, before being sent on to see Major General Stafford Irwin, the 5th Division commander.

On Monday morning, after spending the night as Irwin's guests, Lay and Duer were shoe-horned into a light liaison aircraft and flown to the advance headquarters of the USAAF Ninth Air Force in Normandy. Brigadier General Richard Nugent, the Chief of Staff for operations at the Ninth, was an old friend of Lay's from before the war, so Lay sought him out.

"In spite of my dirty beard, he recognized me and extended a welcome I won't forget," Lay wrote in his memoir. "It was the first time since our 'return to Allied control' that Walt and I were able to positively identify ourselves."

Dinner that night was at the *château* that had been commandeered by Major General Hoyt Vandenberg, commander of the Ninth. Nugent insisted on the practical joke of presenting Lay to Vandenberg without cleaning him up, convinced that the unkempt character was unrecognizable. Lay went along with this prank.

"Beirne!" Vandenberg said, identifying him immediately. "I thought you were dead."

The next day, August 15, Lay and Duer were back in England. Of the only other two men from *Peg O'My Heart* to escape capture, Robert Peterson was at that moment making his way through the Pyrenees between Foix and

Andorra, while Alfred Richter was in Gibraltar waiting for the flight that would take him back to England.

From London, Lay and Duer traveled to their former base at Lavenham, where they were reunited with the men of the 487th Bomb Group. As Lay noted, the new commander, Colonel Robert Taylor III, "had had the 487th for three months, so it was out of the question for me to get my old outfit back. But I won't forget the welcome they gave me when I visited the officer's club."

Before departing for a 30-day stateside furlough, Beirne Lay made good on his promise to Jeanne Gilbert back in Oucques. He sought out and paid a visit to Lord FitzAlan. They enjoyed a drink as they reminisced in his lordship's great home three miles south of Windsor Castle. He told Lay that it was too bad he had not come the day before. King George VI and Queen Elizabeth had "come over for a spot of tea as they often do, and they would have enjoyed your story."

Chapter 44

Hollywood Calling

Colonel Beirne Lay never returned to combat. He left the USAAF in 1946 after a stint in a headquarters staff job at the Pentagon, but remained in the Air Force Reserve. In the meantime, his memoir of his three months in occupied France, *I've Had It: The Survival of a Bomb Group Commander*, was published in 1945, but he would soon be immersed in a much bigger project.

Lieutenant Walt Duer, meanwhile, left the service and went back to California. He got married, settled down in the small Santa Barbara county town of Solvang to raise a family, and pursued a career as a carpenter.

Beirne Lay also went west – back to Hollywood. He reconnected with Sydney "Sy" Bartlett, whom he had gotten to know while at Eighth Air Force headquarters early in the war. Born in Ukraine as Sacha Baraniev, Bartlett had come to the United States at the age of four. He had worked as a newspaperman before coming to Hollywood in 1933 to work as a screenwriter with RKO Studios.

When the Eighth Air Force was formed in 1942, both men served as staff officers in the inner sanctum of the organization. Bartlett worked closely with Brigadier General Frank Armstrong, a bomb group commander who later led the Eighth's 1st Bomb Wing. When Armstrong went to the Pacific to command the B-29s of the 315th Bomb Wing, Bartlett went with him.

In 1946, both Lay and Bartlett were working as screenwriters in Hollywood when Bartlett approached Lay and "literally forced me into joining a venture which I thought foredoomed so soon after the war." The project was a novel based on their wartime experiences in the Eighth Air

Force, with one part being based on Lay's earlier non-fiction article about the August 1943 Regensburg mission.[*]

The novel took shape in Lay's basement over the ensuing two years and was published in 1948 as *Twelve O'Clock High*. The book that Lay feared would be buried in the postwar avalanche of combat fiction broke out of the pack and became a best-seller. It remains a classic of World War II fiction.

In turn, there was a great stirring of interest in the film rights. William Wyler, with whom Lay had worked on the *Memphis Belle* film, was interested in acquiring the property for Paramount, but Darryl Zanuck at 20th Century Fox stepped in to offer the two men $100,000 ($1.2 million in today's dollars), plus a like amount for ancillary rights. Zanuck poured on a lavish Hollywood production, with Gregory Peck as the lead character, General Frank Savage, clearly based on Frank Armstrong. *Twelve O'Clock High* premiered in December 1949 and earned $3.2 million ($37 million in current valuation) in its initial release. The film earned two academy awards, one for Sound Recording and one for Dean Jagger as Best Supporting Actor. A television series based on the film, and also featuring Beirne Lay as a screenwriter, aired on the ABC network between 1964 and 1967.

Through 1963, Beirne Lay wrote several other screenplays and books, while continuing to produce magazine articles. Notably, he collaborated with fellow Eighth Air Force bomber pilot – and A-List Hollywood star – Jimmy Stewart on the 1955 film *Strategic Air Command*, which Lay wrote and in which Stewart starred.

———

While Lay was making it big in Hollywood, the film people in Paris who had cast themselves in the roles of protectors of Allied airmen came out of the shadows.

Drue Leyton, aka Dorothy Tartière, was sought out and interviewed by American journalists who arrived in Paris after the liberation in August 1944. Helen Kirkpatrick, a correspondent with Chicago and Pittsburgh papers, wrote that when American troops arrived at her farm, Leyton and the airmen she was then sheltering "were on the road to greet them." She told Kirkpatrick that she planned to return to the United States. She did,

[*]See Chapter 39.

passing away in Corona del Mar, California in 1997. She never returned to the big screen.

Albert Malhuzier energetically continued his documentary film career. In 1945, he produced *Réseau X: Caméras Sous la Botte* (*Network X: Cameras Under the Boot*), with Robert Gudin, dedicated to the liberation of Paris. After this, he traveled the world, concentrating on nature and outdoor adventure films. For his 1952 film *In Pursuit of the Gorillas*, he took his wife and nine children to Central Africa. Along with Jacques Cousteau and others, he was a founder of the film and lecture series *Connaissance du Monde* (*Knowledge of the World*), which still continues. In 2019, *Connaissance du Monde* launched its own noncommercial television channel.

When Beirne Lay left France in August 1944, he did so planning to return soon after the war to visit those who had helped out when he and Walt Duer were men on the run. Other things got in the way, and he didn't make it, although his brother, Major John Lay of the Ninth Air Force, visited the Paugoy farm in his stead in 1945.

Finally, in 1956, a dozen years after he had been there, and a half dozen since he had become famous with *Twelve O'Clock High*, the self-described prodigal son went back. He was in Britain and France on duty as a US Air Force reserve officer and seized the opportunity. Having commandeered a staff car in Paris, he drove to Oucques, where he looked up Jeanne Gilbert whom he found "sharp and energetic." As he wrote in the book's epilogue, when *I've Had It* was republished in 1980 as *Presumed Dead*, his reunion with her was "ecstatic."

The two old friends then climbed into Lay's car and made their way into the countryside to visit the Paugoys. Robert and Georgette had turned the farm over to their son and were now living in the nearby village. Though he had not seen Lay in 12 years and was not expecting him, Robert recognized his former American lodger immediately. They talked for several hours and drove out to the farm.

Robert Paugoy passed away before they could have a second reunion, but Georgette and Denise made a visit to California in 1971, where they were greeted by both Lay and Walt Duer.

PART EIGHT

LIGHTNING STRUCK TWICE

Chapter 45

Aces Among the Wolves

It was Monday, March 27, 1944 and the bombers of the Eighth Air Force were out in force. It was a major effort against the Luftwaffe air bases across the south and west of France. The Eighth put up 701 B-17s and B-24s against enemy airfields in a great sweeping arc from Cazeax to Pau in the south, from Biarritz to Bordeaux in the west, and from Tours to Chartres, not far from Paris.

The invasion of occupied France was coming and everyone knew it, even those who had not been explicitly briefed as to when and where. The Germans knew it too. It was not hard to guess why their airfields in France were being pounded and pummeled.

But there was more to it than that.

The Eighth had declared war on the Luftwaffe – Hermann Göring's knights of the air, who had been bedeviling its operations and killing its airmen for more than a year and a half. At the end of February 1944, the

Big Week operations had put Eighth Air Force maximum efforts over the Reich almost every day, focusing on the German aircraft industry and the logistical infrastructure that fed the Luftwaffe.

Of course, the Luftwaffe was also out in force on March 27, protecting their airfields and themselves. But the hunters were also the hunted. Along with its 701 bombers, the Eighth sent out 960 fighters – more than on any day so far in the war. Among them were a couple dozen P-47 Thunderbolts of the celebrated 56th Fighter Group. Best known as "Zemke's Wolf Pack," the 56th was led by the renowned fighter ace Colonel Hubert "Hub" Zemke.

Based at Horsham St Faith in Norfolk – but operating out of its future home base at Halesworth in Suffolk on the 27th – the 56th was known at the time for being the home of the highest scoring American aces in the European Theater. Back in the United States, where the public craved stories of war heroes, the names and photos of such aces as Robert S. "Bob" Johnson, Francis "Gabby" Gabreski, Gerald "Jerry" Johnson, and Walker Melville "Bud" Mahurin had been gracing the pages of newspapers all winter long.

On March 27, the Wolf Pack was running with the bombers targeting Tours, 125 miles southwest of Paris. Bud Mahurin, who had received orders promoting him to major just four days earlier, was leading the "A" element of the Pack, while Jerry Johnson was in command of "B." Colonel Dave Schilling, Zemke's deputy group commander, was flying as overall commanding officer for the Pack's activities this day.

As Mahurin wrote in his escape and evasion report, "we circled over the town, waiting for the show [the bomber stream] to pass. As soon as we were relieved by other fighter groups we started looking for airdromes to strafe on our way out [back to England] as we had been briefed, and went as a unit [80 miles northeast] to Chartres."[35]

It was nearing 3:00pm as they passed over a Luftwaffe field about halfway to Chartres. Schilling went in for a strafing attack, while Mahurin remained at 15,000 feet to draw antiaircraft fire away from him.

When Schilling climbed back after leaving at least one German aircraft ablaze, Mahurin reported that he had eyes on a Dornier Do 217 medium bomber. It was in flight at lower altitude, using a straight section of the railway line as a navigation aid and looking like the proverbial sitting duck. Mahurin radioed Schilling to say that he was going after it, to which Schilling replied, "I'll cover you."

The Do 217 gunner, manning an MG 131 machine gun in a rotating turret aft of the flight deck, saw Mahurin diving from behind and opened fire. He poured at least a few 13mm rounds directly into the 18 cylinders of the Pratt & Whitney R-2800 Double Wasp that sat a few feet ahead of Bud Mahurin.

"I started firing from out of range, thinking that he would stop, but he didn't," Mahurin recalled. "Instead of taking evasive action, I came right in and offered a perfect target for his turret. I closed to 400 yards and began to hit him, but he hit my engine. I closed [in on him], broke off, and called to the others, 'lay off, it's mine.' I closed again and fired to beat hell."

As he flashed past the Do 217, Mahurin watched four crewmen escape from the stricken Dornier. He recalled that someone from the 56th who was flying above shouted, "look at her go!"

Mahurin saw the German bomber hit the ground and explode, noting that the crewmen had jumped at minimum altitude. In his escape and evasion report, he mentioned that he had seen no parachutes, though in his later memoirs he wrote that when the crew did open their chutes, they "appeared to be caught in the blast."

Soon it would be Mahurin's turn to feel the need to abandon his ship.

"I started to climb," he remembered. It would not take many hits on those vulnerable cylinders to be fatal to his powerful Double Wasp. "Oil was spattering on the windshield. I could see my shadow on the ground with a column of smoke behind it. I throttled back and took it easy. In about a minute, there was a bang, and the left side [of the P-47] was burning."

"Watch out boy," Schilling called. "You're on fire."

Bud Mahurin's career as an Eighth Air Force fighter pilot had come to an abrupt end. A few moments earlier, the blazing Dornier bomber had brought his score as an ace to 19.75, but now he was about to enter a new life as a man on the run.

***

It had all begun back in September 1941, when a 22-year-old clerk at City Light & Power in Fort Wayne, Indiana quit his job to report for duty as a would-be pilot in the USAAF. Or maybe you could say that it started ten years earlier, when 12-year-old Walker Mahurin took his first airplane ride in a racy new Stinson Reliant owned by a friend of his stepfather.

Over the course of the ensuing decade, Mahurin grew up, enrolled at Purdue University, and started a serious romance with a farmer's daughter named Patricia Sweet. Mahurin had, in the meantime, signed up for the US Army's Aviation Cadet Training Program, which offered free pilot training to men with at least two years of college. Fast forward to September 1941 and Mahurin was sitting in the cockpit of a Fairchild PT-19 outside Chickasha, Oklahoma, where the Wilson-Bonfils Airfield ran a primary flight school for the USAAF.

A year later, Mahurin had passed through many layers of progressively more advanced flight training, and was sitting in the cockpit of a Republic P-47 Thunderbolt. He was now assigned to Hub Zemke's 56th Fighter Group, composed of the 61st, 62nd, and 63rd Fighter Squadrons. Mahurin became a flight leader in the 63rd as the group deployed to England in January 1943 to join the VIII Fighter Command of the Eighth Air Force. They began flying operational missions over occupied Europe in April, mainly "Rodeo" fighter sweeps aimed at luring the Luftwaffe into combat.

Mahurin's early combat career was anything but auspicious. He found himself performing poorly in air battles, and in July he foolishly flew too close to a B-24 over England in an unnecessary close formation stunt that resulted in the tail of his Thunderbolt being chewed off by the Liberator's props. He survived the ensuing crash, but when he got back to Horsham St Faith, it was Hub Zemke's turn to do the chewing. Luckily, Mahurin was not grounded.

Things turned around completely for the cocky young aviator during the great Schweinfurt-Regensburg operation on August 17, 1943. Over Eupen, Belgium at around 4:30pm that day, the 56th Fighter Group was escorting Flying Fortresses back to England from Schweinfurt when the Luftwaffe pounced.

"By God! They're hurting our boys," Mahurin recalled thinking as he watched "German fighter after German fighter flying through the formation, guns blazing."

He dived into the melee, picked a Focke-Wulf Fw 190 and lined up, unseen by the German pilot, on his six o'clock position. Closing to within 500 yards before opening fire, the young American attacked.

"When the ammunition from my eight machine guns hit the German, he sparkled like fireflies from the impact of explosive shells," Mahurin wrote in his memoirs. "His aircraft immediately flipped over on its back and bobbled erratically upside down. Then it gradually began an inverted dive, trailing fire and smoke."

Mahurin pulled up, found himself on another Focke-Wulf's six o'clock and repeated the whole thing. He went home that night with two aerial victories. His friend Jerry Johnson went home with three. Two days later, Johnson added two to become the 56th's first ace. Mahurin got another

Focke-Wulf on September 8 and a confirmed pair of Messerschmitt Bf 110s on October 4 to become an ace himself.

In seven months, the 56th Fighter Group would shoot down 167 German aircraft – 23 of them on November 26 alone. After three in the latter battle and one more three days later, Bud Mahurin was touted in a November 30 dispatch by the Associated Press as "the leading American ace in this theater" with a total of 12. Mahurin retained the top spot well into 1944, though his friend Walter Beckham of the 353rd Fighter Group then crept ahead.

Beckham was shot down during a strafing run near Bergen-Neukirchen in eastern Germany on February 22, and Mahurin pushed his score to 18.75 with three victories on March 8. However, Bob Johnson of the Wolf Pack downed three on March 15 to bring his total to 22.

On March 27, snatching back the lead in the highly competitive "race of aces" was clearly on Mahurin's mind as he opened fire on the Do 217. But the globs of oil on his windshield told him that *his* race had now been run.

Chapter 46

Aces Down

Walker "Bud" Mahurin bailed out of his Thunderbolt at 3,000 feet and yanked the ripcord.

Nothing happened.

Rushing up toward him were the fields and rolling hills of France's Eure-et-Loir Department. He could see people below and hear them shouting.

"I thought I had had it," he remembered succinctly.

He pulled the ripcord again, discovering now that the wire was too long and needed to be pulled farther.

This time it worked, but just in the nick of time. Four or five seconds after his parachute billowed open, Mahurin crashed into soft, plowed dirt in a farmer's field. His Thunderbolt crashed about 50 yards away and exploded in a ball of fire.

Mahurin stood up and began pulling off his heavy flying gear and his Mae West life jacket. He even ditched his necktie and his watch before starting to run toward the nearby woods.

Overhead, Dave Schilling and others came down low, buzzed him, and circled Mahurin's position to confirm that he had survived. Mahurin and Schilling exchanged waves.

Mahurin later wrote in his escape and evasion report that he was "afraid they were going to try and land to pick me up." This would have been a dangerous maneuver considering the uneven terrain. Of course, he also feared that a dozen circling Thunderbolts were a beacon for Germans who searching for him.

Coincidentally, at that same moment, Jerry Johnson of the Wolf Pack had also been shot down. Two other pilots considered landing to retrieve him, but abandoned their efforts when a wingtip clipped a tree.

After about ten minutes, the Wolf Pack flew away and Mahurin was alone in a nearby wood. It was more low underbrush than a stand of trees in which he could conceal himself. He had come down near Boisville-la-Saint-Père, a village of a few hundred people 12 miles southeast of Chartres, but this mattered little at the moment. All he wanted was a place to hide.

"I did not know what to do," Mahurin recalled. "I was getting pretty rattled... I thought that I would fall right into a bunch of Germans and that they would come after me in staff cars and tanks. Actually, I didn't see a German for four days."

Jerry Johnson was not so lucky. He was picked up by a German patrol and spent the rest of the war as a prisoner in Stalag Luft I.

Mahurin tore the insignia off his uniform and dirtied it up, trying to make himself as "tacky as possible," and thereby not easily identifiable as an American airman. He found a stack of cut saplings that he thought would provide a reasonable hiding place and worked his way underneath.

"I knew that it would be daylight for about eight hours more and I was not looking forward to this uncomfortable wait, but I had better stick to the best possible cover," he wrote in E&E No.617. "Every time I moved the bramble bushes crunched and made so much noise that I thought someone was sure to hear. I was careful to move only when the birds were singing and I could assume that no one was around."

As the hours ticked by, he heard a motorcycle pass near his hiding place and then continue out to the crash site of his aircraft. He figured it was a German, but resisted the urge to peek from under his saplings.

As soon as it was dark, Mahurin climbed out and headed southwest toward Spain. He had no plan, aside from that of so many who had found themselves in this predicament. He would walk – or run – southwest until he could approach a civilian and hope for a referral to an organization that could help him find a way to the Spanish border.

As he walked, he came to a small town, probably Boisville-la-Saint-Père, but he decided to circle around it. As dawn was beginning to break in the east, he grew tired, climbed a stack of hay bales in a field, found a crevice, and went to sleep.

Bud Mahurin awoke on Tuesday morning to the sound of a German aircraft circling overhead. He was sure that they were looking for him, but he later learned that there was a Luftwaffe aerial gunnery training field at Voves, southwest of Boisville, and this was probably a trainee going through his paces.

He intended to wait in the relative safety of his hiding place until nightfall, but at around 3:00pm he could no longer stand the inaction, so he crawled out. Surveying the scene, he saw a man working in a garden next to a house, and decided, "it's now or never." If he was going to make contact with someone who was by himself, this was his opportunity.

Mahurin was able to approach the man without being seen, but just as he reached the house, two other people appeared. The airman ducked around the corner and took a deep breath.

"It's now or never," he repeated to himself, and now it was.

Mahurin whistled to the man, who turned with a frightened expression and looked at this strange character who had spent most of the day in a stack of hay bales – and looked it.

"*Je suis aviateur Américain*," Mahurin whispered.

The man replied with a blank stare.

"*Pouvez-vous cachez moi?*" Mahurin continued, trying in his heavy American accent to ask, "can you hide me?"

The man seemed to understand, but was unimpressed when Mahurin brought out his dog tags to prove his nationality.

"*Cachez vous*," the man said at last, confirming that he would hide the American airman.

A second man, whom Mahurin later decided was the local mayor, appeared with some bread and meat, as well as a bottle of wine. They sat down to a late lunch, then went to another house, where Mahurin took a pencil and paper and sketched a series of pictures to explain that he had shot down a German aircraft before he went down himself – and now he wanted to travel to Spain. They proceeded to relieve Mahurin of his ring and his cigarette lighter and showed him to a bed where he could spend the night.

Mahurin was awakened before dawn on Wednesday morning, by a Frenchman whom he later named as "Pierre." He did not understand everything that Pierre said, but he caught the word "*travaillez*."

"I thought that was fine," Mahurin wrote in his 1962 memoirs, *Honest John*, retelling a story that he had earlier mentioned in his escape and evasion report. "I was going *traveling*." It was not until later in the day that he figured out that "*travaillez*" means "work," not "travel."

The American pilot spent the next several days helping a threshing crew to bale straw, cutting wire with pliers, and watching the blisters forming on his hands.

In his memoirs, Mahurin mentioned being introduced to Jean-Baptiste le Curer, the man who seemed to be in charge of the local underground organization, a man whose "thin mustache coupled to a hawklike nose made him look naturally sinister." Curer was a prominent local grain merchant who did business with the Germans while leading a double life as a Résistance leader. He cautioned Mahurin not to be in a rush to get to Spain because there were a lot of downed airmen ahead of him in the queue.

On Sunday, April 2, an English-speaking woman arrived from Paris to interview Mahurin. She explained that he had been put to work on the threshing crew so that the underground organization – unnamed by Mahurin – could keep an eye on him and decide whether or not he was a German sent to infiltrate their organization by pretending to be an American.

She told Mahurin that he had passed their scrutiny, and that a clandestine radio message from London had confirmed his identity. With this, he was taken back to the house where he had had lunch on his first day. A boy was there with two bicycles, and Mahurin was instructed to ride south, following the boy.

Traveling on dirt roads that meandered though the countryside, they rode for about 15 miles to Voves. The boy refused to allow Mahurin to come close to him, pedaling furiously whenever the American did so. At last, they reached a two-story brick building near some railroad tracks that was the home of the Chaurin family, who explained that they had recently hosted members of an American B-24 crew.

For the next week, Mahurin spent his days doing very little other than watching passing trains on the single-track line outside his window. He later noted in his escape and evasion report that there was a lot of traffic, as many as 16 trains daily. The Germans had switched a lot of freight trains traveling between Chartres and Orléans to this less conspicuous single track on account of Allied air attacks on the mainline. He noticed German Reichsbahn freight cars among the French SNCF cars, and saw many older locomotives, which he guessed were being shipped to Germany.

During the week of April 9, shortly after Easter, Curer, the man with the sinister mustache, reappeared with a leaflet that had been dropped over Paris after a recent RAF raid. Printed in French, it carried a photo of Mahurin and Walter Beckham, and appealed to the French public to aid these two valued fighter pilots to escape back to England.

THE ONES WHO GOT AWAY

"Why didn't you tell us?" Curer asked Mahurin through an interpreter. "This would have put you at the head of the list."

Mahurin explained that he had tried, but Curer couldn't understand his attempts to speak French.

Curer now swung into action. He was full of ideas.

Might Mahurin pose as a gendarme and take a train to Paris?

No, his poor command of the language nixed that option.

Could he hop on a train for Marseilles and find his way to the Pyrenees along the Pat O'Leary escape line?

Mahurin was receptive to that idea.

At last, Curer offered to get on the radio and request that Mahurin be *flown* back to England. The Royal Air Force made regular clandestine night flights in and out of occupied France to aid the Résistance and support Britain's own SOE sabotage efforts. As Beirne Lay had discovered when it was too late for him, occasionally – *very* occasionally – they repatriated high value evaders by air.[*]

Mahurin had no idea about the dangerous nocturnal incursions, made by the RAF's Westland Lysander short takeoff and landing (STOL) aircraft, but when he was told, he found the idea of traveling through Luftwaffe controlled air space in a slow clumsy aircraft like the Lysander terrifying.

Curer insisted, and at last Mahurin conceded.

A few days later, a Résistance operative arrived from nearby Châteaudun. He was carrying a large packet that contained detailed drawings and plans of the big Luftwaffe base in that city, and information about Heinkel He 177 long-range bombers of Kampfgeschwader 40 and 100 (KG 40 and 100) that were based there. In fact, Mahurin reported in his escape and evasion report that he had seen these aircraft operating in that area. The man thought that as long as Mahurin was headed back to England, he could easily take this package along with him and deliver it to Allied intelligence.

Mahurin was incredulous. If he was caught by the Germans as a downed airman, he would end up as a POW. If he was caught with this material, he could be executed on the spot as a spy!

[*]See Chapter 43.

The following afternoon, when a car arrived to take Mahurin to catch his flight, he meant to leave the Châteaudun envelope behind, but his hostess, Madame Chaurin, had slipped it into his pocket. She was sure that he wouldn't mind.

By 6:00pm, after a drive of about 20 miles, Mahurin was sitting in the kitchen of a rural home, where several other people were waiting for a BBC radio broadcast that contained some coded information about the flight of the Lysander. It turned out that two of these men were French agents, who had been dropped into their occupied homeland for an espionage mission, and who were now going back to England. As he related in his memoirs, they had several suitcases of purloined documents that made Mahurin's envelope look insignificant.

"The more I learned," Mahurin fretted, "the more frightened I became at the prospect of being caught."

At last, the coded message was heard and they were off, bicycling to another farmhouse near where the Lysander would land at midnight by the light of the full moon. However, when aircraft engines were heard, it turned out to be an RAF nighttime bombing mission to a nearby target, accompanied by the roar of Luftwaffe interceptors coming and going and the rattle of machine-gun fire. This excitement went on for a long time, and when silence again prevailed, it was clear that the Lysander was not coming that night.

The next day, they learned that their Lysander had actually almost made it, but it had crashed or been shot down. When the Germans arrived to inspect the wreckage and found French currency scattered about, they correctly deduced that the aircraft had been part of a special operation gone bad.

With the heat on, Mahurin's handlers decided that they could not attempt another pickup at the present location, so they took a train to Orléans to regroup. Here, they planned to radio their contacts in England for a new strategy.

After a third class ride that Mahurin found unnerving because he felt that his inability to speak French made him stand out, they disembarked at the busy Orléans train station. The place was crowded with German troops, and German fighter aircraft filled the skies.

On Saturday, May 6, after several days at the safe house, another pickup was arranged, and Mahurin was back at the station with his handlers and the French spies. This time, despite the German troops standing nearby, Mahurin made the mistake of attempting to reply in French when declining some food that was innocently offered.

"My French had English written all over it," he admitted. "Even the Germans began to stare at me."

After this near miss, Mahurin's group traveled to the place outside town where another Lysander was due to land. At midnight, as they waited impatiently, they at last heard the rumble of the single Bristol Mercury engine and saw the silhouette of their aircraft against the nearly full moon. Mahurin recalled his consternation as the pilot circled the field several times, with the Mercury reverberating across the landscape, before finally touching down.

"The flight was the damnedest I ever made or hope to make," Mahurin recalled in a colorful story in his memoirs. "It took four and a half hours to fly back to England. Those crazy Frenchmen drank from a bottle of wine and sang crazy French songs all the way. They didn't have a worry in the world. As for me, I was sure we'd be shot down. At ninety miles an hour we were absolute dead ducks."

After landing at an RAF airfield in Cambridgeshire, Mahurin thought that at last he was free, but he was wrong.

"I found myself under arrest back in England," he wrote in his memoirs.

The British were taking no chances. Just as he been sent to work on Curer's farm until the French Résistance people were sure that he was not a German infiltrator, the British had the same worries. Mahurin was taken, under escort, to the Air Ministry in London for "investigation and interrogation."

The British intelligence people betrayed no telltale enthusiasm when he handed them the Châteaudun envelope, but he was gratified when he learned a few weeks later that the Royal Air Force had launched an attack on the Luftwaffe base near that city.

Finally, on May 8, Captain John F. White from the 56th Fighter Group, who knew Mahurin, showed up to sign a confidential certificate confirming his identity.

The erstwhile top-scoring ace was entering a new and unexpected phase in his career.

Chapter 47

Back into Combat

Bud Mahurin was not to be permitted to rejoin the race of aces, of which he had once been a star player. He would have wanted to do so, but he ran into the Eighth Air Force dictum of not allowing recovered evaders back into the skies over Europe because they had information about the French underground that could not be risked if they were shot down again and captured.

He hoped, even assumed, that this order would be modified after the impending Normandy invasion, when France started to come under the control of Allied armies. He was willing to bide his time.

While Mahurin accepted his being grounded from combat operations, he had not expected to be denied a return to the land of the living – at least not right away.

"The colonel in charge cautioned me not to talk to anyone until he gave me a permission," Mahurin griped in his memoirs. "I was not to leave the building unless escorted, and especially not to call outside to any of my friends. [The Eighth Air Force] wanted a proper press release regarding my return."

Mahurin was told that he was a "hot potato," given his minor celebrity status as a leading ace.

Indeed, the Eighth Air Force had waited two weeks to issue their press release about Mahurin and Jerry Johnson being shot down. Even his mother hadn't known right away. She had received a telegram saying merely that he "had been sent on a trip."

Though he returned to England on May 7, the press release concerning this was not issued until May 22. The reasons for the concern came down to the manner of Mahurin's return. He was told that he was only the twelfth Allied airman to date to have been *flown* back to England.

"I was to keep this information confidential, on the pain of court martial," he later divulged in his memoirs. "If word ever spread that pilots could be flown out, all airmen who went down subsequently would demand to return to England by air, or would think that I had been given preferential treatment." He didn't even tell Hub Zemke, his group commander.

Of course, another component of this cloak of secrecy was the Allies not wanting to reveal the clandestine incursions by the Lysanders, which played a vital role in the insertion and extraction of spies and special operations agents.

On May 17, Mahurin was invited to Wycombe Abbey in Buckinghamshire to dine at a tableful of generals headed by General Carl Spaatz, the commander of the US Strategic Air Forces (USSTAF), which incorporated both the Eighth and Fifteenth Air Forces.

"When General Spaatz asked me to tell him of my escape, I figured he was the man running the show and I'd better tell all I knew," Mahurin explained. "It took four hours to satisfy him."

A week after his dinner with Spaatz, Mahurin embarked on an American homecoming that was managed by the USAAF press office. He garnered immense press coverage, with a parade in Grand Rapids, and the realization that the hot potato was now a star. Soon, he was also a lieutenant colonel.

When the commotion died down, the first thing on Bud Mahurin's wish list was to get back into combat, and he managed to secure a job commanding the 3rd Fighter Squadron, 3rd Air Commando Group, which was deploying to the Philippines.

Meanwhile, though, the first thing on the mind of his girlfriend, Patricia Sweet, was a wedding. They disagreed over the sequence of these two events. Pat won. The wedding came in September, the Philippines came in October.

By the fall of 1944, the size of the air forces of Imperial Japan's army and navy had dwindled considerably from their heyday of the previous years, so air-to-air battles of the scale that Mahurin had seen in Europe were rare. Mahurin's single aerial victory in the Pacific came on January 14, 1945, when he downed a Kawasaki Ki-46 "Dinah" twin-engine reconnaissance aircraft.

Most of the operations for the 3rd Commando, flown over both the Philippines and Formosa, were ground attack missions. Antiaircraft fire was intense, and on one mission, Mahurin took so many hits that he had to ditch his P-51D Mustang in the South China Sea. He was picked up by a rescue boat within hours.

After the war, Mahurin stayed in the USAAF as it became the independent US Air Force in 1947, and earned a degree in aeronautical engineering from Purdue University while in the service. He and Pat were now raising two children as his career took him into a desk job, working for the Secretary of the Air Force at the Pentagon.

When the Korean War began in June 1950, however, Bud once again yearned for the aerial combat that had so kindled his adrenaline during World War II. The new air war was a jet war. The US Air Force, which shouldered the lion's share of air operations for the joint United Nations Command, was now flying North American F-86 Sabres as its lead air superiority fighter.

Opposing them were Soviet-made Mikoyan Gurevich MiG-15s flown by pilots from North Korea, the People's Republic of China, and the Soviet Union. Although American pilots listened constantly to Russian-language radio traffic between Soviet pilots and Soviet air controllers, the presence in large numbers of the men and aircraft of the Soviet 64th Fighter Aviation Corps was not officially acknowledged by either side for four decades.

Bud Mahurin, now a colonel, arrived in Korea in December 1951 on a 90-day deployment, assigned to fly Sabres with the 51st Fighter-Interceptor Wing (FIW) out of the K-13 air base at Suwon. The 51st was one of two wings in the US Air Force's Far East Air Force (FEAF) to be flying the Sabre in combat. The other was the 4th FIW, which had been operational since October 1950.

At the 51st, Mahurin found himself reunited with Colonel Gabby Gabreski with whom he had flown in the 56th Fighter Group in World War II, and who had ended the war as the highest-scoring USAAF ace in the European Theater. Together, they developed the tactics that would make the 51st effective in air-to-air combat with Soviet and Chinese MiG pilots.

One of the most difficult obstacles faced by American fighter pilots was the rules of engagement imposed by their own United Nations Command that did not permit them to enter Chinese air space during operations over North Korea. The enemy, meanwhile, operated freely on both sides of the border, and their biggest air base in the region – untouchable for US Air Force pilots – was at Antung, within sight of the border. Nevertheless, though they were hamstrung by these rules of engagement, the Sabre pilots prevailed over the MiG-15 pilots in the Korean War by a rate of eight-to-one.

Bud Mahurin scored his first aerial victory in a Sabre on January 6, 1952. He followed up with one each in February and March, plus a shared victory to bring his jet total to 3.5 by the time that his 90-day tour of duty ended in March.

As he was packing his bags to go stateside, Mahurin received a message from Fifth Air Force commander Major General Frank Everest ordering him to unpack them and assume command of the 4th Fighter-Interceptor Group (FIG) of the 4th FIW.

Mahurin now had to tell his wife, who was expecting him imminently after a three-month absence, that "I'm not going to be home for a while."

Mahurin stepped into his new job at the K-14 air base at Kimpo, near Seoul, on March 18, 1952. Using the call sign *Honest John*, which had been established earlier as the appellation for 4th FIG leaders, Mahurin continued to fly as many F-86 missions as possible, though he did not add to his score while flying with his new outfit.

In May 1952, according to Mahurin, the 4th FIG began to find the enemy "markedly reluctant to challenge us in the sky as we patrolled up and down the Yalu." To address this issue, and to "force the Russians to send MiGs our way," Mahurin suggested that the 4th FIG should exploit the bomb-carrying capability built into the Sabre. There were attachment points which could be used to carry bombs, but these were being used instead to attach auxiliary fuel tanks. On May 8, the Sabres of the 4th FIG began ground-attack operations over North Korea carrying one bomb and one fuel tank. If challenged by MiGs, Sabres could respond more effectively than other types of strike aircraft.

On May 13, Mahurin was leading a bombing mission against railroad yards about 65 miles north of the North Korean capital of Pyongyang, and around 150 miles north of Kimpo. After a successful bomb run, all of the Sabres turned for home.

Recalling that "the most dangerous thing a pilot can do on a ground attack mission is to fly back over the target," Mahurin failed to follow his own advice. As he foolishly turned around for his second pass, he saw a truck on a nearby road and decided to go down for a strafing attack.

"I just knew they couldn't lay a gun on me," he wrote in his memoirs. "I had been through my share of bad luck through the years and I was now leading a charmed life. So what the hell, let's get the truck."

Chapter 48

Déjà Vu, Again and Again

That lone Russian-built truck on a North Korean highway on May 13, 1952 was like that Dornier Do 217 hugging the railroad tracks over Eure-et-Loir on March 27, 1944. It was a target too far, and a somber marker of a turning point in the life of Walker Melville Mahurin.

Each time, there were the streaking embers of tracers swarming around his aircraft, and each time, there came the jarring impact of projectiles striking the fuselage and ripping into the engine. In 1944, hemorrhaging motor oil obscured his windshield, and in 1952 it was the boiling cloud of smoke that filled the cockpit.

"This can't be happening to a nice guy like me," he later remembered thinking. "What the hell am I going to do?"

"Hey Ted, I've been hit," he said over his radio to Major Ted Coberly, a member of his flight who was the pilot of the last Sabre he had seen before he attacked the truck. "I think I'm on fire. Can you see me?"

By now, the rest of the flight was out of the area, and were, as Mahurin later recalled bitterly, "halfway back to the officers' club." No one had eyes on the stricken Sabre.

"*Honest John*," Coberly replied. "Switch to emergency channel while I set up air-sea rescue." With that, all radio communications ended abruptly. The systems within the F-86 Sabre with the call sign *Honest John* were falling apart. The General Electric J47-GE-13 turbojet engine was still functioning, but overheating so badly that Mahurin had to throttle back "to keep from burning off the tail."

"What the hell am I going to do?"

What indeed?

It was impossible for the damaged aircraft to make it back to base. Using his ejection seat to escape by parachute was not an option. After his folly of going low to chase the truck, he did not have the altitude. The only viable choice was to head toward the coast, hoping to ditch the stricken jet on the salt flats at the edge of the Yellow Sea.

In 1944, the goal for American pilots who could not make it home was the Spanish border. In 1952, it was the Yellow Sea. If he could ditch in or near the sea, there was a good chance of being rescued. American air-sea rescue helicopters and fixed wing aircraft were the Westland Lysanders of the Korean War, and they were skilled and practiced in the art of saving pilots who went down offshore.

Mahurin kept the Sabre aloft and pointed it west, racing down the valley of the Chongchon River, watching the tops of mountains that rose above him. He wished that he had more altitude, but was glad for what he had.

He guessed that he was about 60 miles from open water. The F-86E variant of the Sabre, which Mahurin flew, had a stall speed of 123mph and a top speed of 679mph at sea level. Even if he had throttled back roughly to the midpoint between the two, he had at least ten minutes to get to a place where rescue was a reasonable hope.

On his way down the Chongchon Valley, he had to enter the heavily defended air space above the cities of Anju and Sinanju. He found these skies awash with tracers and felt the jolt of antiaircraft rounds hitting his fuselage. As he passed through the hailstorm over Sinanju, his fire warning light came on and he felt the Sabre losing altitude.

He saw rice paddies ahead and glimpsed the sea in the distance. As his nose pitched up, he gritted his teeth for the impact. His right wing clipped a telephone pole and suddenly he felt the fuselage hit the ground – probably at around stall speed, but frighteningly fast. As the muddy surface absorbed the impact, the Sabre's wings sheared off and the fuselage began to corkscrew, rolling and tumbling through the rice paddies.

Bud Mahurin came to a stop with his cockpit upside down. After what had just happened, he had no reason to still be alive. But he was.

With great difficulty, he extricated himself from the cockpit and looked around. It was déjà vu all over again, and as he had eight years ago when he was last a stranger in a strange land, he ran for his life. He had suffered a broken arm, but at least his legs still worked.

He ran toward the Yellow Sea, visible in the distance, hoping to buy time for the rescue helicopter that he assumed would be coming for him.

American pilots had been successfully recovered from the Chongchon Delta before, and they could be again.

For a moment, the only sounds were the ringing in his ears and the sloppy sucking sound of his footsteps in the mud. Then he heard voices in the distance. They were coming closer.

Sooner than he had hoped, he found himself surrounded by North Korean farm workers. He smiled and tried not to appear threatening. They looked at him curiously and asked if he was a "Russki." In 1944, Mahurin had been the one to pick the moment of his first contact with a civilian. In 1952, the moment picked him.

In 1944, he had not seen a German soldier for four days, and then at a safe distance. In 1952, two armed, uniformed men reached him within minutes. One wore the uniform of North Korea, the other that of the Chinese People's Volunteer Army (PVA), the designation under which units of the China's regular army, the People's Liberation Army (PLA), operated in Korea. The twosome represented the dual authorities of which he was about to become a pawn.

In the sky there were no helicopters. He later learned that rescue efforts had been concentrated inland, near where he had reported being hit. The course of Bud Mahurin's entire life had changed.

For his first few hours in North Korea, Bud Mahurin was an object of curiosity. He was taken to a radio shack and questioned by several PVA and North Korean officers in an uncoordinated way – as though they didn't know quite what to do with him. He was given some civilian clothes and was able to change out of his wet flying suit. After dark, he was hauled back to the crash site so that they could extract the gunsight from his Sabre.

Over the next several days, he got his broken arm set, and was taken to a series of military camps, where he continued to be grilled. He worried about what his family had been told, and he worried about what would happen to him next. Those worries would be with him every day for a year and a half. When he was told that his family did not know where he was, it was one of the few bits of accurate information that he received.

The next several weeks melted one into the other, punctuated by continued interrogation, mainly by Chinese officers with varying degrees of English fluency. They wanted to know about radio frequencies and radar, and were especially interested in contrails left at high altitude by American jets.

He had expected to be put into a POW camp along with other Americans, but this never happened. Because of his rank as a colonel, he was considered to be a prisoner with valuable information that required extraction by extreme measures. As the months passed, the questioning devolved into a long dark night of psychological and physical torture. Mahurin was moved several times, and his experiences included 45 days of sensory deprivation underground in a coal mine.

Christmas came and went – uncelebrated – and 1952 faded into 1953. The winter temperatures descended as low as minus 50 Fahrenheit, and he started to lose circulation in his legs. A month of solitary confinement alternated with long periods where he was harangued for hours every day. He spent 33 days seated on a stool.

It got so bad that he slashed his wrists with a small piece of broken knife blade that he had salvaged while sharpening a pencil to answer written questions. His captors found him nearly dead from blood loss, but revived him.

Almost from the beginning of his ordeal, the Chinese had demanded that Mahurin confess to "crimes against the people of the world," without elucidating specifics. Finally, several months in, they decided to use the ploy that the US Air Force had been conducting "germ warfare" against North Korea. He was told repeatedly that if he did not confess, he would be killed.

As early as 1951, the Chinese had told the world that outbreaks of cholera, smallpox, and even bubonic plague that were occurring in North Korea were caused by deliberate American action, claiming that it was linked to the World War II-era Japanese Unit 731 biological and chemical weapons research program. This theory, proclaimed as fact, was widely repeated in Soviet bloc media, and even discussed in the West.

Given sanitary conditions as they existed at the time in North Korea, a natural occurrence of these diseases was certainly probable, but admitting this would have been an embarrassment, so external forces had to be blamed. The United States and the United Nations Command issued denials. The UN Security Council tried to get the International Red Cross to investigate, but the Soviet Union vetoed this plan.

By the time that Mahurin was in their clutches, the North Koreans and Chinese had decided that F-86s under his command were among those aircraft that had carried disease-laden insects in their external fuel tanks. He argued that the fuel tanks contained fuel, adding that insects could not survive at F-86 operational altitudes.

As time went on, the pendulum of psychological torture inflicted upon Mahurin swung back and forth between sadistic bad cops and sympathetic good cops, but the message was the same – a signed confession or a bullet in the head. Even the good cop who paid him regular visits after April 1953 assured him that because the Chinese had never declared him as a POW, he was not subject to the Geneva Convention. This man, whom Mahurin called "Happy Hal," said that he could be kept indefinitely and no one in the outside world would ever know.

In June 1953, Mahurin finally settled on a strategy. He would write a confession, but fill it with such preposterous inaccuracies that anyone in the Air Force who read it would recognize it as pure fiction. He also decided to drag out the process for as long as possible. He finally finished the "confession" on August 10, not knowing that the armistice concluding all hostilities in the Korean War had been signed two weeks earlier on July 27.

Mahurin remained in custody until September 3, when he was finally allowed out of his cell. In turn, he was allowed to speak freely with a pair of fellow American prisoners, his first such contact with American servicemen in 16 months. It turned out that both Marine Colonel Frank Schwable and Air Force Colonel Andy Evans had also been coerced into signing confessions.

Evans was a 1941 West Point graduate and a six-victory ace who flew with the 357th Fighter Group in World War II. At the time he was shot down, he was flying F-84 Thunderjets as deputy commander of the 58th Fighter-Bomber Wing. Of the three men, Evans, who had been in captivity for just six months, was in the worst shape. Mahurin weighed barely 100 pounds, but was in generally good health. Evans had lost about half his body weight and was down to 88 pounds. He was noticeably emaciated and haggard in appearance.

Their Chinese jailers gave the three men clean uniforms and told them that they were to be released. However, in one last surreal act, the Chinese turned them over to the North Koreans, who sat the "confessed criminals" down before a tribunal.

The Americans feared now that they would never be released, but after being rebuked loud and long by a panel consisting of three North Korean officers, they were told that they were being given leniency for their crimes and were promptly loaded into the back of a dump truck.

Chapter 49

A Haunted Life

On September 6, 1953, after a grueling three-day drive, the truck carrying Bud Mahurin, Andy Evans, and Frank Schwable reached the compound at Panmunjom, where the armistice had been signed in July. They blinked with disbelief as they began seeing American troops and the American flag flying. Suddenly, Mahurin's 16 months of mostly solitary confinement ended abruptly and he found himself surrounded by a swirling crowd of American service personnel and American reporters.

They had all known he was coming. Mahurin was greeted by Brigadier General Ed Underhill, vice commander of the Fifth Air Force, and he recognized other faces in the crowd. The reporters piled on the World War II ace who had commanded a fighter wing before he disappeared, badgering him with trivial questions about how he felt.

Almost immediately after reaching the American controlled area, the man who had spoken to almost no one but Chinese interrogators for more than a year found himself seated next to Andy Evans at the head table in front of 350 reporters and newsreel cameramen. Schwable did not appear.

"I was not quite prepared for what happened," Mahurin wrote in his memoirs in a comment that was an understatement most extreme. Where he intended candor and transparency in his personal revelations at the press conference, his words displayed human frailties that did not fit his public image as a World War II hero.

"I was so anxious to get the word across and stop the damage done by the false confessions that I couldn't think of anything else," he later explained. No one in the outside world had yet heard about these confessions, so he might have done well to direct media attention more positively – on how glad he was to be free, for example.

In retrospect, the Air Force should have had handlers on hand to debrief and counsel both Mahurin and Evans, instead of scheduling a press conference before the men had even had a chance to take a shower! The media narrative spun out of control. An Associated Press bulletin issued immediately after the September 6 press conference reported that "two Air Force colonels with brilliant records said today they had broken under relentless communist mental torture and made false statements that they had dropped germ bombs on North Korea."

The media narrative of Mahurin's release, which might have centered on a returning hero who survived captivity, instead focused on his "being broken under torture." In turn, the Air Force compounded the negative spin. Having failed to allow him to decompress on his first day out of North Korea, they next overcompensated by returning him to the States on a slow boat ocean voyage rather than flying him home. For 16 days, Mahurin was at sea and unable to explain his actions and address the growing controversy. *En route* home, he came to realize how ill prepared the Air Force really was. "Little by little it dawned on me that the United States had not, after all, developed a positive course of counter propaganda," he reflected in his memoirs. Indeed, neither were they were prepared for the type of cunning psychological trauma induced by the Chinese inquisitors, nor did the press and public have any comprehension of the depth of the cruelty they had endured.

The deliberate fallacies that Mahurin had put into his "confession" made it obviously false, but to the layman, these were too technical. It was the mere fact that he had "confessed." US Senator Richard Russell, a Democrat from Georgia and the ranking member of the Senate Armed Services Committee, told Secretary of Defense Charles Wilson that he thought Mahurin and other "signers of false confessions should be immediately separated from the services under conditions other than honorable."

The Air Force officers who knew him, many of whom were now in command leadership positions, greeted him as a returning colleague, and job offers were forthcoming. Mahurin accepted a desk job from his friend Brigadier General Don Hutchison, commander of the 27th Air Division of the Western Air Defense Force at Norton AFB in California.

However, farther up the chain of command, his September 6 revelations and the fact that he had put biological warfare squarely on the agenda made him an embarrassment. The man who had described himself at a "hot potato" in 1944 was back in that role. Déjà vu – again.

He was investigated by the Air Force Office of Special Investigations and told them his whole story. In April 1954, he was called before an AFR 36-2 Board (Officer Personnel Administrative Discharge Procedures), where he related his whole story yet again. It was another strange déjà vu for the man who had been through the interrogations by the Chinese.

He passed his inquisitions, and the Air Force seemed satisfied, though the career of Colonel Walker Mahurin had topped out.

In 1956, he left the service to take a job as Director of Military Relations at Northrop Aircraft in Hawthorne, California. At first, things went well. The Mahurin family adapted to civilian life – until they didn't. The money, although a third better than his Air Force salary, was just not enough. At work, he discovered that "without realizing it, I was not fitting into industry." In his memoirs, he admitted, without naming names, that he was asked to leave.

Eventually, he landed a job selling electronic equipment, but after about two and a half years, he was hired by McDonnell Aircraft of St Louis to set up a small West Coast office. It was an auspicious moment in aerospace history because it was the threshold of the space program and McDonnell was the prime contractor for the Mercury and Gemini spacecraft.

The renounced confession still wore heavily on Mahurin's mind. It cast a dark shadow over his autobiography, entitled *Honest John*, which was published in 1962. "This story has been difficult for me to tell," he wrote on the first page. "I decided to tell the whole story as plainly, simply and truthfully as I could remember it... the title *Honest John* has a double meaning."

He went on to say that he would not have done things differently in his life "with one exception. Should events unfold so that I face capture by the same enemy [Communist China], I will never let myself be captured alive."

Mahurin's ensuing years were filled with changes. He left McDonnell, and by 1967, he was head of the Space and Information Systems Division of North American Aviation. His marriage to Pat Sweet ended in divorce, and he remarried. He and Joan Gill Mahurin stayed together until his death.

Meanwhile, the career of Gerald "Jerry" Johnson, Mahurin's fellow 56th Fighter Group ace who was shot down on the same day in 1944, had taken different turns. He had languished in a German stalag while Mahurin was fighting in the Pacific. Like Mahurin, he remained in the postwar US Air Force, but he did not go to Korea.

Johnson became part of the Strategic Air Command and led the 305th Bomb Wing as it was setting speed records in the 1960s with the B-58

Hustler supersonic bomber. He rose to the rank of lieutenant general and commanded the Eighth Air Force during Operation *Linebacker II*, the strategic air offensive against North Vietnam in 1972.

Andy Evans also remained in the Air Force, flew F-4 Phantoms over Vietnam, and retired as a major general. He died in 2001. Johnson and Mahurin passed away two years apart, in 2008 and 2010 respectively. All three men were interred at Arlington National Cemetery.

The germ warfare tales that so haunted Bud Mahurin long ago faded from conventional memory, though they are still part of the Chinese and North Korean narrative of the Korean War, and they do pop up once in a while on obscure conspiracy theory websites.

PART NINE

BETRAYAL AND TRIUMPH

Chapter 50

Dobie's Boys

Through 1942 and 1943, the Germans and their collaborators in Belgium, as in other occupied countries, had been working to develop means and methods to infiltrate and disrupt the escape networks. By 1944, they had finally managed to spin an unseen spider web of deception and betrayal across the city of Brussels.

Airmen on the run in Belgium would soon learn the hard way of a unique snare fashioned by their enemies to disrupt paths which had successfully carried earlier evaders to freedom.

On Friday, February 4, 1944, the Eighth Air Force launched 373 heavy bombers against the great German rail hub at Frankfurt am Main, while another 260 bombers roamed across the Reich picking off targets of opportunity. As part of the Frankfurt strike, the B-17 Flying Fortress known as *Dobie*, assigned to the 349th Bomb Squadron, 100th Bomb Group, lifted off from Thorpe Abbots in Norfolk at 6:00am with 2nd Lieutenant John William "Bud" Brown at the controls and 2nd Lieutenant Albert Fitzpatrick in the right seat.

Over Frankfurt, they took a brutal mauling from German flak, and as they turned for home, Brown and Fitzpatrick had to struggle to stay with the rest of the squadron. Gradually they fell behind, and by the time they reached Belgian air space, *Dobie* was alone. Three Focke-Wulf Fw 190 interceptors rose to meet them and the Fortress's number one engine was blown to bits. When the Focke-Wulfs knocked out two more engines, Brown had no choice but to sound the bail-out alarm.

Bud Brown's eleventh mission came to an end at around 1:30pm on that day as he was the last out of the stricken Fortress. Falling from 8,000 feet, he struggled with the ripcord, imagining that his life was also about to end.

Finally, after free falling for more than a mile through the icy air, his parachute blossomed and he looked down at the snow-covered fields near Kasterlee, Belgium, five miles south of the city of Turnhout. As he descended, he watched *Dobie* crash in a ball of fire not far away.

All but one of *Dobie*'s crew managed to successfully escape the bomber. One of the gunners, Staff Sergeant William Kemp, was found near the crash site, where he'd been thrown on impact. He had survived, but was badly injured and passed away before he could be taken to a hospital. It had been his first mission. Kemp was one of five of gunners aboard *Dobie* that day who were not part of her regular crew, but last minute fill-ins substituting for men who had been sick that day.

Because this slice of Belgium lay beneath the aerial corridor through which the American bombers generally flew, it was air space in which the Luftwaffe interceptors lurked in force for prey. At the same time, it was a corridor beneath which members of Belgium's underground also lay in wait to lend helping hands. Brown was picked up almost immediately and hustled off to a safe house.

Dobie's navigator, 2nd Lieutenant Theodore "Ted" Kleinman, landed some distance away. He had been injured by shrapnel in his right arm, but this did not impede his movements. A group of Belgians took him in at around 3:15pm.

Others of "*Dobie*'s Boys" were not so lucky. Kemp was the only one to die that day, but copilot Fitzpatrick broke his leg when he landed, and was helpless to escape when the Germans made a beeline for his parachute.

Others were likewise swept up in an efficient German dragnet. Among the crew, only Brown and Kleinman got away, escaping in separate directions. The two 24-year-olds with home addresses just half a mile apart in Eugene, Oregon would not see one another again for seven months.

That night, Kleinman laid his head at the home of Franz Verstraaten in Turnhout, where he would remain until March 27. Brown, meanwhile, spent the night near Kasterlee, and set out on his own on Saturday, planning to head for Brussels to make contact with Comet Line operatives.

At around 10:00am, a man on a bicycle appeared. He slowed as he stared at Brown, looking him over curiously. At last, he asked whether Brown was an American, though this was pretty evident by the looks of Brown's uniform.

When the American had confirmed the obvious, the man led him a short distance to the tiny hamlet of Sint-Josef-Olen, and introduced him to Louis Govers and Louis Mertens, who gave him a change of clothes and put him up for the night. They both spoke English, and were associated with the underground Belgian White Brigade.

On Sunday morning, with Brown now dressed in less conspicuous civilian attire, his new friends drove him about 40 miles south to a White Brigade safe house of Philippe Vossels at 85 Chaussée de Gand in the Brussels suburb of Molenbeek, where Brown would spend the next four weeks. During that time, he recalled meeting "a great many black market people," an English-speaking man who "talked about his brother in New York," and "a man who claimed to be the head of the Belgian Red Cross." This man was interested in casualty information, but Brown had little to say since he'd had no contact with the other *Dobie* crewmen since the crash.

Around March 14, Bud Brown was abruptly told to go to a cafe and await further instructions. As he wrote in his escape and evasion report, Brown "went to the cafe, stayed about seven hours, and was picked up by a strange guide from the center of the city."[36]

The "strange guide" took him to Chaussée Romaine on the north side of Brussels, after which he passed through several other safe houses. While at the home of Madame Amélie Guyaux, he was visited by a brother and sister calling themselves "Henri and Simone," who were possibly Henri Maca and his sister Marie Maca of the Comet Line organization.

After being burned so often by Gestapo double agents, Henri began asking a lot of questions to establish whether Brown was a genuine American airman. They hit a stumbling block when Bud Brown could not name all the members of *Dobie*'s crew. This was understandable, because five of them were substitutes who stepped in the morning of the mission. Brown had never flown with them before. Henri excused himself and did not reappear for three weeks.

When Henri finally reconnected with Brown on April 8, he introduced him to 23-year-old 1st Lieutenant Bill Grosvenor of Colfax, Iowa. Having flown with the 61st Fighter Squadron, 56th Fighter Group – Colonel Hub Zemke's famous Wolf Pack – Grosvenor had been in Belgium since November 30, 1943, when his prop had hit a telephone pole while he was strafing a train near Lippelo, about 20 miles north of Brussels. He had managed to bail out of his P-47, named *Charming Ellen* after his fiancée, at an altitude of barely 150 feet. In a terse summary in his escape and evasion report, Grosvenor replied to the question that asked about the "nature and extent of damage" to his aircraft by writing simply, "Propeller destroyed. Engine stopped."[37]

With Grosvenor having confirmed that Brown was an authentic American airman, Henri handed both of them off to one of his men, Marcel van Buckenhout, aka "Marcus," at a three-story brick townhouse at 226 Boulevard Emile Bockstael. A close associate of Anne Brusselmans, the famous organizer of safe houses, van Buckenhout worked with her on a number of projects. One of these involved "liberating" a large stock of Belgian flour that had been confiscated by the Germans. This was then being distributed to safe houses all over town. As he told Anne at the time, "we are only taking back what was stolen from us in the first place."

Van Buckenhout moved Brown and Grosvenor from house to house numerous times over the coming weeks. On May 3, he delivered them for a four-week stay to the safe house at 147 Avenue du Cimetière de Bruxelles in the suburb of Evere. It was run by Madame Jeanne Frix-Claes, an enterprising widow who ran a cafe and flower shop. This being near the cemetery, Madame Claes had a side job trading in tombstones.

In early June, van Buckenhout moved Brown and Grosvenor across town to the apartment of Jean van den Eede and Madeleine "Midge" Fontaine in an art deco building at 188 Avenue Houba de Stooper. It was upstairs from the Café La Terrasse, which today operates as Brasserie de l'Expo. On June 6, three days after the move, news came of the long-awaited Allied invasion of Normandy. With the Allies now on the ground in occupied Europe, Brown and Grosvenor were anxious to hear the daily updates on the BBC, so they asked van Buckenhout to move them *back* to Madame Claes's house as she had a radio.

It was a bad decision.

At 6:00am on June 20, there was a banging on Madame Claes's front door. In burst two Germans with the insignia on their uniforms of the Geheime Feldpolizei (GFP), the secret police arm of the Abwehr, German military intelligence.

She managed to shout a warning, but it was too late.

Brown recalled in his escape and evasion report that he and Grosvenor "tried first to get out a bedroom window, then went on the roof from an attic window. A rifle bead was drawn upon [us]."

As it turned out, the German raid was just a fluke. "The Germans had apparently not come searching for evaders," Brown reported. "Madame Claes thought that her sister-in-law, with whom she did not get along very well, had turned her in for putting flowers on American graves in the cemetery."

Chapter 51

A Valuable Asset

For nearly two months, while Bud Brown was being shuffled around Brussels, Ted Kleinman, *Dobie*'s navigator, had remained at Franz Verstraaten's house in Turnhout, only five miles from where his parachute had landed. As he recalled in his escape and evasion report, E&E No.2101, Kleinman was visited during his time at Verstraaten's by a man known only as Jacques, who was a member of the Belgian underground. He may have been the same "Red Cross man" whom Bud Brown met in February, because Kleinman reported that he was compiling "casualty information." It was from him that Kleinman learned about Bill Kemp having been fatally injured in the crash. Because Kemp was one of the substitutes flying on that mission, Kleinman did not even know him.

At last, on March 27, it was Kleinman's turn to move on. Verstraaten's wife took him to Brussels by train. Here after several nights in safe houses, the American was told that he was soon going to Liège, about 80 miles to the east, and then on to Spain via the Comet Line.

However, on April 8, while Kleinman was staying with a man named Victor and his wife at their Brussels apartment, a crisis suddenly arose. Victor's wife walked in, telling Kleinman that her husband had just been picked up by the police on a minor charge apparently unrelated to underground activities. She told Kleinman that he was now in danger, and that he should wait while she contacted a man named Max Varley of the White Brigade who could accelerate Kleinman's exit to Liège.

This plan was also about to go sideways.

While she was talking to Varley and his wife at a nearby cafe, the Belgian police swooped in to arrest a man from a *different* underground organization who was also coincidentally named Victor. By accident, the wife of the *first* Victor was pointed out as "Victor's wife." Thinking that she was married to the *second* Victor whom they had just detained, the police arrested her as well!

Amid the confusion, the Varleys slipped away and raced to the apartment to collect the fugitive American. Kleinman was stashed at a safe house in Molenbeek until May 1, when he was loaded into the back of a truck headed for Liège.

It is unclear what fate befell either of the Victors, or indeed the first Victor's wife.

For more a month and a half, Kleinman bided his time at his Liège safe house, waiting for word on when he might be going to leave for Spain. When the Allies invaded Normandy on June 6, 1944, and underground groups throughout France and Belgium refocused their attention on direct action, the process of helping evaders to escape slowed.

In the meantime, Kleinman met a man named Edgard Delbecq, who "seemed to be engaged in sabotage work." As he wrote in his escape and evasion report, this greatly interested Kleinman, who "wanted to do sabotage work also, but was not permitted to." Evaders were discouraged from activities that could get them shot on sight as spies or saboteurs – but he would soon have his chance to take an active role in the underground.

On June 16, Kleinman moved again – not toward Spain, but about 100 miles west to the small town of Basècles near the French border. In Basècles, Ted Kleinman's safe house was the home of Carlos Bernard and his wife, a two-story brick building on the edge of town. Of this situation, he wrote that the "house was near the wireless for the [local underground] group, which was located on top of a kiln in a nearby quarry. I offered to serve as radio operator and was accepted."

After a few days, however, Kleinman "became a little uneasy about the job." As he explained, this was because he was told to go to the kiln at prescribed times, and "such regularity was likely to be noticed."

He finally convinced the chief of the underground group, Achille Battiste, to at least relocate the wireless set to a less conspicuous place. Three days after they moved it, a German patrol discovered the spot at the kiln where it had been.

As July turned to August, Ted Kleinman was still in Basècles, plying his new trade as a radio man for the Belgian underground. His presence of mind to suggest moving the radio site just ahead of the German raid made him something of a local hero. It certainly cemented Kleinman's value in the eyes of the Belgian underground.

He also got the attention of Fernand Barbaix, a powder merchant who did business with the quarry at Basècles, and who was also an underground chief at Lessines, about 20 miles to the north. He sought Kleinman's counsel, and the two became confidants, regularly comparing notes on underground activities. Barbaix frequently took Kleinman's advice on operational matters.

Over the course of his two months in Basècles, Kleinman made it clear that he was still anxious to get out of occupied Europe and get back to England. Finally, "instructions came through" that the next step in Kleinman's odyssey had been arranged. He was no longer going to Spain as earlier briefed, but was now told that he would "go to Brussels and on to Switzerland using a Belgian passport somehow secured for a Swedish alien."

It was about August 25 when Ted Kleinman returned to Brussels, where he was picked up in a car and driven to the townhouse at 16 Rue Forestière. He did not know that he had just stepped into a spider's web.

Chapter 52

Jake and *Marty*

On Monday, May 22, 1944, as Ted Kleinman was biding his time in Liège, he heard the thunder in the sky of low-flying American fighter-bombers. The Eighth Air Force had dispatched 130 P-47 Thunderbolts to attack bridges and other targets of opportunity in the area. The Thunderbolts had a successful day. A great deal of infrastructure that served the German army was damaged or destroyed, and all of the aircraft returned to base – except one. This was the P-47 from the 351st Fighter Squadron, 353rd Fighter Group out of Raydon in Suffolk that was piloted by 1st Lieutenant Jack Terzian. He had named her *Marty*, after his girlfriend, Martha Tait, who was waiting for him back in Manhasset on New York's Long Island.

Terzian, who went by the name "Jake," had been down low when he took a barrage of ground fire that fatally damaged *Marty*. He rode her in, cracking up in a field and injuring his ankle in the process.

This was not the first time that Jake Terzian had lost a P-47 named *Marty*. Back on April 9, the 353rd had been flying an escort mission with Eighth Air Force bombers on a deep penetration mission into eastern Germany. On the way back, Terzian had run out of fuel and had to bail out over the North Sea. Fortunately, an Allied air-sea rescue aircraft had plucked him out of the frigid waters that time.

Today, in the rolling hills of Belgium, there would be no rescue. Jake Terzian was on his own.

The road that led him to this turn in his life had begun almost 25 years earlier, in a place far closer to Belgium than Long Island. In 1919, Jake had been born Kegham Terzian in Adana, Turkey, the third child of Paul and Sirouhi Terzian. Turkey's vast Ottoman Empire had been imploding since the turn of the century, and was going through convulsions of ethnic and class violence. Armenians like the Terzian family had lived in Adana for generations, but their Ottoman Turk government had turned on them. After the Adana Massacre of 1909 and the seizure of Armenian property in 1923, life had become untenable. The Terzians left for America in 1924.

When the United States entered World War II in December 1941, Jake had been in the USAAF for nine months, and he was assigned to the 351st Fighter Squadron in March 1943. His air-to-air combat had been limited. His only successful duel with the Luftwaffe had been a shared victory over a Focke-Wulf Fw 190 on March 2, 1944, although he was credited with aiding in the destruction of several German aircraft on the ground during March.

As he crawled out of the cockpit of the second *Marty* on May 22, his thoughts were on how a man who could barely walk would get away. Fortunately, Belgian civilians were nearby. In his escape and evasion report, E&E No.1789, Terzian credits a man he called "LeClerc" from the nearby town of Burst as being the first on the scene to help.

Much more detail about those who came to his aid is provided by Lancelot van de Putte, who researched wartime resistance activities in the area for a 2008 dissertation for his degree from the University of Ghent in Belgium. From this, we know that Terzian was aided by 22-year-old Florent de Clercq and his older sister, Lucienne Elza de Clercq – and many others. First on the scene of *Marty*'s crash landing were Norbert van Herrweghe and Cyrillius Eloot, both members of the Organisation Militaire Belge de Résistance (Belgian Military Resistance Organization). They took him to the home of Henri van Boven in nearby Hillegem.

After several days, Florent arrived with Roger van Boxtael, a White Brigade operative, who transported the American to the home of de Clercq's parents, where Terzian's ankle was treated by a doctor named Willy Bernard. At some point around the first of June, Florent drove Terzian at least part of the way to Brussels. Here he was taken in by Charles Leman of the communist Front de l'Indépendance, and later by Guillaume "Willy" De Keyser of Groupe Zero, a White Brigade affiliate.

In the wee hours of Monday, May 29, while Jake Terzian was staying with Henri van Boven in Hillegem, he awakened to the rumbling in the sky of four

Pratt & Whitney R-1830 Twin Wasp engines. They belonged to a B-24D Liberator known as *C for Charlie*, flying that night on a secret mission.

With two starboard engines shot up and the wing tanks on fire, 1st Lieutenant Henry "Hank" Wolcott ordered the crew to abandon ship at an altitude of about 6,000 feet. The bomber continued in a northwesterly direction, crashing near Ashage, about six miles from Ninove.

The crash site was only about a mile from where Jake Terzian was recovering from his injured ankle, and he no doubt heard the crash. Terzian did not know it yet, but nine weeks later, he would meet members of the crew under very tumultuous circumstances.

Chapter 53

Running Through the Woods

The secret mission of Hank Wolcott's *C for Charlie* that night was part of a clandestine operation known as *Carpetbagger*. As the men and women of the underground organizations throughout occupied Europe worked to aid the escape and evasion of Eighth Air Force airmen, the Eighth was returning the favor with airdrops of weapons and materiel. Such operations had been ongoing since 1940 by the British SOE in cooperation with the Royal Air Force. Now, General "Wild Bill" Donovan's American Office of Strategic Services (OSS) had gotten into the same act in cooperation with the Eighth.

Specifically, the Eighth contributed the 482nd Bomb Group, containing the 35th and 406th Bomb Squadrons. The 482nd was withdrawn from combat, given a provisional designation as the 801st Bomb Group, and earmarked for *Carpetbagger* airdrop missions.

At around 11:00pm on May 28, at Harrington in Northamptonshire, an isolated location befitting covert activities, Hank Wolcott took the controls beneath a quarter moon – bright enough to be helpful for the mission at hand, but not so bright as to be helpful to German night fighters lurking over Belgium. In the right seat next to Wolcott was 1st Lieutenant Robert Auda, his copilot.

In the bombardier's position in the nose was 2nd Lieutenant Wallis Cozzens, though the "hands-on" for the dropping the payload of supplies for the resistance would be the hands of top turret gunner Tech Sergeant Dirvin Deihl – pushing the payload out manually. *C for Charlie*'s navigator was 1st Lieutenant William Ryckman, but tonight he had an understudy. A novice at nocturnal navigating for *Carpetbagger* missions, 2nd Lieutenant Carmen Vozzella was along to learn the ropes.

In the back of the aircraft, Tech Sergeant Dale Loucks was the radio operator, while Staff Sergeant Frederick Tuttle manned the waist gun position and Staff Sergeant Richard Hawkins was in the tail turret.

At last, they were cleared for takeoff, and Wolcott pushed forward the four throttle levers. By midnight, the aircraft was over the English Channel and headed toward its drop zone south of Brussels. At about 2:30am on Monday morning, as they circled this drop zone, they received no radio signal from the people on the ground. Wolcott aborted the mission and turned toward home.

As the Liberator was over Ninove, about 15 miles west of Brussels, it came under fire from the cannon of a Messerschmitt Bf 110 night fighter piloted by Hauptmann Josef Krahforst. The German ace was flying with the Luftwaffe night fighter wing Nachtjagdgeschwader 4 (NJG 4) out of Florennes, Belgium, and *C for Charlie* would be one of his 11 kills.

As the big aircraft went down near Ashage, a mile from where Jake Terzian was, nine men escaped, though only eight parachutes blossomed. Richard Hawkins was killed as he hit the ground near the crash site. In their book *'40-'45 Above the Schelde, Dender and Durme*, Cynrik de Decker and Jean-Louis Roba quoted André de Rijck, who witnessed the crash. "I went with a friend to look at the wreck," he recalled. "Next to the aircraft was the body of a crew member. We then continued to look for other crew members in the surrounding fields, but found nothing."

That night, Hawkins was taken to the tiny chapel of Sint-Nicolas in the nearby village of Aaigem, just as German soldiers arrived. Their officer stripped the rings off Hawkins's fingers and ordered his body to be buried immediately.

"The Germans had not given permission to organize a church service," De Rijck griped. "The priest then held a ceremony at the grave. There were four of us standing around." Among them was Georges de Cooman, who was one of those who had helped wrap Hawkins in his parachute. Hawkins was survived by his wife of eight months, Virginia Kennedy Hawkins, of Marion, Ohio.

Deihl, Tuttle, and Vozzella landed within sight of one another, were safely picked up by the underground, and were taken to the home of Roger Schollaert in Sint-Lievens-Esse, where they were joined by Dale Loucks.

In his escape and evasion report, E&E No.1877, Hank Wolcott, the pilot of *C for Charlie*, gave no information about his first days in Belgium, but he is mentioned in the account written by 2nd Lieutenant Al Sanders of the 486th Bomb Group in his escape and evasion report, E&E No.1595. These men – two B-24 pilots who had been shot down half a day apart – met a few days later at the farm of Caban Albert near Nederhasselt.

Henry Walbridge Wolcott III, aged 25, from Royal Oak, Michigan, had been a chemistry student when he enlisted in the USAAF in early 1942. Alfred M. L. "Smokey Al" Sanders from Kentwood, Louisiana, who grew up running barefoot through the piney woods, had been a track star at Louisiana State University. He had a tiger painted on his B-24 and named the aircraft *Mike, the Spirit of LSU*, after his school's mascot. When he enlisted in 1942, Sanders had recently graduated and just married his girlfriend, Mildred "Millie" Allen.

Sanders and *Mike* had flown 11 missions with the 832nd Bomb Squadron, 486th Bomb Group, when they headed for the Wintershall refinery in Lützkendorf, Germany on May 28. Over the target, antiaircraft fire was intense, and the lead bomber was shot out of the sky. Confusion reigned as the deputy group commander took over and did not order the bomb release. By this time, *Mike* had been hit and had lost an engine, so Sanders ordered bombardier Daniel O'Connell to jettison their bombs into the inferno which the refinery had become, thanks to earlier waves of bombers. Exiting the target area, Sanders struggled with *Mike* for 350 miles, but 20 miles south of Brussels, he had to order the crew to abandon ship.

Sanders broke his ankle when his parachute brought him down hard, but was quickly picked up by a Belgian nobleman named Melchior Deseau who drove him away in his 1940 Ford station wagon.

Taken to a place where he was hidden in the back of a fish truck, Sanders was given a change of civilian clothes, including a pair of high-topped shoes that supported his ankle. He passed through a series of safe houses and farmyards over the next few days, not knowing that Millie had given birth to their son two days after he was shot down – and that she had already received the dreaded telegram telling her that the boy's father was missing in action.

Around the first of June, soon after Sanders and Wolcott met at Albert's farm, they were joined by three Russian soldiers in German uniforms. This strange circumstance was explained by their having been commandeered into the Wehrmacht after being captured on the Eastern Front – but they had since deserted. Fortunately, one of them was a veterinarian, and he set Sanders's ankle.

The Russians and Americans barely had a chance to size up one another when an energetic 20-year-old Belgian chemistry student named Alex arrived, identifying himself as the "chief" of one of the many underground organizations operating in the area. He added that they would soon be joined by more "comrades." These turned out to be 15 more Russians.

These Russians and Americans comprised a band of stepbrothers thrown together by circumstance on the eve of the Allied invasion of France on June 6, and who were about to share harrowing adventures. As the Allied troops fought their way ashore in Normandy, they found themselves 250 miles to the northeast, spending their days helping Alex build land mines and booby traps with which the underground would harass the Germans.

One day, their monotony was broken when a teenage girl showed up at the farm to breathlessly warn of a German patrol nearby. They had already killed a man while searching a farm for Allied airmen. It was time to run. Alex and the others piled into trucks and were driven ten miles south to Bierghes, where they took refuge with a man named Georges Tondeur.

On June 18, the Germans arrived at Tondeur's farmhouse and proceeded to tear the place apart, smashing furniture while searching for the evaders, who managed to hide under the floorboards without being seen. Not so lucky, Tondeur and his farmhands were all arrested and hauled away. When they were sure that the coast was clear, the "stepbrothers" crawled out, grabbed one of Tondeur's trucks and drove south to another farm near Rebecq that Alex knew about.

After four days here, when they received word of *another* impending German raid, some White Brigade operatives grabbed Wolcott and Sanders and hustled them off to the village in Trop, where they spent the night in the hilltop *château* of a steel mill owner drinking Heidsieck champagne. It was a curious contrast to hiding under floorboards with a platoon of Russians.

Around July 1, the Americans were taken to the Victorian *château* of a couple named Rowart, where Sanders became a fast friend of the household's Scottish terrier. Throughout the war, the Rowarts had sheltered many people, from evading airmen to Jews escaping from Germany and beyond.

———

On Thursday, August 10, Melchior Deseau reappeared with a man whom Walcott identified as Claud, "the chief of partisans in Rebecq." The two men proceeded to outline a plan by which Claud would drive Wolcott and Sanders "to Switzerland tomorrow." When Friday came, Deseau now told the Americans that "another car would come to take them to Brussels."

Soon after Deseau drove away, the other car came. Sanders vividly described the driver as "a very dark, pock-marked man of 40 years whose jaws were sunken as though he had no teeth and who wore a black cloth over the thumb of his right hand."

In Brussels, the man drove Wolcott and Sanders to the house at 16 Rue Forestière in the Anderlecht district. Unbeknownst to them, this was one of the most dangerous addresses in Brussels.

Chapter 54

Into a World of Intrigue

Bill Ryckman and Wallis Cozzens were together when they were found by Belgian resistance people after *C for Charlie* went down on May 29. They were taken to the home of Remi Diependaele in Grotenberge, about four miles west of the crash site. It was here that they were told about a deceased airman who had been found near Aaigem and shown a photo that had been taken from his survival kit. It was substitute gunner Richard Hawkins.

The two 21-year-old *Carpetbagger*s, Ryckman from Fresno, California and Cozzens from Eldorado, Texas, remained with Diependaele until June 20, when a man named George de Vrieste took them to a farm near Herzele. A week later, while they were still there, they had a scare when someone ducked in to warn them that German troops were coming. They scrambled into a wheat field to hide, but soon learned that the Germans had gone to a different farm instead. After this close call, De Vrieste decided to move them to the village of Woubrechtegem, where he put Ryckman and Cozzens in the care of people associated with the White Brigade.

Among these new acquaintances was a striking, black-haired young woman named Bertha. She claimed to have been born in Long Beach, California, and said that her father was still there. Bertha went on to mention that she and her mother were waiting for De Vrieste's organization to get them out of Belgium. As Ryckman explained in his escape and evasion report, Bertha said "she knew a man in Brussels to whom she had turned over soldiers after Dunkirk. She promised to try and reach him [to help us]. After a day she returned declaring that she had made contact."[38]

On Tuesday, July 4, Bertha and the two Americans bicycled to Aspelare, where her mother owned a small grocery store. Here, they met a man named Arsene Priells who had come down from Brussels to get them.

The following day, Arsene, Bertha, and the two Americans arose early and biked to Ninove, where they boarded the 5:00am train into Brussels.

By the time they reached the capital, Arsene had outlined a plan by which the evaders would be taken to Switzerland, rather than to Spain. Ryckman found this idea "suspicious," but he and Cozzens went along with it.

They walked to a three-story building in the Anderlicht district, which Cozzens, in his escape and evasion report, E&E No.1916, pinpointed as being at 45 Rue Jorez. On the top floor was a well-appointed four-room apartment belonging to Bertha's aunt Alvier (or Elvir by Cozzens's spelling) Willemsen. It was here that Bertha left them. Ryckman noted "she apparently had suspicions about the move and wanted to make sure that [we] were going to be in good hands."

People seemed to be arriving all the time, many bringing liquor, and soon a party atmosphere prevailed. A "wealthy-appearing, dark-haired woman" named Germaine Leheys appeared. According to Ryckman, she had known "some Belgian consul before the war and somehow this person could fix it up so that [we could go to Switzerland] by car... [but] something went wrong so that [we] could not leave as quickly as anticipated. None of this story seemed to make any sense."

Ryckman's misgivings were only intensified with the arrival of "a tall slender Chief about 40 with a small moustache and dark silky hair." As drinks were being served, this man warned them that they should not be caught on the street with "anything that looked suspicious." He relieved them of the cloth maps that airmen carried, and Alvier took their hacksaws. They let Ryckman and Cozzens keep their compasses.

The two Americans remained at Alvier Willemsen's apartment until the afternoon of July 14, when Germaine Leheys came to get them. Followed by men whom Ryckman described as "two thugs or bodyguards of some sort," they walked through the meandering streets until around 4:30pm, when a car pulled up and they were motioned to get in.

At the wheel was a gray-haired man with glasses, whom Ryckman described as having a "rather heavy build, little finger missing from his right hand, coarse shredded black hair flopping in his eye, gray in streaks, a very dark grayish face, moustache covering his whole lip." Ryckman added that "this man seemed to become quite excited about the two thugs who were following."

After "about ten or fifteen minutes of the most labored turning" they reached their destination – 16 Rue Forestière.

Chapter 55

A Safe House Most Unsafe

At first glance, the building at 16 Rue Forestière seemed typical of the anonymous three-story townhouses around Brussels that were used as safe houses. However, it was different. As the airmen who arrived here would all discover, albeit not immediately, this was not the safe house they expected, but a house most *unsafe*.

In his description of the place, later narrated to the Military Intelligence Service (MIS) back in London and included in his escape and evasion report, Bill Ryckman said that when he and Wallis Cozzens arrived on July 14, they "went in the front door and up the marble stairs. To the left were three steps going down to a living room below street level. Beyond, through French doors was the kitchen, which opened into a raised patio with a large fence. On the next floor were two rooms separated by a curtain. In them were a lot of chairs and English maps."[39]

Ryckman added that the "Chief with the silky hair," whom they had met earlier at Alvier's apartment, was here, though "the house seemed to be run by a very good looking, dark haired woman named Jacqueline."

That evening, Ryckman and Cozzens sat down to drink cognac with Jacqueline and the Chief, who spun a fanciful tale about having "spent part of his life in India. He had been in El Paso, Texas and up in Canada. He seemed to know Canada well enough to make Canadians believe that he was Canadian. He gave a story about being a British agent."

As they sipped their cognac and listened to the Chief's imaginative stories, Ryckman and Cozzens continued to feel the same uneasiness that they had at Alvier's apartment.

There was good reason.

As the house at 16 Rue Forestière was not as advertised, neither was the Chief. His real name was Prosper DeZitter, and he was one of the most diabolical antagonists of unwitting downed airmen in the annals of escape and evasion. With his dark, slicked back hair, his thin mustache, and a missing finger, he looked the part of a villain, yet his cunning and convincing manner seduced many into falling for his deceptions.

DeZitter's inner circle included "Jacqueline," whom Ryckman mentioned, and whose real name was Florentina Girault. She was DeZitter's mistress and the Spanish wife of Belgian merchant Paul Dings. There was also a Russian named Nicolas Fetisoff who had a skin condition that had left him with a pock-marked face. He was the same man who would drive Hank Wolcott and Al Sanders to Brussels in August.

Among the other supporting characters at the house were the men whom Ryckman referred to as "bodyguards." One of them was a man whom Ryckman described as "blond, with slicked back hair, who stood nearly six feet tall," and who introduced himself as "Charlie." He spoke English with a German accent, which could have been explained as a Flemish accent to allay suspicions. American or British airmen were unlikely to know the difference.

Belgian-born, DeZitter was a sociopath who began his career as a petty criminal at an early age, and graduated quickly to more serious prevarications. Some of what he told Ryckman and Cozzens was true. He *had* been to Canada, having fled there in 1913 to avoid going to jail after being convicted of raping a minor – a fact that he omitted. He returned unreformed to Belgium in around 1926, and went back to his familiar life as a malefactor and con man. Through the years, he worked as a used car salesman while being in and out of jail for various criminal schemes from forgery and embezzlement to *escroqueries au marriage* (marriage fraud).

When the Germans occupied Belgium in 1940, DeZitter offered his services – at a price, of course – to the Geheime Feldpolizei (GFP). As with their rival, the Gestapo, the GFP knew that many Allied airmen were crossing occupied Europe, and capturing them was a priority.

The scheme that DeZitter sold to the GFP was the creation of a false escape line, complete with faux safe houses that were anything but safe for evaders. The building at 16 Rue Forestière, known in the later lore of escape and evasion lines as the "Dog House," was the Brussels hub for DeZitter's operation. Well paid by the GFP, he and Jacqueline had utilized a number of unsafe houses around Brussels. Before the Dog House, their hub had been the "Boarding School" on Avenue A. J. Slegers in Woluwe-Saint-Lambert on the east side of Brussels.

Operating for the GFP as one of their *Vertrauensleute* or "V-Leute," men of confidence, DeZitter was also a prolific betrayer of fellow Belgians, as well as Allied airmen. He and his accomplices appear in numerous accounts of evaders being double crossed by fraudulent Belgian underground operatives.

Ted Kleinman crossed the threshold of 16 Rue Forestière about six weeks after Ryckman and Cozzens had passed through the Dog House. After two months in Basècles as a radio operator and consultant to underground leader Fernand Barbaix, he was pleased when "instructions came through," albeit from an unspecified source, that he was to be taken to Switzerland by way of Brussels. He was picked up in a car by "a Russian named Nick," obviously Nicolas Fetisoff, and driven to 16 Rue Forestière.

As Kleinman described it, the car "drove to the back of the house while two men from the street jumped onto the running boards and gave instructions to go around to the front of the house to enter." Inside, one of these men, "a tall dirty blond with hair combed straight back, blue-green eyes set close together, a gray suit," introduced himself as "Charlie" and gave Kleinman a form to fill out.

Charlie introduced Kleinman to "the Chief," whom the airman described as a man with a mustache, who "spoke French with an accent, claimed to born in India." He was, of course, Prosper DeZitter. In his escape and evasion report, Kleinman also wrote of being greeted by a dark-haired woman in her early thirties, who was certainly Florentina Girault, aka Jacqueline.

Kleinman later told the MIS that he was "suspicious of his company" and told the Chief as much – not knowing who DeZitter really was, and what he represented. With great irony, Kleinman also related a story that he had heard in Basècles about an organization supposedly aiding evaders which was actually turning them over to the Germans. With tongue in cheek, DeZitter consoled Kleinman, giving him "the most reassuring reaction of incredulousness at such a tale."

There were several RAF airmen, as well as two other Americans, at the Dog House during the third week of August, but Kleinman met the latter only briefly, because they departed the day after he arrived. One of them was Sergeant Hugh Bomar, who had been the right waist gunner of a 493rd Bomb Group B-24 shot down on June 14, and with whom Kleinman would cross paths about a week later.

———

For each of these men, as for every airman who passed through its doors, DeZitter's Dog House was a way station on the road to a very unpleasant surprise.

On Tuesday, July 18, after four days at 16 Rue Forestière, Bill Ryckman and Wallis Cozzens were told that they were about "to go to France and then the Swiss frontier traveling the whole way by automobile." The two airmen climbed into a 1936 Dodge with five "guides," and drove away, not toward France, but across Brussels to a tall office building on Avenue Louise – which turned out to be the administrative epicenter of the German occupation of Belgium!

Ryckman and Cozzens were a bit suspicious as they were taken to a room on the third or fourth floor – but nothing could have quite prepared them for what they saw when they entered the room. On one wall was a large map of Brussels, but on the opposite wall were large framed portraits of Adolf Hitler and Luftwaffe boss Hermann Göring.

Behind the desk in the center of the room, wearing the uniform of a Luftwaffe officer and surrounded by others in uniform, was the man whom they knew from 16 Rue Forestière as Charlie.

Ryckman later wrote that Cozzens grabbed one of the Germans in the room by the lapels, while another shouted at him to sit down. He did. There was no questioning who was in charge. As is often done as an interrogation technique, Charlie relaxed Ryckman and Cozzens by playing a "good cop" role. He calmly told them about himself. He said that he was originally from Bremen, but he had worked in the air conditioning business in the United States and in South America. When this strange recounting of Charlie's life in the Americas was through, the two Americans were loaded back into the Dodge.

This time, their next stop was a prison cell.

———

One by one, two by two, the evaders left 16 Rue Forestière with a promise of a drive to Switzerland, but they all ended up at the building on Avenue Louise that was just 800 yards, or a ten-minute walk, from the Dog House.

Avenue Louise (or Louizalaan in Flemish) is a broad tree-lined boulevard in an elegant neighborhood just south of central Brussels. By the late 1930s, a number of modern multi-story office buildings and luxury apartment houses had been constructed here, and in 1940, several of these had been taken over by various German occupation agencies, including the Gestapo, the Luftwaffe, and the Abwehr's GFP – the paymaster of Prosper DeZitter. The basements of these buildings became infamous as torture chambers under the German occupation.

The Gestapo originally set up their headquarters in the stylish, 12-story, art deco Résidence Belvédère at 453 Avenue Louise – though they moved to 347 Avenue Louise in 1943 after their first headquarters was strafed by Jean de Sélys Longchamps, a Belgian nobleman flying with the Royal Air Force.

Bud Brown, the pilot of *Dobie*, and fighter pilot Bill Grosvenor had reached Avenue Louise about a month earlier without visiting the Dog House – having been arrested as collateral damage in the GFP raid on the apartment of Jeanne Frix-Claes. Brown and Grosvenor were taken to Avenue Louise for their audience with Charlie, whom Brown described as "tall [with] dirty blond hair combed straight back."

With Jeanne Frix-Claes in custody, dangerous fissures were rippling through the organization of which she was a part. In his escape and evasion report, Brown mentioned that during his interrogation, Charlie showed him photos of Jean van den Eede and Midge Fontaine, as well as Marcel van Buckenhout and his wife. Charlie assured him that they had all been taken into custody. Perhaps at that very moment they were enduring the third degree in a concrete room in the basement of the same building.

As he did with most of the evaders who came his way, Charlie told Brown and Grosvenor that since they were "caught in civilian clothes, they would go to a regular criminals' prison [rather than a POW stalag] until [we] could tell a story to prove our identity." This threat was clearly a lie – if the Germans didn't believe they were airmen, why were they taken to Luftwaffe headquarters?

After about eight hours in separate cells in the dingy basement at Avenue Louise, Brown and Grosvenor were taken to the infamous Saint-Gilles Prison.

Gradually, the other evaders also took the elevator ride at Avenue Louise. On Sunday, August 13, Hank Wolcott and Al Sanders were waiting at

16 Rue Forestière for Nicolas Fetisoff to pick them up and "take them to Switzerland." Instead, a "short, blond man" showed up, took their dog tags and proceeded to drive them around the city. They were taken "to a house off a courtyard," where their identification papers were checked before they were driven by truck to Avenue Louise.

As with Wolcott's fellow crewmen, Ryckman and Cozzens, three weeks earlier, they were stunned by the sight of the Hitler and Göring portraits on the wall – but especially unnerved at the sight of Charlie in full uniform, behind the desk. With a dramatic flourish, he proceeded to lay his pistol on the desk, telling his American friends, "I suppose you now know that you are prisoners of German intelligence."

On August 30, after a few days at the Dog House, it was Ted Kleinman's turn. His hosts were going through the motions of preparing false identity papers for him and two RAF airmen, when someone said that one of them needed a headshot photo to be taken. For some reason, it was decided that all three evaders would make the run to the photo booth. As Kleinman later recalled in his escape and evasion report, they climbed into a large Ford sedan, and took off with Charlie riding outside on the running board. Kleinman recalled that this "seemed to the passengers rather curious."[40]

They drove straight down Avenue Louise, where Charlie and the driver escorted them upstairs, straight into the same Luftwaffe office where so many evaders had stood before.

During his interrogation at Avenue Louise, Kleinman admitted to Charlie in a rambling account of his time in Belgium that he had been in Turnhout and Liège, but did not mention Basècles. Kleinman recalled that Charlie "saw that he was making no headway, declared that he could not afford to waste time," and dismissed Kleinman to call in another prisoner.

Kleinman never saw Charlie again. He was taken to Saint-Gilles Prison almost immediately.

Chapter 56

A Dungeon Most Medieval

For each of the evaders whose luck ran out so dramatically at Avenue Louise, the next stop was Saint-Gilles Prison, a gothic citadel located at 106 Avenue Ducpétiaux on the south side of Brussels. Deliberately designed by its architects to strike fear and hopelessness into anyone who passed through its foreboding gates, the prison was completed in 1884 in the style of a medieval fortress.

Inside, the design philosophy was for solitary confinement in small cramped cells. When the prison was taken over by the Germans in 1940 to be used mainly to incarcerate political prisoners, the Nazi jailers readily adapted the existing accommodations as the dreaded "dark cells," where lonely inmates were denied even light. Built with five wings of 120 cells each, Saint-Gilles had a maximum capacity of 600 inmates – but by 1944, it held around 1,400, including an increasing number of Allied airmen.

In his 1989 book, *Child At War*, author Mark Bles told the true story of Hortense Daman, a teenage girl from the Belgian underground who was imprisoned here during the occupation.

"Prisoners would be taken into the courtyard and the massive timber gates would be closed behind them," wrote Bles. "They lived in small cells like bare stone caves standing off narrow cast-iron galleries rising in tiers above the hard tiled floor. The prisoners lived like so many troglodytes in lofty, vaulted tunnels which rang constantly with the sound of steel and smelt sickly of cabbage and urine."

When they arrived here on June 20, Bud Brown and Bill Grosvenor knew it was going to be bad, but no one could have guessed how bad. Brown later wrote in his escape and evasion report that "special recognition should be shown to 1st Lieutenant William Grosvenor who suffered much torture in the hands of the Germans for not giving information… Grosvenor was kept in black cells for some 31 days. The Germans used whisper recordings to break him down."

Another man who landed in Saint-Gilles without a stay at the Dog House was Jake Terzian, the P-47 pilot who had named his aircraft *Marty* after his girlfriend. Brought to Brussels during the first week of June by Guillaume "Willy" De Keyser, Terzian had been taken under the wing of Anne Brusselmans, who placed him with Josse van Craenenbroeck in a three-story gray brick safe house at 16 Place du Conseil in the Anderlicht district of Brussels. Terzian was still here on July 12 when the safe house was betrayed, and the Gestapo hauled him off to Saint-Gilles by way of their headquarters at 347 Avenue Louise.

In his escape and evasion report, Terzian recalled that he was "put in a solitary and dark cell for four days," then isolated for three weeks.[41] "They took my dog tags and forced me to pop to attention every time an NCO came to the door," he wrote. "There was no soap or cigarettes… I was put in with some Germans who were in jail for stealing. They smoked in front of me but never gave me any cigarettes. Then I was in with Belgians who had deserted the German army after four days."

On July 18, shortly after Terzian's arrival, Bill Ryckman and Wallis Cozzens came through the gates. Stripped to their underwear, they were told that they would be charged as spies, despite their having military dog tags. After one night inside, Ryckman was separated from Cozzens, taken to an administrative office, frisked, and moved into a cell with several British and American airmen, including Captain Richard "Dick" Scott.

A 1942 West Point graduate, Scott was a P-38 pilot with the 385th Fighter Squadron, 364th Fighter Group who had gone down over Baarn in the Netherlands on March 15, 1944 when his left wing hit an electrical transmission tower.

He told Ryckman that he had been picked up by the Dutch underground and had made it to Brussels, where he fell in with a group promising to get him out of occupied Europe via Switzerland. At this point in the conversation, things began to sound awfully familiar to Ryckman! Ryckman probably did not know whether to laugh or cry when Scott told him about meeting a man who claimed to be a British intelligence officer who "had spent most of his life in India," and who introduced him to his wife Jacqueline. Like so many others, Scott had been duped by DeZitter and Girault.

It was around August 3, after the men in Ryckman's cell had been on what he called a "starvation diet" for some time, that Dick Scott was pulled out to be sent to Stalag Luft III at Sagan in eastern Germany. He would survive his ordeal and was liberated in 1945.

Ryckman was then moved to a larger cell filled with Luftwaffe deserters, as well as a Belgian and a Frenchman who had joined the German Army early in the war, but who had since deserted. At the end of August, Ryckman, like many of the airmen in Saint-Gilles, was dragged back to Luftwaffe headquarters, where Charlie was once again his inquisitor.

As Ryckman later explained to MIS, the airmen at Saint-Gilles "had decided to follow the tactics of talking to the interrogators on any subject to keep them off interrogation." For Ryckman, this included "going about two hours gradually covering... V-1s, the Russian front, Normandy, South America, the United States."

Finally Charlie took out a dossier on Ryckman and "began to insist on knowing the details of what had happened to Ryckman since he had been down. It is worth noting that [Charlie] did not seem to remark at all [about] the 801st Bomb Group [the secret *Carpetbaggers* organization, though the group was] listed on the form."

When Ryckman refused, Charlie told him that he was going back to the "dark cells." However, when he returned to Saint-Gilles, Ryckman learned that all of the dark cells were "full up," so he was put back into the same cell where he had been that morning.

On August 26, Ryckman was finally moved to a four-by-six-foot dark cell, "with a high ceiling and no light except for three small holes in the door. A bucket served for a toilet. There were no blankets." Here he remained for five days without water.

Ryckman's pilot, Hank Wolcott, accompanied by Al Sanders, crossed the Saint-Gilles threshold from Avenue Louise on August 13. They were strip-searched and their dog tags taken away. Next, they were told that they could be executed as spies because they had no dog tags!

Chapter 57

Sleight of Hand

Beyond the walls of Saint-Gilles, beyond the narrow streets of Brussels, events were taking place that were sending ripples of concern through the lives of the jailers at Saint-Gilles, the interrogators at Avenue Louise, and the whole German occupation establishment.

After four long, unbearable years, the *Allies were coming*.

Until the Allies achieved their breakout from the Normandy beachheads on July 25, 1944, ending a grueling six-week stalemate, it seemed as though they would never come. Since that date, though, great progress had been made. On August 25, elements of the US First Army, along with attached French units, liberated Paris, giving hope to the people of Brussels. After the British Second Army's breakout from Normandy, its XXX Corps component, under Lieutenant General Brian Horrocks, was spearheading the advance toward Belgium.

From his citadel in Brussels, all of this was being watched intently by SS-Generalleutnant Richard Jungclaus. He had commanded all Gestapo and other SS police units in Belgium and northeastern France since 1942, and as of the summer of 1944, he now also commanded the Wehrmacht and its Geheime Feldpolizei (GFP) in this region.

By late August, though, Jungclaus was feeling an emotion new to him – trepidation. The clock was ticking, and he found himself between the rock of the Allied advance from the west and the hard place of the demands coming at him from Berlin, where Heinrich Himmler was insisting that he accelerate the transfer of prisoners from Saint-Gilles to concentration camps inside Germany.

The last days of August at Saint-Gilles were a frenetic scene of inmates being dragged out of their cells and taken away to be loaded into freight trains. On August 10, for example, 827 of them, mainly Belgian political prisoners, were sent to Buchenwald, followed by 2,084 similar unfortunates aboard overflowing trains on August 30.

———

By late on Friday, September 1, preparations were being made for the next shipment from Saint-Gilles. The Germans had shunted 32 freight cars onto a railway spur line near the Bruxelles-Midi, or Brussels-South, railway station in preparation for an early departure the following day. Among the 1,370 names on the SS prisoner manifest for Saturday morning were around four dozen Allied airmen – estimates vary from 41 to 52. A review of the Eighth Air Force after-action reports indicates that 28 were Americans; the rest were mainly from Britain's Royal Air Force.

The train was scheduled to depart at 8:30am, carrying these poor souls to Neuengamme concentration camp near Hamburg. At 1:30am, the guards began rousting the chosen inmates from their cells, and by 4:00am they were being jostled into the trucks that would take them two miles north to the station. On the streets, people were out to bear witness to this transfer. As the trucks passed one corner, there was a throng of women singing the Belgian national anthem. Little scraps of paper fluttered from inside the trucks and were quickly gathered up by onlookers. Each one contained an address and a message for a loved one.

Would any of those messages drifting from the trucks ever reach its intended recipient? Would the sender ever know?

Bill Ryckman recalled that the men from his truck reached the station around 8:00am, "and were put into a baggage car, some 42 strong, all airmen except for a red-haired Frenchman who was supposed to have parachuted on the continent a couple of years ago and was condemned to death."

At the station, armed German troops patrolled Platform 14–15 as men and women were kicked, shoved, and *locked* into the sweaty, rolling torture boxes that would take them to Germany. Jungclaus assumed that his men were in complete control of this whole process, but things would soon be slipping out of balance, things Jungclaus did not see and could not yet imagine were possible.

———

Rail transport within Belgium, as in all of occupied Europe, was under German management, but day-to-day operations remained in the hands of the national railways. In Belgium, this was the Société Nationale des Chemins de Fer Belges (or Nationale Maatschappij der Belgische Spoorwegen in Flemish), the SNCB/NMBS. The Germans had installed their own station managers at major rail stations to ensure that trains serving the occupation or the Wehrmacht received the highest priority, but routine operations of trains, locomotives, and railyards were run day-to-day by Belgian personnel. For four years, these rail workers had been intimidated into compliance, but this was about to change.

For his 1985 book, *Des Bâtons dans les Roues* (*Sticks in the Wheels*), author Claude Lokker interviewed a number of SNCB/NMBS employees who were on duty on Saturday, September 2 when the tacit acquiescence of railroad personnel disintegrated.

At 7:40am, by Lokker's account, Léon Petit, the SNCB/NMBS station manager at Bruxelles-Midi, began alerting railway workers in his network – from dispatchers, to switchers, to yard and repair shop workers – that the time had come for a vast and confusing sleight of hand that would baffle and perplex their Nazi masters.

First, word came in that the locomotive coupled to the 32-car prisoner train had developed "mechanical difficulties." The Germans were assured that it was just a minor glitch. These things happened all the time – especially in a rail system hindered by wartime shortages. A replacement locomotive was finally summoned, though not until 9:15am. A streamlined 4-4-2 Type 12 steam locomotive, No.1202, painted in the dark green, gold-striped livery of the SNCB/NMBS, it was destined to become the centerpiece of a vast shell game. This began when it was learned that No.1202 had a broken air brake pump. The exasperated Germans sent in some of their own railroad mechanics to handle repairs, but as they worked, the engineer went missing and German troops were sent to find him. Growing impatient, the Germans in charge then told the search parties to bring back *any* crew they could find.

By 3:15pm, the schedule had slipped nearly seven hours when engineer Louis Verheggen and fireman Léon Pouchet were delivered to No.1202 at gunpoint. By 4:15pm, Verheggen and Pouchet had brought the locomotive to Platform 14–15, and had coupled onto the 32-car prison train. SS guards climbed into the engine cab to make sure that the two Belgian operators behaved. At least another 150 German troops boarded the train as guards, and an antiaircraft car was attached. Its guns were positioned so that the gunners would have a clear field of fire to hit any point on the exterior of the train in the case of an escape attempt.

When Verheggen and Pouchet were ordered to depart at 4:50pm, the SS guards did not notice, amid the maze of tracks in the railyard yard, that the train had been switched onto a slow sidetrack. Instead of going north on the mainline toward Germany, it chugged toward the yard at Vorst, two miles south of Bruxelles-Midi, where the assistant station master followed official protocol, leaving the train sidetracked to allow a 72-car German freight train to pass on the mainline. Everyone knew that under the occupation, German supply trains *always* had the right of way.

At 5:45pm, when Verheggen insisted to the SS guards that he needed to go find a yard engineer to help him get on the correct track, the SS men called his bluff and ordered him to get the train moving immediately. The exasperated SS smelled a stall tactic. Under other circumstances they would have probably shot Verheggen – but they needed him to run the train.

Nine hours had passed since the originally scheduled departure time, and the train was barely ten miles from where it had started. They should have been in Germany by now. By 11:00pm, they had reached Mechelen, about 25 miles north of Bruxelles-Midi, when they stopped for a red signal light. Verheggen knew that this light was malfunctioning, but he managed to convince the SS that he should walk to a nearby yard telephone and call the yard master for permission to continue. The SS boss reluctantly agreed, but Verheggen made the call with a gun to his head.

While all this was going on, and as No.1202 was stopped and idling, Verheggen left the steam valve open, causing the loss of a great deal of water that was necessary for the locomotive's boilers. Knowing nothing of locomotive operation, the SS men never noticed. Finally, Verheggen showed the water levels to the Germans. Verheggen wasn't lying. They needed more water now. Unfortunately, damage done to the Mechelen yard by Allied air attacks meant that they had to backtrack several miles off the mainline to Muizen. It was not until 5:30am on Sunday morning that the water tanks were replenished and the train was finally *almost* back on the mainline in Mechelen.

What Verheggen and his SS tormenters did not know was that bigger events had unfolded through the night – events that made No.1202 and its 32-car train among the lesser of the worries for Richard Jungclaus. He knew that the Allies were coming, but he now learned they were coming sooner than expected – much sooner.

Late on Saturday, September 2, the spearhead of the British XXX Corps, the Guards Armoured Division under General Allan Adair, had reached the French city of Douai, about 35 road miles from the Belgian border. As he followed their rapid progress on maps, Adair's boss, Lieutenant General Brian Horrocks, the commandeer of XXX Corps, noted that Adair was only about 100 miles from the Belgian capital.

Barring serious opposition, of which none was anticipated, Horrocks knew that Adair could easily reach Brussels within a week, but this was not good enough. He ordered Adair not simply to cross the Belgian border on Sunday, but to make a high-speed dash all the way to Brussels!

Chapter 58

Improbable Twists of Fate

Engineer Louis Verheggen had been a part of the subtle shell game that unfolded all night long and past dawn on Sunday, September 3, 1944. The skillful sleight of hand being executed by him and the SNCB/NMBS dispatchers had essentially made the train disappear. It was 21 hours behind schedule, and barely 25 miles from where it started, but no one in the office of Richard Jungclaus had a firm grasp on exactly where it was – or how it had been shuffled.

The German railroad commander at Bruxelles-Midi may even have assumed that it was well on its way to Germany, but he had a lot of other fish to fry on that Sunday morning. Trains had to be mustered to transport German personnel escaping in advance of the approaching British Army. He was also trying to schedule the departure of a hospital train that was evacuating wounded Wehrmacht troops to Germany.

In the cab of No.1202, Louis Verheggen had only one fish to fry, and he had been frying all night. As he was bringing No.1202 back toward the mainline at Mechelen from the water tank at Muizen, everyone in the cab felt it start to skid on a curve.

What happened?

Again, Verheggen showed the irritable SS guards what the problem was. The boxes that released sand to provide traction were malfunctioning. The German in charge could see this. He swore at the train, and he swore at Verheggen, but he could see the problem with his own eyes. Again, as with the water tanks, the Belgian engineer was not lying. He had just not explained that he had deliberately dumped the sand.

They inched onward to the nearest phone box where Verheggen was permitted – again, with a gun to his head – to phone a dispatcher to request a different locomotive. Verheggen was told to make his way to the Klein-Eiland yard in Brussels for the locomotive swap.

As No.1202 chugged slowly southward, rumors were sweeping the railyards and the city. The British advance was more rapid than expected. Everything had started to unravel. Belgian rail workers were disappearing up and down the line, leaving the Germans to fend for themselves. At the same time, German discipline in the city was collapsing into disarray. Germans were commandeering automobiles and trucks to take them east away from the Allies. Even Richard Jungclaus was packing his bags.

By 9:10am on Sunday, the locomotive had passed back through Bruxelles-Midi – where it started – and had arrived in Klein-Eiland. When No.1202 was uncoupled from the train, Verheggen stepped out to inspect it, gave the SS the slip and disappeared into the confusion of the railyard. Next, fireman Léon Pouchet also vanished into the confusion.

By that same time, the German commander at Klein-Eiland had found a replacement locomotive, but he could find no one to operate it.

Across town that Sunday morning, Ludwig Mayr-Frankenberg, the veteran German diplomat who had been the representative of the Reichskommissariat (Reich Foreign Ministry) in Belgium since 1943 – the *de facto* ambassador – was visited by the consuls of neutral Sweden and Switzerland. They were not strangers to his office, having been here several times over the previous week or so with futile pleas for the release of political prisoners.

Today, Mayr-Frankenberg had better news. Though no one at the railyards yet knew it, Richard Jungclaus had just reluctantly authorized the release of all the political prisoners in 31 of the cars of the prisoner train.

The Allied airmen, however, were *not* to be released.

When the neutral diplomats reached the railyard and located the train, they found themselves in a bitter argument with the Germans on site, who refused to release the prisoners. It was afternoon before clarification was relayed from Jungclaus's office, and the 31 cars filled with political prisoners were finally opened.

Through the slats in the wall of the one car not emptied, Bud Brown recalled seeing Jeanne Frix-Claes, Midge Fontaine, and Marcel van Buckenhout amid the people escaping from the train.

As the airmen remained imprisoned, chaos and confusion reigned all around them. The Belgians had abandoned the offices, shops, and switches of the railyard, and the German railway workers were also running away. Bill Ryckman recalled that the Germans had begun "looting trucks and German soldiers full of cognac were going around riotously... There were general disturbances outside [the car.]"

Jake Terzian wrote that he "noticed that one SS officer had changed his uniform to Wehrmacht." The SS knew that they were deeply disliked and often mistreated by Allied front line soldiers, while captured Wehrmacht troops received more respect.

According to a rumor that Bill Ryckman heard at the time, "there was some effort [being made] to turn the airmen over to the Belgian Red Cross." Sergeant Hugh Bomar, the B-24 crewman whom Ted Kleinman had met at the Dog House, heard it differently.* He wrote in his escape and evasion report that "an effort was made to turn the POWs over to the Red Cross but they refused to take the responsibility of accepting us."[42]

Bomar went on to paint a vivid picture of the scene in the railyard, adding that "nobody seemed to know what was happening and the political prisoners were looting the cars."

The tumult was compounded by the problem of the trainload of wounded German troops being evacuated to Germany. By some accounts, their locomotive had struck another train, and the medevac train was brought back by a switcher to be coupled to a different road locomotive.

Ryckman reported another rumor going around that the Germans were so fearful of the medevac train – which the airmen called the "Red Cross" train because it was marked with red crosses – being blown up that they "had arranged with the Armee Blanche [White Brigade] to let the hospital train through, granting in return the release of all political prisoners."

Bomar's account concurred. He wrote that the prisoners were told that the underground "had given their word that one Red Cross train could go through the lines in return for the release of all political prisoners."

*See Chapter 55.

But the Allied prisoners were not out of the woods. In fact, they were headed back in!

———

Amid the chaos, the efficient German war machine almost took a step which would have once again condemned the airmen to a disastrous fate. One can imagine their astonishment and helpless alarm as they felt their car being detached from the other 31 cars and attached to the Wehrmacht medevac train with a fresh locomotive.

Nothing now stood between them and the German border.

"We started out of the station again but soon stopped," Hugh Bomar recalled. "There was the noise of explosions and tanks, then we backed into the yard [at Schaarbeek, after traveling five miles]… two of the cars were derailed so the cars behind them were abandoned. The Germans in these cars all piled into the first few cars and they went off. We POWs were left there and everything was quiet."

Sergeant Maurice Muir of the Royal Air Force, who was a crewman on a Halifax bomber shot down on May 28, wrote in his MI9 after-action report, No.2885, that as the train was getting under way at 2:00pm, "three POWs were able to get out of the carriage." Bill Ryckman reported the same incident, writing that the "red-haired Frenchman then opened the door of the baggage car" and five men jumped out. If the Frenchman did have a death sentence hanging over his head, as he claimed, this was his lucky day.

One of the men who jumped was former LSU track star Al Sanders, who had been on the run with Hank Wolcott of *C for Charlie* for two and a half months before they were taken to Saint-Gilles. Wolcott later recalled that he was about to join Sanders but changed his mind at the last moment, fearing the German patrols that were still in the area.

"Al hit the ground running," his daughter Winkie Sanders Ruiz wrote in an article about her father which she coauthored.[43] "It was probably the fastest quarter mile in the history of man for this track star from LSU! Bullets were flying, but in the dark they missed their mark. Al found himself in a sports park and could hear the dogs behind him. He ran on and reached a street and a canal. Not knowing which way to go from there, he ran in the opposite direction from the Germans with their lights. He saw a barge on the river and took his chances. He jumped onto the deck and rapped on the door to the cabin. Inside, Mr. and Mrs Wijs, thinking it was the Germans or a burglar were terrified. But when they heard Al speaking English they opened the door. Al ingeniously whispered, 'President Roosevelt,' and Mr. Wijs responded with 'Queen Wihelmina,' the name of the reigning monarch of the Netherlands."

Sanders spent his first night of freedom aboard the Wijs barge on the Bassin Vergote, an extension of the Brussels-Scheldt Canal that runs through Brussels.

Back at the car that had been their jail, most of the men stayed put through a sleepless night. Jake Terzian reported "much shunting to and fro, and our particular car was switched off, derailed, and left there." He added that most of the men "lay low until [Monday] morning fearing a trap."

As quiet descended over the Schaarbeek railyard late on Sunday, September 3, elsewhere there was a great commotion. Just two miles to the south, in the center of Brussels, Allan Adair and the British Guards Armoured Division had arrived and were pressing toward the Royal Palace through a great mass of jubilant citizens, who greeted them and climbed aboard their vehicles.

Against minimal German opposition, Adair's Sherman tanks had overcome all obstacles and covered about 100 miles before the sun set on Sunday.

Chapter 59

Mornings After

On the morning of Monday, September 4, 1944, the citizens of Brussels, along with the escaped political prisoners and the Allied airmen, awoke to a city devoid of German troops.

Bill Ryckman wrote that "about daybreak it was agreed that any man who wanted to leave could." Jake Terzian added that "the 39 remaining airmen" in the car "escaped in small groups during the early hours of the morning."

Bud Brown of *Dobie* and P-47 pilot Bill Grosvenor, who had been on the run together from early April until they landed in Saint-Gilles, headed out together, accompanied by Ted Kleinman from Brown's crew.

A makeshift Allied headquarters had already been installed at the prestigious 250-room Hôtel Métropole on Place de Brouckère in the center of Brussels – where many a German officer had resided until just a few days before. Hearing this, Anne Brusselmans, the helper of so many evaders, went there and sought out a British intelligence officer. Introducing herself, she explained that "I have 54 downed airmen scattered all over this city. What do you want me to do with them?"

Her young daughter Yvonne, who wrote of this day in her memoirs, recalled that the lieutenant replied, staring in disbelief, "I suggest you round them up and bring them here."

"All right, I shall," she replied crisply. "In the meantime, you arrange for these men to be flown back to England as soon as possible. They are eager to be reunited with their families. Some of them have been hidden in Brussels for the last nine months!"

In turn, a message was broadcast over Belgian radio requesting that people housing evaders bring them to the Métropole, an undertaking that would have been unthinkable just 48 hours earlier.

The men staggering forth from the derailed car, tired, hungry, and thirsty, had no radios, of course, but word was spreading quickly. Al Sanders awoke on the barge, thanked his hosts, and made his way toward the center of town. He wrote in his escape and evasion report that at the Métropole, he "turned himself in to an American colonel," who got him a room upstairs.[44]

Jake Terzian remembered that he and several others ran into a group of Belgians from the White Brigade as they were walking through the streets of Schaarbeek that Monday morning. Not immediately recognized as Allied airmen, they "were suspected of being Germans and taken to police headquarters, cleared, and then the party started."[45]

The party to which Jake Terzian referred was memorable. As the evaders and their helpers arrived at the Métropole, they began to recognize friendly faces. Suddenly, the realization washed over everyone that they could show their own faces without fear or caution, and that they could speak with others without whispering. There was an explosion of euphoria.

Yvonne Brusselmans, who was there with her mother, later wrote that "the ambiance inside the hotel was exhilarating. Champagne was flowing at tables, around which sat airmen and helpers. Addresses were exchanged, promises of return visits were made, anecdotes were recounted. Suddenly, Mother heard a sentence which made her jump out of her seat."

Someone had said "bring another bottle of champagne, and charge it to Madame Anne."

Though he was probably kidding, Anne Brusselmans noticed the number of bottles already consumed and panicked.

"I want you to take these men off my hands right now," she told the first military intelligence officer she saw. "There is no way I can treat them to such extravagant expense."

As she was leaving the hotel, she was approached by a haggard old man walking with a cane, whom she did not immediately recognize.

"Monsieur van Buckenhout, is it really you?" Anne asked of her friend Marcel van Buckenhout, who had been at Saint-Gilles since June. In her memoirs, Yvonne Brusselmans said that it was like her mother had seen a ghost.

"The *Boches* beat my feet with a rifle butt," he replied. "However, I have come out better than some of them."

Airey Neave of MI9, who had arrived in Brussels with Allan Adair's troops, was in the Métropole bar that day himself. He too recalled the vast quantities of champagne that flowed. In his memoirs, he wrote of joining "100 airmen and 100 Comet Line helpers" in the bar as they toasted the liberation. He added that he intervened and saw to it that the bar tab was forwarded to the Supreme Headquarters Allied Expeditionary Force (SHAEF). As Neave recalled, General Eisenhower's staff paid the bill.

Three members of the crew of Hank Wolcott's *C for Charlie*, the *Carpetbagger* B-24 that went down on May 29, were nowhere near Brussels that morning. Nor had Dirvin Deihl, Fred Tuttle, and Carmen Vozzella ever endured the misery of German incarceration.

Given the fiendish efficiency of the DeZitter operation, it's a wonder that any downed airmen passed through Brussels in the summer of 1944 without having been snared at his infamous Dog House, but this trio was among many who had.

Evading together since the night that *C for Charlie* went down, these three men from that aircraft had eventually made their way into Brussels, where they made contact with a man named Jacques Delhaye who stashed them for a time in a narrow red brick safe house at 14 Rue de Scheutveld, about three miles west of the Dog House. On June 30, Deihl went to the home of Claire de Veuster, while Tuttle and Vozzella were turned over to Yvonne Bienfait, a nurse at the hospital in Schaarbeek.

While several of their fellow crewmembers were invited to go for a car ride to freedom via Switzerland, only to wind up at Saint-Gilles, Deihl, Tuttle, and Vozzella took automobile rides into the countryside that brought them to wholly unexpected sanctuaries. These were the camps in the mountainous Ardennes region that had been established under the auspices of Airey Neave's Operation *Marathon*, a plan to hide airmen in remote forests until Allied troops arrived.

Of the three, Deihl was the only one who gave details in his escape and evasion report. He wrote that on July 4, he was picked up by a man named Henri Pompier and driven about 80 miles south, through Namur, to the village of Wépion. From there, he was taken by bicycle to a camp deep in the nearby woods. He recalled "about 30 airmen staying there."[46]

Deihl added that he next "went to some woods at Porcheresse and stayed there for about a month." He did not mention Vozzella, who was also at the camp.

Deihl wrote that when news came of the Allies advancing toward the Belgian border, the men from Porcheresse "walked to a camp near the French frontier, and were there about a week when we were found by an advanced American patrol."

In his escape and evasion report, Deihl complimented the people he had met in Belgium, writing that "I was in the hands of the organization all this time and never doubted for a minute that I wouldn't be brought back to safety."[47]

In Brussels, things were moving quickly. British Field Marshal Bernard Montgomery, commander of the Allied 21st Army Group, the parent organization of the British Second Army and XXX Corps, would be having lunch with the mayor of Brussels on Thursday, September 7, and the Belgian government in exile would return from London the next day to strike the phrase "in exile" from their title.

The US Army moved quickly to airlift its recovered airmen back to England. On Tuesday, September 5, Bill Ryckman was taken to Amiens in France, where freed POWs were being gathered. On Wednesday, he took matters into his own hands, sought out a USAAF transport pilot, and hitched a ride to England. Al Sanders also flew back on September 6.

Ryckman and Sanders were the first of the men whom we have followed in this narrative to leave Belgium, and both were debriefed in England by MIS in the manner that had become routine for returning evaders since 1942. The others were debriefed in Brussels by an organization called IS9. Known for its intriguing "three witches" insignia, this MI9 spinoff was a little-known joint Anglo-American intelligence entity created to debrief former POWs liberated by the Allies. Airey Neave had brought the first of many IS9 agents with him that week, and they promptly opened offices in a six-story Victorian apartment house at 218 Avenue de Tervueren in the Brussels suburb of Woluwe-Saint-Pierre, four miles east of the Hôtel Métropole. By September 9, Bud Brown, Wallis Cozzens, Dale Loucks, Fred Tuttle, and Hank Wolcott had been interviewed by IS9, while Bill Grosvenor and Carmen Vozzella were debriefed the next day.

Ted Kleinman remained in Belgium longer than the others. He followed up with the people down in Basècles with whom he had worked as an underground radio man two months earlier. What he found was not a happy ending. Kleinman learned that Fernand Barbaix, the powder merchant and underground boss in Lessines with whom he had spent many hours in conversation, had been picked up in the aftermath of an attack on a German convoy and summarily executed by a firing squad.

Kleinman checked on Carlos Bernard and his wife, whose home had been Kleinman's first safe house in the area. He learned they had been arrested by the Gestapo. Under interrogation, Madame Bernard had defiantly refused to answer questions and was brutally kicked and beaten. She died six months later of kidney failure.

In Brussels, Kleinman had also offered to take a Belgian Army team to the infamous Dog House. They kicked down the door at 16 Rue Forestière and found no one at home. As the Allies approached, Prosper DeZitter and Florentina Girault had climbed into his 1936 Dodge and escaped to the only place in Europe where they would be welcome – Hitler's Germany.

SS-Generalleutnant Richard Jungclaus was among those who also raced eastward out of Belgium during the first week of September. He would pay the price for relenting, in a moment of weakness, to humanitarian pressure and releasing those prisoners aboard that last train. His boss, Reichsführer-SS Heinrich Himmler, was furious. On September 16, the seething Himmler demoted Jungclaus and exiled him to Croatia, then a German puppet state, to battle the partisan insurrection consuming the Balkans. Fighting with the 7.SS-Freiwilligen Gebirgs-Division "Prinz Eugen," Jungclaus was killed in action on April 15, 1945, three weeks before the war ended.

DeZitter initially found sanctuary with friends in Würzburg, and there are stories of him peddling his services to Allied intelligence services in the aftermath of the Nazi defeat, but the clock was ticking. Belgian authorities caught up with him and he was arrested in June 1946. Ironically, the man who had sent so many to the foreboding Saint-Gilles Prison was sent into one of its dark, cramped cells himself. He was tried, convicted, denied clemency by the royal family, and finally executed by a firing squad on September 17, 1948. Florentina Girault was also caught. On June 4, 1949, she became one of the last women sentenced to death and executed in Belgium.

Saint-Gilles Prison, certainly a villain, albeit inanimate, of this narrative, still exists, and as late as the third decade of the twenty-first century, it was being used as a prison by the Belgian Justice Ministry. In 2017, the annual report of the Belgian Direction Générale des Établissements Pénitentiaires (General Directorate of Penitentiary Institutions) reported that Saint-Gilles had a capacity of 579, but held 896 prisoners. As of November 2021, it had 903 inmates.

The Hôtel Métropole, meanwhile, is only a gilded memory. Having survived two world wars, it continued for many decades as *the* opulent five-star luxury hotel in the heart of Brussels before closing its doors in April 2020 after 125 years. Its bar, where the evaders and helpers partied on the day after liberation, is still in operation as the Café Métropole.

Chapter 60

Years After

On September 7, 1944, Millie Sanders received a phone call at her home in Louisiana from Western Union claiming they had a telegram for her from a Lieutenant Alfred Sanders.

"*That isn't funny!*" Millie shouted at the operator, angrily slamming down the receiver. Millie was in no mood for practical jokes. A little over three months earlier she'd received the dreadful "missing in action" telegram, and she'd heard nothing since.

As related by Al and Millie's daughter, Winkie Ruiz, the operator called back and, finally, Millie agreed to listen to the message, which read "Dearest, I am safe and well. Will be home soon. Letter following."[48]

Millie's husband had gone overseas weighing 175 pounds and came home to her weighing 130, thanks to life on the run and the starvation weeks at Saint-Gilles. He also came home to learn that Millie had given birth to their son, Mike, two days after he was shot down.

Sanders remained in the US Air Force until 1962, including three years at Ramstein AB in Germany. While he was in Europe, he went back to Belgium and looked up some of the people who had aided him while he was a fugitive. Among them, he called on the Rowerts in their Victorian *château*, where he enjoyed his reunion with their little black terrier. The Scottie recognized his old friend with great excitement – on both sides.

Sanders went on to earn his master's degree in vocational education from Florida State. He taught electronics and engineering at Brevard Junior College in Rockledge, Florida for 17 years. He and Millie made their home in Florida until 2012, when they moved to North Oaks, Minnesota to be near their daughter, Winkie Ruiz, and her family. Millie passed away in 2013 and Al died in 2017, at the age of 98.

As with Al Sanders, many of the airmen from this narrative stayed in the service and had postwar careers in the US Air Force. Promoted to captain, Bud Brown moved from bombers to transports, and flew with the 86th Troop Carrier Squadron, 374th Troop Carrier Wing during the Korean War. On September 27, 1951, his Curtiss C-46, *en route* from Atsuji to Tachikawa in Japan, crashed into Mount Tanazawa. There were no survivors. Brown was only 31. He was buried in the Golden Gate National Cemetery in San Bruno, California.

Ted Kleinman returned to the States in 1944 and was assigned as a USAAF flight training officer. He left the service after the war to work for his father-in-law in Oregon, but went back on active duty during the Korean War. He stayed in the Air Force, specifically in the Strategic Air Command, where he served as a KC-135 navigator instructor at various locations, including SAC headquarters. He ended his career at Vandenberg AFB, having transitioned to SAC's Titan II and Minuteman ICBMs.

Hank Wolcott, the pilot of the *Carpetbagger* B-24 named *C for Charlie*, who had evaded for two and a half months with Al Sanders, went home to Lansing, Michigan, where he worked as an accountant for 30 years. His obituary mentions him as having been "a pioneer in the early stage of the computer age." He and his wife Rosemary retired to Niceville, Florida in 1987.

Wolcott and Sanders stayed in touch through the years, but while Sanders went back to Europe to revisit old haunts soon after the war, Wolcott did not. Through the years, though, he was haunted by a memory of that night in May 1944 when *C for Charlie* went down. Everyone in the crew had bailed out successfully and had survived – except one man, Sergeant Richard Hawkins.

"I never did really know for sure that I didn't do something wrong that he couldn't get out," Wolcott told Bill Kaczor of the Associated Press in an interview 57 years later.

Finally, in March 2001, Hank and Rosemary went back to the places south of Brussels where he and Sanders had hidden, and he "was treated like a returning hero." They and other family members were greeted as dignitaries and toasted with champagne. They visited the chapel of Sint-Nicolas in the Belgian village of Aaigem, where Hawkins had been surreptitiously buried in the predawn darkness on May 29, 1944 while four Belgian civilians looked on. His body had long since been moved to the Ardennes American Cemetery in Neuville-en-Condroz, Belgium, where the Wolcotts also visited.

Kaczor reported that Wolcott met Georges de Cooman, who was there at Aaigem on that early morning in 1944 when Hawkins had first been laid to rest. He gave Wolcott mementos and a letter he had written to the Hawkins family. De Cooman said he "had kept the items for more than five decades waiting for someone from the crew to return."

When he got back to Florida, Wolcott set out to track down the other members of *C for Charlie*'s crew, and Hawkins's widow, Virginia Kennedy Hawkins. "I think of a young married man killed when he was 22 years old, the pain that they suffered," Wolcott told Bill Kaczor. "I want to tell them that I had some of the pain."

According to the Associated Press, Wolcott's searches were unsuccessful. Virginia had moved, and no forwarding address was found. Hank Wolcott passed away in Lansing in 2011 at the age of 92. Rosemary died in 2017.

Jake Terzian, who had named his P-47 Thunderbolt *Marty* after his girlfriend, Martha Tait, went back to the States and married her in October 1944.

For almost 70 years, Marty was with the man she called "the wild Armenian who stole my heart." Jake remained in the US Air Force until 1963, retiring as a lieutenant colonel at Dyess AFB outside Abilene, Texas. Jake and Marty settled down in Abilene and he took a job with the New York Life Insurance Company.

Terzian was an active member of the Air Force Escape and Evasion Society and the P-47 Thunderbolt Association, one of whose ball caps became a signature part of his wardrobe. Indeed, his obituary began with the line "on Tuesday, June 18, 2013 Jack (Jake) Terzian, 93, put on his infamous P-47 cap for the last time." He was laid to rest in Arlington National Cemetery.

Through the years, Terzian had attended many of the reunions in England of his 353rd Fighter Group. When it came time for their "Last Hurrah" reunion in 2015, Marty sent a message telling his old comrades and friends that "as long as there is a member of Jake's family around, you and your families will always be remembered and loved."

She concluded by telling them that Jake had gone away to "fly sorties with those of you already departed."

These words are a fitting epitaph for so many.

Notes

1 E&E No.849 (now in NARA Record Group 498). Captain Smith's handwritten draft of these comments is reproduced in this book as Picture EE-024.

2 E&E No.8.

3 E&E No.9.

4 E&E No.14 and No.20.

5 E&E No.10.

6 E&E Nos.8, 9, and 10 respectively.

7 E&E No.10.

8 E&E No.10.

9 These reports were compiled and written jointly in a single document as E&E Nos.31 and 32.

10 These records are posted on the group website (303rdbg.com).

11 E&E No.44.

12 E&E No.44.

13 Arthur B. Ferguson, "Origins of the Combined Bomber Offensive," in Craven, Wesley Frank and Cate, James Lea (eds). *Army Air Forces in World War II, Volume II Europe: Torch to Pointblank August 1942 to December 1943; Part IV: Toward Overlord; Chapter 20: Pointblank*. Washington: Air Force Historical Studies Office, 1948. Page 685.

14 E&E No.170.

15 E&E No.170.

16 E&E No.320.

17 E&E No.320.

18 E&E No.332.

19 E&E No.224.

20 Newsletter of the Air Forces Escape and Evasion Society (AFEES), November 2017.
21 E&E No.224.
22 E&E No.224 and No.225.
23 E&E No.328.
24 AFEES newsletter, November 2017.
25 These records are cited by Dutch researcher Jacobus "Co" de Swart on the *Aircrew Remembered* website (www.aircrewremembered.com).
26 E&E No.230.
27 In a May 2, 2006 oral history interview with Pattie Johnston that is on file with the Lawrence, Kansas Public Library, Grodi clarified that his name was pronounced "Grow-dye."
28 E&E No.229.
29 Yvonne Daley-Brusselmans in her memoir *Belgium Rendezvous 127 Revisited*. Manhattan, Kansas: Sunflower University Press, 2001.
30 E&E No.156.
31 E&E No.230.
32 E&E No.849.
33 E&E No.846.
34 E&E No.1036.
35 E&E No.617.
36 E&E No.1841.
37 E&E No.1881.
38 E&E No.1591.
39 E&E No.1591.
40 E&E No.2101.
41 E&E No.1789.
42 E&E No.1593.
43 Newsletter of Waverly Gardens, the retirement home in Minnesota where Al and his wife moved in 2012, August 2017 issue.
44 E&E No.1595.
45 E&E No.1789.
46 E&E No.1668.
47 E&E No.1668.
48 Waverly Gardens newsletter.

Bibliography

At the heart of this narrative are the stories of the evading airmen, including direct quotes from them. These were taken directly from the escape and evasion reports of each individual, which were written in 1942, 1943, and 1944 as the events occurred. They were compiled at that time by the Escape and Evasion Section (MIS-X) of the Military Intelligence Service (MIS), a component of Headquarters, US Forces, European Theater. They were transferred to the US National Archives and Records Administration (NARA) between July 1945 and March 1947 by the Administration Branch of the US Forces, European Theater. They now reside with the US National Archives as part of NARA Record Group 498 (RG 498), Records of Headquarters, European Theater of Operations, US Army (World War II). These constitute the primary source for this work.

The specific escape and evasion (E&E) reports from which direct quotes are drawn, and the names of the persons quoted, are as follows:

E&E No.8 (1943): Gilbert Schowalter

E&E No.9 (1943): Jack E. Williams

E&E No.10 (1943): John R. "Johnny" McKee

E&E No.14 (1943): Norman Peter Therrien

E&E No.20 (1943): Frederick A. Hartung

E&E No.31 (1943): William A. Whitman

E&E No.32 (1943): Iva Lee Fegette

E&E No.44 (1943): Harry Edwin Roach Jr.

E&E No.95 (1943): John White

E&E No.156 (1943): Wilmont C. "Bill" Grodi

E&E No.157 (1943): John K. Hughes

E&E No.158 (1943): Adelbert D. "Dell" Kneale

E&E No.159 (1943): Melvin L. Frazier

E&E No.160 (1943): Denver M. Canaday

E&E No.162 (1943): Claude Sharpless

E&E No.169 (1943): George S. Monser

E&E No.170 (1943): Robert Elmer Nelson

E&E No.171 (1943): Raymond A. Genz

E&E No.224 (1943): Joseph J. Walters

E&E No.225 (1943): Kenneth P. Fahncke

E&E No.229 (1943): Martin G. Minnich

E&E No.230 (1943): Henry P. "Hank" Sarnow

E&E No.320 (1943): Otto F. Bruzewski

E&E No.328 (1944): William Claxton "Billy" Howell

E&E No.332 (1944): Thomas R. Moore

E&E No.339 (1944): Beirne Lay Jr.

E&E No.508 (1944): William P. Kiniklis

E&E No.617 (1944): Walker Melville "Bud" Mahurin

E&E No.846 (1944): Gilbert M. Stonebarger

E&E No.849 (1944): Joel White McPherson

E&E No.940 (1944): Walter Armstrong Duer

E&E No.1036 (1944): Alfred H. Richter

E&E No.1511 (1944): Robert Peterson

E&E No.1591 (1944): William G. Ryckman

E&E No.1593 (1944): Hugh Bomar

E&E No.1595 (1944): Alfred M. L. Sanders

E&E No.1668 (1944): Dirvin Davis Deihl

E&E No.1789 (1944): Jack "Jake" Terzian

E&E No.1841 (1944): John W. "Bud" Brown

E&E No.1877 (1944): Henry Walbridge "Hank" Wolcott III

E&E No.1881 (1944): William D. Grosvenor

E&E No.1915 (1944): Robert F. Auda

E&E No.1916 (1944): Wallis O. Cozzens

E&E No.1917 (1944): Frederick A. Tuttle

E&E No.1918 (1944): Dale S. Loucks

E&E No.2101 (1944): Theodore H. "Ted" Kleinman

Other reference works and recommended reading include:

Bishop, Patrick. *The Man Who Was Saturday: The Extraordinary Life of Airey Neave*. London: William Collins, 2019.

Bles, Mark. *Child At War: The True Story of Hortense Daman*. London: Hodder & Stoughton, 2013 (originally published in 1989).

Blumenson, Martin. *United States Army in World War II, European Theater of Operations: Breakout and Pursuit*. Washington, DC: Center of Military History, United States Army, 1961.

Coffey, Thomas. *Decision Over Schweinfurt: The US Eighth Air Force Battle for Daylight Bombing*. New York: David McKay Company, 1977.

Coffey, Thomas M. *Iron Eagle: The Turbulent Life of General Curtis LeMay*. New York: Random House, 1986.

Crahay, Lieutenant General Baron Albert. *20 Heroes de Chez Nous (20 Home Town Heroes)*. Bruxelles: J. M. Collet, 1983.

Craven, Wesley Frank (Princeton University) and Cate, James Lea (University of Chicago), editors. *Army Air Forces in World War II*, 3 volumes. Washington, DC: Office of Air Force History, 1947, 1948, 1951.

Daley-Brusselmans, Yvonne. *Belgium Rendezvous 127 Revisited*. Manhattan, Kansas: Sunflower University Press, 2001.

Darling, Donald. *Secret Sunday*. London: William Kimber, 1975.

Darling, Donald. *Sunday at Large, Assignments of a Secret Agent*. London: William Kimber, 1977.

De Decker, Cynrik and Roba, Jean-Louis. *'40–'45 Above the Schelde, Dender and Durme*. Erpe: De Krijger, 1996.

De Ridder Files, Yvonne. *The Quest for Freedom, Belgian Resistance in World War II*. Santa Barbara, CA: Fithian Press, 1991.

D'Udekem D'Acoz, Marie Pierre. *Andrée de Jongh. Une Vie De Résistante*. Brussels: Racine, 2016.

Dupont Bouchat, Marie Sylvie. "de Jongh (Dédée)". In Gubin, Eliane (ed.). *Dictionnaire Des Femmes Belges XIX et XX Siécles*. Brussels; Editions Racine, 2016.

Ferguson, Arthur (Duke University). Chapters regarding the strategic air war in the European and Mediterranean Theaters. In Craven, Wesley Frank and Cate, James, Lea (eds). *Army Air Forces in World War II: Europe*. Washington, DC: Office of Air Force History, 1951.

Freeman, Roger, with Alan Crouchman and Vic Maslen. *Mighty Eighth War Diary*. London: Jane's, 1981.

Freeman, Roger. *The Mighty Eighth: A History of the Units, Men and Machines of the US 8th Air Force*. London: Cassell, 1979, 1986, 2000.

Fruythof, August. *Via het Vagevuur naar de Hel (From Purgatory to Hell)*. Weelde, Belgium: Uitgeverij Ten Berge, 1980.

Gillot, Jean-Jacques. *L'Epuration en Dordogne selon Doublemètre (Purification in the Dordogne According to Doublemètre)*. Perigueux, France: Pilote 24 Editions, 2002.

Goodall, Scott. *The Freedom Trail: Following One of the Hardest Wartime Escape Routes across the Pyrenees into Northern Spain*. Banbury, Oxfordshire: Inchmere Design, Ltd., 2005.

Hughes, Richard D'Oyly. *Memoirs, Volume VIII* (unpublished). Typed manuscript in the collection of the Air Force Historical Research Agency, Maxwell AFB, Alabama as Call Number 520.056-234.

Jackson, Julian. *France: The Dark Years 1940–1944*. Oxford: Oxford University Press, 2001.

Jouan, Cécile. *Comète. Histoire d'une ligne d'évasion*. Veurne: Editions de Beffroi, 1948.

Lay Jr, Beirne. *I've Had It: The Survival of a Bomb Group Commander*. New York: Dodd, Mead & Company, 1945.

Lay Jr, Beirne. *Presumed Dead: The Survival of a Bomb Group Commander*. New York: Dodd, Mead & Company, 1980.

LeMay, Curtis E. with MacKinlay Kantor. *Mission with LeMay: My Story*. New York: Doubleday, 1965.

Lokker, Claude. *Des Batons dans les Roues (Sticks in the Wheels)*. Brussels: MIM Fonds Ortelius, 1985.

MI9 after-action report No.2885 (1944): Sergeant Maurice Muir (RAF).

MacDermott, Alasdair. "Cométe, a World War II Belgian Evasion Line." In Coekelbergs, Roger, et al. (eds). *Livre mémorial Agents de Renseignement et d'Action [Memorial Volume of Intelligence and Action Agents]*. Antwerp: Livre Mèmorial, 2015.

Mahurin, Walker "Bud." *Honest John: The Extraordinary Autobiography of the Famous World War II Ace Who was Brainwashed by the Communists*. New York: G.P. Putnam's Sons, 1962.

Maurer, Maurer. *Air Force Combat Units of World War II*. Maxwell AFB: Office of Air Force History, 1983.

Neave, Airey. *Little Cyclone*. London: Hodder and Stoughton, 1954.

Neave, Airey. *Saturday at MI9: A History of Underground Escape Lines in Northwest Europe in 1940s by a Leading Organizer at MI9*. London: Hodder and Stoughton, 1969.

Neave, Airey. *The Escape Room*. New York: Doubleday & Company, 1970.

Nothomb, Jean-François. *"Le réseau d'évasion Comète."* Brussels: Bulletin de l'ANRB, 1984.

Ottis, Sherri Greene. *Silent Heroes: Downed Airmen and the French Underground*. Lexington, KY: University Press of Kentucky, 2001.

Parton, James. *Air Force Spoken Here: General Ira Eaker and the Command of the Air*. Bethesda, Maryland: Adler & Adler, 1986.

Penaud, Guy. *Histoire de la Résistance en Périgord*. Périgueux, France: Pierre Fanlac, 1985.

Shiber, Etta. *Paris Underground*. New York: Charles Scribner's Sons, 1943.

Speer, Albert. *Inside the Third Reich*. London: Orion Books, 1969.

Tartière, Dorothy (Drue Leyton). *The House Near Paris: An American Woman's Story of Traffic In Patriots*. New York: Simon & Schuster, 1946.

Van de Putte, Lancelot. *The Resistance in Erpe-Mere during World War II*. Ghent: University of Ghent, Faculty of Arts and Philosophy Department of Latest History, 2008.

Verhoeyen, Etienne. *"La Ligne d'évasion Comète (Août 1941 Février 1943),"* *Jours de Guerre*. Brussels: Jours de Guerre, 1997.

Yenne, Bill. *Big Week: Six Days That Changed the Course of World War II*. New York: Berkley/Caliber, 2013.

Yenne, Bill. *Hit the Target: Eight Men Who Led the Eighth Air Force to Victory Over the Luftwaffe*. New York: Berkley/Caliber, 2015.

Zemke, Hub, and Roger Freeman. *Zemke's Wolf Pack*. New York: Orion Books/Crown Publishers, 1988.

Index

References to images are in **bold**.

About the Author

Bill Yenne is the San Francisco-based author of more than two dozen books on military and historical topics. He is a member of the American Aviation Historical Society, and he has contributed to encyclopedias of both world wars. His work has been selected for the official Chief of Staff of the Air Force Reading List, and he is the recipient of the Air Force Association's prestigious Gill Robb Wilson Award for his "most outstanding contribution in the field of arts and letters, [for his] work of over two dozen airpower-themed books, and for years of effort shaping how many people understand and appreciate airpower."

Walter J. Boyne, the former head of the Smithsonian National Air and Space Museum, has recommended Mr Yenne's work, writing, "I can guarantee that you will be engaged by his master storytelling from his opening words to the very last page."

Mr Yenne's book *MacArthur's Air Force: American Airpower Over the Pacific and in the Far East, 1941–45* was described by Brian Sobel, author of *The Fighting Pattons*, as "a revelatory and groundbreaking chronicle."

Aviation biographies penned by Mr Yenne include *Hap Arnold: The General Who Invented the US Air Force*, which General Craig McKinley, president of the Air Force Association, described as "a superior job helping the reader better understand General Arnold" and his dual biography of Dick Bong and Tommy McGuire, *Aces High: The Heroic Story of the Two Top-Scoring American Aces of World War II*, which was described by pilot and best-selling author Dan Roam as "the greatest flying story of all time."

Mr Yenne has appeared in documentaries airing on the History Channel, the National Geographic Channel, the Smithsonian Channel, ARD German Television, and NHK Japanese Television. His book signings have been covered by C-SPAN.

Visit him on the web at BillYenne.com.